INTERNATIONAL FASCISM
1919–45

Cass Series: Totalitarian Movements and Political Religions
Series Editors: Michael Burleigh and Robert Mallett
ISSN: 1477-058X

This innovative new book series will scrutinise all attempts to totally refashion mankind and society, whether these hailed from the Left or the Right, which, unusually, will receive equal consideration. Although its primary focus will be on the authoritarian and totalitarian politics of the twentieth century, the series will also provide a forum for the wider discussion of the politics of faith and salvation in general, together with an examination of their inexorably catastrophic consequences. There are no chronological or geographical limitations to the books that may be included, and the series will include reprints of classic works and translations, as well as monographs and collections of essays.

Faith, Politics and Nazism: Selected Essays by Uriel Tal
With a Foreword by Saul Friedlander

Totalitarian Democracy and After: International Colloquium in Memory of Jakob L. Talmon
Yehoshua Arieli (ed.)

Contrasting the French and Italian Communist Parties: Comrades and Culture
Cyrille Guiat

The Italian Road to Fascism
Emilio Gentile, translated by Robert Mallett

International Fascism, 1919–45
Gert Sørensen and Robert Mallett (eds.)

International Fascism
1919–45

Editors

Gert Sørensen
Robert Mallett

FRANK CASS
LONDON • PORTLAND, OR

First published in 2002 in Great Britain by
FRANK CASS PUBLISHERS
Crown House, 47 Chase Side
London N14 5BP, England

and in the United States of America by
FRANK CASS PUBLISHERS
c/o ISBS, 5824 N.E. Hassalo Street
Portland, Oregon 97213-3644

Website: www.frankcass.com

British Library Cataloguing in Publication Data

International fascism, 1919–1945
1.Fascism – History – 20th century
I.Sorensen, Gert, 1948– II.Mallett, Robert, 1961–
320.5'33'09042

ISBN 0-7146-5301-2 (cloth)
ISBN 0-7146-8262-4 (paper)
ISSN 1477-058X

Library of Congress Cataloging-in-Publication Data

International fascism, 1919-45 / edited by Gert Sørensen and Robert Mallett.
    p. cm.
Includes bibliographical references and index.
    ISBN 0-7146-5301-2 (hardcover) — ISBN 0-7146-8262-4 (pbk.)
    1. Fascism—History. 2. Fascism—Italy—Historiography. 3. World ld
politics—20th century. 4. Europe—Politics and government—20th
century. 5. Ideology. I. Sørensen, Gert, 1948- II. Mallett, Robert,
1961-
D726.5.I48 2002
335.6'09'041—dc21
                                                                  2002001716

This group of studies first appeared in a Special Issue on
'International Fascism, 1919–45'
of *Totalitarian Movements and Political Religions*
(ISSN 1469-0764) 2/3 (Winter 2001) published by Frank Cass.

Printed in Great Britain by Antony Rowe Ltd, Chippenham, Wilts

Contents

Foreword

ROBERT MALLETT

Fascismo was, at heart, a revolutionary creed as opposed to the mere maintainer of an existing social and political order, as some academics would have us believe. This much became all too evident when the Mussolini regime banned all political opposition and imposed dictatorial rule in 1926. Thereafter, the godfather of Fascism, largely unobstructed by monarchy, Church or political, military and economic élites, frequently repeated that he would transform Italy, and return the Italian people to the greatness of their Imperial Roman ancestors. No one could claim that Mussolini was not ambitious. Italy, at that time not a full-time member of the exclusive Great Powers' club, lagged way behind its European neighbours the British and French. In economic terms Italy was much poorer, in military terms decidedly more backward, while socially the Italian people remained split between a comparatively affluent north and a desperately impoverished and unstable south. Yet Mussolini's movement, its strange pseudo-Roman cultural and artistic idioms and its increasingly successful endeavours to subvert the international political order, particularly after the rise of Hitler, did make its mark on Italy and the wider world. Even if Mussolini claimed that Fascism was not for export, this was patently not the case.

As this collection of articles shows, the Italian Fascist movement left an indelible imprint on the inter-war period. Trine Kjeldahl succintly examines the Mussolini regime as part of a broader analysis of Raymond Aron's work on 'totalitarianism'. For Kjeldahl, Aron's contribution to his field was incontrovertible. Not only did he identify the 'religious' dimension of the various inter-war regimes, but he was also able to establish the link between totalitarian ideology and revisionism in terms of international relations. In his excellent study of the Danish reactionary Right, Adam Holm argues that, while Denmark was never a country likely to endorse political extremism, the advent of Fascism in Italy sparked much furious debate within that country. The very existence of parliamentary democracy came under intense scrutiny, although the Danish radical Right fortunately believed that dictatorship suited the Latins but not the more sedate north Europeans. Denmark, thus, was spared revolutionary government, or at least until the Germans arrived in 1940. Morten Heiberg's analysis of Mussolini's intervention in the Spanish Civil War and Franco Savarino's essay on Fascist policy toward Latin America, and Mexico in particular, emphasise the pro-active attempts of the regime to disseminate fascist ideological ideas. In turn, both demonstrate the limits of Mussolini's influence. Franco, a resilient character, rebuffed the senior dictator's efforts to impose an Italian-style fascist regime on Spain. He would fight the Spanish war, and run Spain, his way. Across the Atlantic, in Mexico, Rome went to considerable lengths to win over native Italian émigrés to the fascist ideal, and thus to help shift a turbulent Mexican society toward its own fascist revolution. Here, too, Mussolini's efforts fell on stony ground. Italian immigrants preferred integration into Mexican society to intimate bonds with the Fascist dictatorship, while the Mexican establishment itself resented Mussolini's crude attempts to impose the Roman cultural heritage on a country already enriched by native and Hispanic traditions. Mogens Pelt extends the analysis to Greece. Examining the Metaxas dictatorship in detail he shows how Greek 'fascism' ironically clashed, for geopolitical reasons, with its Italian counterpart. In turn Metaxas identified closely with German National Socialism which, he believed, might eventually prevent Italian aggression against his country. This proved an ambitious idea, given the nature of Italian–German relations, and ultimately failed.

The *Duce*'s attempts to carve out a Fascist empire in the Italian *mare nostrum* – based fundamentally upon the ancient Roman model – may seem laughable to many today, but during the 1930s they were taken very seriously and, moreover, contributed hugely to the international disorder that eventually led to war in 1939. Steen Bo Frandsen examines this fascinating subject not through the papers of Rome's military archives, but through Mussolini's rhetoric. In particular, Frandsen's excellent essay shows how Fascism's reclamation of the Pontine Marshes was converted by the regime into a symbol of Mussolini's endeavour to reconquer the lands of Roman antiquity. Fascism succeeded in establishing Pontinia, but failed dismally to rebuild the empire. Lucio Ceva explains why. The Fascist government may well have spent liberally on building up its armed forces, but while these proved by and large effective in combating Libyan rebels, the Ethiopian armies, Spanish militiamen and Albanian tribesmen, widespread corruption within the regime prevented effective armaments production. The result was that Italy became fatally reliant on the success of German arms once Mussolini declared his much more ambitious war against Britain and France in 1940. Fascist militarism and imperialism, the very soul of the entire ideology, therefore quickly became exposed as hollow dreams, amply exemplified by the disastrous Italian offensive against Greece.

Finally, this volume looks at the Fascist regime's relationship with the Vatican and the Italian Crown. John Pollard expertly compares the performance of Benedict XV during the First World War with that of, in the words of John Cornwell, 'Hitler's Pope', Pius XII two decades later. Pollard rightly challenges Cornwell's accusations against 'Papa Pacelli'. Pius XII was in no way sympathetic toward Nazi barbarism and, furthermore, acted as go-between for the Allies and those German generals who aimed to overthrow Hitler in 1940. Pacelli also tried to prevent Mussolini plunging Italy into war, but in vain. Gert Sørensen's challenging article invites us to think again about the nature of the state in Mussolini's Italy. It is more relevant, he argues, to see Fascist Italy as a 'dual state' in a permanent state of emergency rather than, as Mussolini himself termed it, a diarchy. The latter term, in the words of Sørensen, does not permit us to 'embrace the complex reality of the subordinated role of the king'; a question that strikes at the very heart of Mussolini's *modus operandi*.

At their genesis each of the articles included here was first aired at the international conference on *Fascism in an International Context, 1919–1945*, held at the Danish Cultural Institute in Rome in June 2000. The conference, organised jointly by the Department of Romance Languages and Literature, University of Copenhagen, and the *Centro Falisco per li Studi Storici* (CEFASS), saw much debate on these crucial arguments. We are much indebted to the CEFASS research director, Professore Michele Abbate, for organising an intellectual event of such breadth and depth. In sharing the pleasure of those moments with a wider readership we hope that the debate may now be fruitfully extended.

1

'Opposing the past':[1]
Danish Radical Conservatism and Right-Wing Authoritarianism in the Inter-War Years

ADAM HOLM

Introduction

'Fascism', Helmut Franke, a German nationalist, wrote in 1924, 'is little else than the synthesis between conservatism and modernism'.[2] Having been to Italy to witness the new phenomenon with his own eyes, Franke was certain that the movement, under the charismatic auspices of Benito Mussolini, was chiefly interested in putting an end to political unrest and restoring law and order. His interpretation of the ideological nature of Fascism,[3] so obviously at odds with the bulk of later scholarly knowledge, is however an interesting example of what many contemporary observers wanted Fascism to be.

In the context of the turbulent years after the First World War, the political dichotomies were clear-cut: those who advocated a fundamental change of the established social structures were revolutionary and lumped together as communists, while those who opposed this 'red peril' were considered champions of the existing social institutions and norms, in effect conservatives, disregarding that they may have called themselves something else. Although Fascism was never a static concept, it is still hard to come across leading Italian Fascists who expressed a desire for conservatism, let alone who intended to conserve the prevailing state of affairs.[4] Yet in the period when 'European conservatism turned nasty',[5] many conservatives around Europe looked to Italy with barely concealed hopes for the future. There are several examples in Danish newspapers and popular magazines of Mussolini being praised for his 'great personality', his ability to steer his country safely through the dire straits of crisis, and his 'unpolitical' dedication to the faith of his countrymen. Mussolini was, for a substantial period of time, even after the heavily critised murder of Matteotti in 1924, seen as a right-wing conservative, much in the mould of the so-called 'diehard' tradition within the British Tory Party.[6]

The numerous punitive expeditions in the rural areas and violent incidents in the cities, however, caused a serious distortion of the picture of Fascism as a law-abiding force of order. Great effort was made to differentiate between the 'good' Fascism personified by the *Duce*, and the 'bad' Fascism of the *squadristi*, who were considered the very negation of the valiant and just leader; in short, proletarian, anarchistic and unruly. The notion of many foreign journalists covering Fascism was clear, as has been noticed in the case of the conservative British press: 'The papers hoped that the "good" fascists would triumph over the "bad" and create a real Italian Conservative party'.[7] So firmly rooted was this line of interpretation that one leading British fascist, Arnold Leese, even referred to his branch of fascism as 'conservatism with knobs on'.[8]

Having merely scratched the surface, the above examples show that conservatism and fascism have often been considered twins, with the latter being the more aggressive and activistic of the two.[9] Or, as the historian Karl Mannheim puts it, 'Indeed, for many Rightists, fascism was simply a more "dynamic" form of conservatism'.[10] According to this assumption, they are the products of similar circumstances, they react to the same tendencies, and their ideal society looks almost identical. Sharing the same instincts meant that both conservatism and fascism, in the wake of the Bolshevik revolution, turned against communism and wanted to repress organised trade unions or social protest movements, which challenged the acclaimed unity of the nation and thus disturbed the organic order, and cultivate nationalism and patriotism.

As king and church were still standing as solid pillars of society in Fascist Italy, conservatives around Europe felt reassured that there were strong mutual bonds between these two authoritarian ideologies. Harbouring a pronounced fascination with the 'strong man' and the 'simple solution', many conservatives either tacitly supported or even themselves resorted to radical actions in the face of the chaos they perceived all around them.[11]

Adhering to a simple yet meaningful dividing line between pro-

and anti-liberal forces of the Right, this paper looks at these two faces of conservatism. I shall briefly begin by providing a rough sketch of the political situation in inter-war Denmark. The basic question is: why no fascism in Denmark? I will then proceed by discussing the relationship between conservatism and radical conservatism in a general theoretical framework, and by exemplifying the Danish version of radical conservatism through different themes. Because of the obvious limitations of time and space, the present article will concentrate geographically and chronologically on Denmark between 1928 and 1940. I take the year 1928 as my starting point – in a comparative European perspective rather arbitrarily – because it was that year when the most influential Danish radical conservative magazine, *Det nye Danmark*, first emerged.

The main argument is that conservatism needs to be studied more carefully, at least in relation to the democracies during the inter-war years, in order to grasp its highly ambiguous ideological content. It can hardly be denied that Danish political culture, with a few notable exceptions, successfully navigated through the stormy waters of anti-democratic ideas. Not only did it survive, but it did so without suffering any major crisis; the government, a Social Democratic-Social Liberal coalition headed by the same Prime Minister, Thorvald Stauning, was in office for eleven years, from 1929 to the German occupation in 1940. In a contemporary European perspective, stability, if anything, seems the most fitting epitaph for that part of modern Danish history. In their best electoral performance the anti-democratic Right, consisting of numerous parties, including several minuscule Nazi parties, gained six per cent of the vote in the national elections of August 1939, which left them with three mandated seats in Parliament. Prior to this, the electoral support in favour of these parties varied from between two and four per cent. The communists would poll even less. All included the declared opponents of the liberal democratic state and, irrespective of ideological beliefs, never approached a stage where they could effectively pose a menace to the parliamentary system they so intensely loathed.

However, this does not mean that the concept of democracy was universally accepted or uniformly interpreted. The 'organised, centralised, authoritarian democracy'[12] which Mussolini outlined in his *Fascist Doctrine* as late as 1932 had, for a long time and in different permutations, been part of the conservative scene not only in Denmark but in several other European countries.[13] The opposite of democracy, namely dictatorship, might not have been in vogue among Danish conservatives and right-wing radicals – after all, it was considered 'un-Danish' to let one man alone dictate the state of affairs – but the existing democracy was far from respected at face value. The picture of the schism between democracy and dictatorship needs to be redrawn at certain points in order to allow for the subtleties to appear more visibly. Not being a staunch believer in totalitarian practices, as was the case with most conservatives, was not the same as holding an uncritical acceptance of democracy in practice, let alone the ideal of democracy. Danish historian Henrik S. Nissen has summed up the general dissatisfaction with the 'system' in this way:

> It is worth bearing in mind that parliamentary democracy was a rather novel form of governance in inter-war Denmark. Many people were raised at a time when it was still an explosive political issue if popular franchise was to become the new constitutional law. How many thought this should never have happened? And how many believed that it might originally have been a good idea which, however, was taken much too far?[14]

This was where radical conservatism and right-wing authoritarianism entered the picture. Before turning to radical conservatism, a brief word on the right-wing authoritarian fascination: here it is taken to understand the rejection of the class struggle, above all with the Social Democrats, who were seen as the domestic enemy, whereas the Soviet Union stood out as the foremost international enemy. The term also implied a very critical attitude toward liberalism in its political (parliamentarism) and economic (capitalism) embodiments. Right-wing authoritarians also preferred a strong centralised state, corporatism, an organic and unified nation, a strong military machine, patriotic and nationalistic values, and reverence for the church and Christian morality, as well as the encouragement of discipline and order. The term right-wing authoritarian carried a certain looseness, since all types of right-wing belief inevitably contained very strong elements of authoritarianism. I use the term to describe a diffuse mode of thinking. Right-wing authoritarianism was, therefore, in many respects close to radical conservatism because they shared a number of affinitive notions and objectives. Radical conservatism in this interpretation will be considered as the more conscious of the two. Having said this, it should be remembered that the boundaries between the different typologies of the anti-constitutional or anti-democratic right-wing were not clearly drawn. The essential positions primarily exist as abstract categories designed for definitional practice. In real life (that is, history as we can observe it), the neat separations between one platform and another simply did not exist. Fascism, as Kevin Passmore rightly observes, emerged 'out of a crisis of conservatism', but this does not mean that conservatism was sapped of all radical potential.[15] In Denmark an extra-parliamentary opposition developed within conservative and liberal-rural supporters which gave rise to a string of small anti-parliamentary leagues. Like their fascist counterparts, they believed themselves to be on the threshold of a new and demanding era. This was what radical conservatism was about.

No Laboratory for Fascism: Denmark as a Case for Comparison

Even though this article is explicitly not about fascism, it would seem a useful starting point to begin by defining fascism and placing it in a Danish context, the reason being that fascism clearly had a momentum in the inter-war years. Not merely an intellectual idea, fascism acquired its shape through various movements and regimes in Europe. Fascism, or some closely resembling configuration of right-wing radicalism, stood out as the predominant point of reference for the non-moderate Right. Before dealing with the structural barriers which fascism faced in Denmark, an operational definition of fascism should be given. It is fairly straightforward. It refers to those movements which in terms of members and activity were significant in the inter-war period, and which advertised their allegiance to the creed by calling themselves fascist, since they, in the words of Martin Blinkhorn 'present no taxonomic problem'.[16] Such groups were rather few in Denmark. Those that actually existed, for instance *Nationalt Ungdomsforbund*, *Nationalkorpset* and *De Jyske Fascister*, manifestly sported the symbol of the *fasces* and took Mussolini and the *camice nere* as their model of inspiration.[17] They petered out, however, as early as the 1920s.[18]

As for Nazism, which was more successful in Denmark, it will be considered as a German variant of Fascism, but with a stronger emphasis on *volk* and blood. Admittedly this is not an original interpretation, but little else in terms of ideology separated Fascism from Nazism other than the issue of racism.[19] In this respect, one could argue that Nazism was more radical than Fascism, whereas the opposite could be contested in relation to their respective visions for the organising principles for the state. Thus considered, Fascism, at least in theory, had a more revolutionary approach than Nazism. I shall not venture further into this discussion for fear of falling into the dark pitfalls of the many cases where theory does not match with reality. As all students of right-wing radicalism will discover, sooner rather than later, one is most fragile when protected behind a supposedly impenetrable shield of theory.

The point of issue is the simple fact that there was no successful fascism in Denmark at a time when nearly every other European country, with a handful of notable exceptions in northern and western Europe saw 'an accelerating, increasingly catastrophic retreat of liberal political institutions'.[20] Why, then, did Danish inter-war fascism fail?

Context was of enormous importance, for fascism in Denmark had to operate in a climate which both politically and economically offered far less promising terrain than existed in many of the war-torn countries, among them some of the newly formed independent states. Swedish historian Ulf Lindström offers a comparative examination of the main reasons why fascism (not excluding Nazism) never seriously took root in the three Scandinavian countries.[21] He finds three particular reasons for this: (i) an efficient political effort to combat the socio-economic crisis in the 1930s; (ii) the assimilation of potentially radical sectors of the population, such as farmers and the 'national' youth, into conservative and agricultural parties, thus demonstrating the flexibility of the established party system; and (iii) the organised trade unions managed to recruit rather than lose members during periods of high unemployment. This leads Lindström to conclude that the strength of fascist organisations and leadership is inversely related to the strength of pluralist democracy. I shall not object to the findings in the above, merely provide a few additional remarks on the Danish case.

The dislocation of war, defeat and the discrediting of the established order that led to the toppling of monarchies in Germany, Austria-Hungary and Russia, along with the threat of a revolutionary *putsch*, were not part of the reality in Denmark. Nor had the country been subjected to dismemberment. Quite the opposite had taken place, since part of the state's territory, which had been annexed by Prussia in the war in 1864, went back to Denmark after a referendum in 1920 following the Versailles Treaty. In short, there was none of the humiliation and profound disillusionment which made ex-servicemen in their thousands join the ranks of the fascists.[22] Naturally, Denmark was exposed to the rigours of international economic competition, but the country had come out of the war in a solid position, not least owing to its considerable exporting of agricultural goods to both sides during the First World War. Denmark thus emerged from the great European cataclysm as a neutral country with a highly stable constitutional monarchy, in which the principal traditions and values of liberal democracy were widely regarded, albeit not of particularly longstanding stock. Denmark had a functioning system of political representation, which accompanied the process of urbanisation and industrialisation. Mass democracy was accepted, at least nominally. A popular franchise – women under 30 and men under 25 excepted – had been introduced. Consequently, the political system was to a large degree able to absorb, and deal with, the interests of various social groups without witnessing the same destructive social and cultural conflicts which were at play in a number of other countries.

While listing the structural and historical hindrances to a fascist breakthrough one should also bear in mind the absence of a strong and large Communist Party. Without reverting to Ernst Nolte's somewhat apologetic analysis of the dialectical relationship between Left and Right,[23] the attitude of the one cannot be dissociated from that of the other. Fascism was therefore to some extent *also* influenced by the presence of virulent groups of anarchists and communists, even if they, in many cases, presented neither a numerical match to the Right nor a revolutionary threat to the political institutions as such.

There is a tendency to forget, in Brian Girvin's phrase, that 'to the extent that parliamentary democracy collapsed, this was in every case occasioned by the Right rather than the Left: whether by fascists, authoritarian nationalists or by the military or an amalgam of all these'.[24] That said, it should be noted that the relatively weak left-wing in Europe was further made unattractive to the hard-pressed middle-classes because conservative parties in the democratic states appealed to national interests, demanded economic stability, sometimes combined with notions of social reforms, wanted actively to fight inflation, and stood out as heralds of traditional cultural and religious values. The lesson to draw from this is that conservatism – here taken to mean the nineteenth century merger between traditional conservatism and liberalism – presents a strong bulwark for democracy under the circumstances briefly touched upon in the above.

In a Danish context many observers, both inside and outside the conservative camp, consider the staunch dedication to democracy by the conservative leadership as ultimately important in obstructing a potential radicalism among conservatives, thus also stemming the general tide of right-wing radicalism. The Conservative People's Party was headed for most of the troubled 1930s by John Christmas Møller. His role in this process has been particularly emphasised because he performed, successfully as it turned out, a delicate balancing act between being in opposition and not searching for extra-parliamentary solutions. He did not want the animosity of conservatives towards the Social Democratic Party, aired most violently by young conservatives, to translate into excessive calls for state models inspired by many of the southern European countries.[25]

The above factors, sketchy as they are, need to be taken into account when describing the restraining of fascism and Nazism in Denmark. What is thus of interest is to draw the line between the conservatism, classical or conventional, which stayed on the 'white' side of democracy, and the radicalised version which moved into the grey zone *en route* to the black and brown wings of the political spectrum.

Conservative Typologies

The concepts of the Right and conservatism are often taken as given. Although superfluous to mention, this is an erroneous assumption. For practical, political purposes we need to have a series of stereotypes, but the definitions show a peculiar tendency of becoming, shall we say, 'slippery' when removed from their original historical setting. Conservatism is perhaps the least exact of the classical ideologies, even eschewing the benchmark, or as some conservatives would have, the stigma, of ideology. Conservatism displays a particular quality for flexibility. Taken at face value conservatism, according to Chateaubriand's dictum, strives to preserve '*les saines doctrines*'[26] irrespective of the historical prerequisites and national conditions. Accordingly, conservatism can be both a cultural feature and a psychological disposition, which in both cases refers to a reluctance towards change. Labelling conservatism as a reactionary or traditionalist force is not a far cry away when read in this manner. But conservatism, in order for it to acquire a political meaning, is more than an attitudinal way of life, something that comes closer to a traditional behaviour that is almost always reactive. By definition the word 'reaction' is semantically incompatible with conservatism.[27] The reactionary mentality is characterised by a negative, automatic response to anything that cannot be fully identified; that is things, places, persons, institutions that signify 'uncertainty'. Unable to come to grips with the present, which to the reactionary is nothing but the most recent stage of social decay, the reactionary optic is a forced romantic transfiguration of the past. The present is devoid of meaning to the reactionary.

Conservative behaviour on the other hand is meaningful, and moreover, as Karl Mannheim teaches us, 'is meaningful in relation to circumstances which change from epoch to epoch'.[28] One could argue that conservatism is the articulated defence of certain values undertaken by a 'traditionalism' which is aware of its place in history, thus recognising the temporal cycle outlined by Edmund Burke in his *Reflections on the Revolution in France* (1790), between the living, the dead and the yet unborn.

Whereas the 'tree of history' (a traditional conservative metaphor) was only impressive in ancient times according to the reactionary viewpoint, the conservative recognises the slow growth of the tree that to his mind is the surest sign of life. As long as the roots are kept alive and nurtured, the stem will stand tall and erect, gradually growing and producing branches and leaves. This is the organic growth metaphor which conservatives place in contrast to the created growth of liberalism.[29] Social and political institutions, as well as aesthetic values and moral norms, are best guarded in this way, but, moreover, also ensured the best development if allowed to progress step by step. As is well known, conservatism is tied up with the 'articulate response'[30] to the French Revolution and the ideas inherent in the Enlightenment. Their role as monarchical defenders has inevitably – and not entirely unfoundedly – placed conservatives as the epitome of power preservation or 'social exclusionary closure'. The *raison d'être* of conservatism has been seen as the defence of the ruling strata of society, the nobility and later the upper middle class. That is, protecting the institutions on which the social divisions were founded and upholding the demarcation against the advance of alternative and competing standards in the political sphere.[31] This scheme of interpretation is best summed up in Samuel Huntington's words: 'Conservatism is the ideology that reminds men of the necessity of some institutions and the desirability of the existing ones'.[32]

When examining Danish conservatism in the inter-war period, three strands of 'Rightism' stand out, by and large equivalent to those in other European conservative traditions, notwithstanding their different mentalities, clienteles and cultures. The first can be identified as a traditionalist position that attempted to reconcile authority with a degree of democracy. This position was influenced by *Højre* (literally 'the Right'), which was succeeded in 1915 by *Det konservative Folkeparti* (Conservative People's Party). The representatives of this line had reluctantly come to accept aspects of liberal economics and political openness in the shape of democracy, the latter being considered a necessary evil.

The second strand was the strongest; namely the liberal-conservative tradition which since the 1880s had been signified by urbanisation and which had adapted itself more and more to a liberal set of values. On the other hand, without being as reserved as the first strand, the liberal-conservatives were still 'conservative' enough to be wrestling with fundamental conflicts between an abstract commitment to the sovereignty of the people, and the desire for class protection and a fear of the powers of modern mass politics. The first strand would be considered more backward looking, more stern and fundamentalist than the second strand. The latter was, as implied, by far the most common, and was propagated by the party chiefs.

The third position, which existed predominantly among young conservatives and a few, influential heretics within the maternal party, was the one which qualified as 'radical conservatism'. As already noted it is hard to identify a single characteristic properly to define the Right throughout the whole period. The three strands were made up of a great variety of inspirations which quite often merged with each other. Consequently, radical conservatism showed elements of both the 'reactionary' impulse in the traditionalist conservatism, and the economic aspects of the more liberal-élitist conservatism.

What made radical conservatism differ from the two more centrist positions was its realisation that strong institutions were desirable, but new ones were needed. The typical belief among radical conservatives, whether they belonged to the 'conservative revolution' in the Weimar Republic, *Action Française* or *Croix de Feu* in France, the Portuguese *Lusitanismo*, or the core of Danish young conservatives, was that the 'processes characteristic of modernity have destroyed the valuable legacy of the past for the present'.[33]

Radical conservatives who, in plain words, were best understood as a radicalisation of classical conservatism, detected a fatal proclivity in structural, 'status quo' conservatism to bow to the pressures of the modern world. By failing to counter the different innovations (that is, the inability to relate to these in a sceptical and self-conscious manner), structural conservatism, basically equivalent with the two strands mentioned above, reduced itself to a mere function of delaying the novelties, rather than rejecting them if they were considered worthless. This was a starting-point for radical conservatism, since it was tied up with value-conservatism.

When such values as nation, authority, stability, religion and courage were threatened by the contemporary situation – the inter-war years being exemplary evidence of this – then value-conservatives had two options at hand, according to Swedish sociologist Göran Dahl: they either resorted to apocalyptic cultural pessimism, or embarked upon a voluntarist radicalisation. For the radical conservatives, it became 'necessary to use radical means to serve the value-conservative ends'.[34]

The idealisation of an action oriented way of life heavily fused with a cult of violence (evidently more pronounced in those countries with recent war experience), which was a central component in radical conservatism, clearly separated it from the liberalised versions of conservatism. Violence as another word for 'change' was not an end in itself, at least not for the Danish radical conservatives, but a symptom of what they rejected about liberalism. More than communism and social democracy, liberalism was the prime enemy of radical conservatism. If the most sensible line in political terms should have been drawn between the supporters and the opponents of liberalism,[35] then radical conservatism parted company with conventional conservatism.

The radical conservatives regarded liberalism as a broad synonym which covered everything from Jacobinism to capitalism over parliamentarism to Bolshevism. In short, all phenomena that had a disruptive effect on the highly acclaimed unity of state and nation were attacked. Democracy with its demand for equality, capitalism with its exploitative nature, modernism in the arts with its extreme stylistic experiments, and American popular and domestic culture gaining increasing access to European markets, were among the 'evils' that helped spark off radical conservatism. Perhaps the most salient mobilising myths of the radical conservatives were those of the 'new' nation, the 'new' era, the 'new' man and so on. Bearing this in mind it is tempting to propose the view that the young conservatives in, for instance, Denmark and Sweden – represented by *Konservativ Ungdom* (Conservative Youth, KU) and *Sveriges Nationella Ungdomsförbund*[36] (National Youth League of Sweden, SNU) respectively – were fascists because they fused a paramilitary style with a 'palingenetic myth'. Their radicalism, which made them also fall out with the conservative establishment, gave them an air of anti-conservatism.

With the currently most powerful one-sentence definition of fascism, at least in the English idiom, namely that advanced by Roger Griffin,[37] it is virtually impossible to refer to the concept of national rebirth outside of a purely fascist context. But a direct translation of the technical phrase 'palingenetic ultra-nationalism' into Danish fits well with the description of the so-called *'genrejserbevægelser'*. They have been lumped together as one, but they did, in fact, cover a range of different groups, as mentioned earlier. The Danish radical conservatives, or radical conservatism in general, had the national rebirth as their most central theme. For all the qualities of Griffin's theories this one is not sufficient when tried on radical conservatism. Or radical conservatism, one might reply, was really fascism.

This, though, is not the case. Four differences can be pointed to. First, although radical conservatism showed signs of being anti-conservative, both in its quest for a new order, and in its defiance and sometime mockery of 'bourgeois conservatism', the radical conservatives were not sufficiently radical to cut their links with the past. The inspiration of the iconoclastic movement of futurism in Fascism is on the other hand evident. Of course there are several architectural examples of Fascism leaning heavily on the past, but this was in sheer terms of iconography and symbolism. While radical conservatism wanted to do away with the institutions of the present, or at least all of those it considered to be infested with the liberal disease, it was, at the same time, set on rescuing the 'spirit' of either a real or mythologised past. Griffin correctly states that the radical conservatives, or as he calls them 'abortive fascist movements', were generally 'insufficiently radical in their populism to destroy traditional ruling elites, and in their ultra-nationalism to destroy the existing political system, and hence never place[d] themselves in a position to translate their visionary words into revolutionary deeds'.[38]

Second, religion played an important part in radical conservatism, which was less the case in Italian Fascism where religion was mainly advanced in the 'sacralisation' of politics.[39] Third, totalitarianism was perhaps the very essence of fascism's political ambitions. While also strongly pro-statist (that is, centralised state dirigisme), the radical conservatives did not speak with the same zest as did the fascists about the omnipresent state. Fourth, whereas fascism with its parades and marches ultimately relied on the mobilised masses, radical conservatives – often considered aristocratic intellectuals – were more ambiguous about this aspect. The Conservative Youth in Denmark expressed the importance of countering the 'red hordes', for which purpose a strong political phalanx based on a broad element of the population was needed, while other radical conservatives shied away from such 'plebian' activities. In the last case a reminiscence of traditional conservative epistemological scepticism of the common man is seen.

The radical conservatism that we are looking at here was not aiming at a fundamental overthrow of the system. The threat to the liberal-democratic system did not, in the Danish context, stem from the likelihood of its complete abolition, but mainly from a partial destabilisation of the liberal political and cultural climate. When dealing with radical conservatism one is, therefore, foremost preoccupied with the nuances of anti-system criticism, rather than the all-out warfare conducted by fascism.

Radical Conservatism in Practice: In Pursuit of National Unity

The revolutionary may have convinced himself that where nothing was seen as important enough to be preserved and reformed, and where quality was seen as missing, new institutions and a new ethos would have to be created. The radical conservative embarked on this in a slightly less radical way. As the German author Arthur Moeller van den Bruck put it in 1923 in his highly influential book *Das dritte Reich*: 'Conservative Man is now a necessary keeper and creator at the same time. He asks the question: what is worthy of preservation? However, he also intends to catch on to the past, not just to break off like revolutionary Man ... Being Conservative means creating things which are worth preserving'.[40]

The underlying premise of this quotation is that there were things not worth preserving. According to a general radical conservative interpretation, the deadly virus of liberalism spread the ills of society, an interpretation that they inevitably shared with the entire radical Right. This disease would acquire many shapes, such as socialism, communism, feminism, pacifism, anarchism, modernism, internationalism, universalism, Americanism and so forth. How healthy a society was depended on the degree to which these bacteria had been successfully quelled. Basically all liberal democratic states were infested with several of these diseases, bearing fatal consequences for the notion of the organic society and hence the unity of the nation. That was the radical conservative diagnosis.

In order to rid the 'body society' of its ailments, a drastic cure and an effective prophylaxis were needed. To stretch this medical metaphor just a little further, the imbalance in society's central nervous system could only be repaired if all efforts were concentrated on the task. Translated into the political realities of the inter-war years, radical conservatives began their search for solutions to redress the balance of the nation. What they were in pursuit of was national unity. Such was the desire that one Danish right-wing party, formed in 1936, even lent its overall ambition to its name: Danish National Unity.[41] Unity was another term for the organic and corporative views of how to organise society which were common on the right-wing scene. A society in which the head was separated from the rest of the body and the body itself further dismembered was not just malfunctioning; it was dead.

It was a general belief among radical conservatives that the will of the people could be embodied solely by those forces which respected the indivisible totality of the people, and hence the unity of the nation. The intellectual establishment, the saturated bourgeoisie, and the socialist or communist part of the working class, were presented as the key opponents. The conservative élite also took a blow for being too weak and constantly on the retreat. This was one reason why conservatives in opposition to the faint conservatism made sure to stress that they were not ordinary conservatives but *radical* conservatives, or else *national* conservatives, *social* conservatives or *revolutionary* conservatives. Traditional conservatism, or perhaps rather the way official conservatism worked, had degenerated into a poor show of old rituals with very little substance. One famous literary critic and radical conservative, Harald Nielsen, wryly noted that the only difference between liberalism and conservatism was that adherents of the latter only caught up with the latest fashion when it was no longer in vogue. But other than that they were now a pair of 'ugly twins', as he remarked. In the absence of a responsible conservatism, capable of commanding respect from all social strata, there was no force strong enough to fend off the advancing enemies, whether liberals or socialists. The overall fault of parliamentary conservatism, the way radical conservatives saw it, was that it ceased to play the important role of the intermediary in society, the reason being that conservatism had become indistinguishable from liberalism. With conservative parties playing the liberal card – to some radical conservatives even the creation of a party was a sign of liberalism's corruptive effect – there was no alternative to constant political conflict, and perhaps collapse, other than the reintroduction of strongly authoritarian methods. There was nothing intrinsically fascist or experimental about the proposed authoritarian arrangements. However, with the notion of social and political order – essentially a religious or metaphysical derivative with the nation as the uniting feature – being severely shaken, actions had to be taken. 'If the nation is ever going to breathe freely again, the heavy burden on its chest must be removed', a leading conservative newspaper editor wrote.[42] Although himself not a genuine radical conservative (he was, after all, the main speechwriter of the chair of the Conservative People's Party), he responded sympathetically to the call for national 'salvation'. What constituted this heavy burden? In the following section I will provide some brief examples of how some representative Danish radical conservatives looked at this question.

The most imminent danger to the nation was considered to be the class struggle. Although the revolutionary Left in Denmark hardly exercised any practical parliamentary importance during the 1930s, the animosity toward communism, rising to unprecedented heights during the Spanish Civil War and the Finnish–Soviet War (1939–40), made communists the epitome of the class struggle. Many radical conservatives realised that the chimera of a revolutionary takeover was blown out of proportion. Still, they never wavered in their belief that communism should not be allowed one single acre because it would soon strike roots and then grow at quick pace. Communism, seen as the 'rationalistic child of the French Revolution'[43] and hence the offspring of Jacobinism, was the ideology of the masses. The advance and eventual victory of mass society, as was described by José Ortega y Gasset, for instance, in his hugely influential book *La Rebellión de las Masas* (which was widely translated and read), instilled fears into many conservatives, whether of moderate or radical leaning, because the masses were portrayed as a faceless, dangerous and uncultured mob, completely ignorant of the importance of maintaining a social hierarchy. Notwithstanding the revolutionary danger with which communists were associated, the international nature of communism, frequently referred to in the barely concealed, anti-Semitic euphemism as 'cosmopolitanism', was the main incentive for considering communism a heavy burden on the shoulders of the nation.

One of the leading Danish radical conservatives, Karl Bøgholm, an academic turned journalist, conceded in one of his lengthy articles on social conservatism that reformist socialism, in fact even communism, displayed a certain sense of social awareness which could not be brushed off that easily. It was bound to leave a certain impact on those parts of society in most need of a helping hand. Consequently conservatism, or as it was in Bøgholm's terminology, 'national social conservatism', should step in and offer its hand. Bøgholm argued that the real danger of socialism and communism was their ability to rally popular excitement, and thus to bring forth the potential 'mass psychosis' of the people. The weakness of these two ideologies, according to Bøgholm, was their utter inability to guide a country. Much as they may try, Bøgholm scornfully remarked, they were bound to fail because the pill they wanted the people to swallow was too bitter. Even when they called their system democratic, thereby trying to tempt the electorate, they could not hide that they were unable to perform the duty required. The '"democratic regimes"', Bøgholm noted, 'have left us with nothing but economic anarchy and financial chaos'.[44] Not only were socialists and communists, usually placed under one banner, considered odd defenders of democracy, they were also seen as an ineffective and incompetent leadership. Rather than providing security for the people, the government, so the argument ran, looked for short-term solutions to the immediate satisfaction of their own parties. The aspect of partiality inherent in parliamentary democracy never proved acceptable to the radical conservatives. A national recovery of the sort deemed necessary was unachievable as long as the political and economic power-holders demonstrated a lack of concern about the decisive historical role they had to play, that of keeping the nation united. Danish right-wing intellectuals would point to Germany during the Weimar Republic or pre-Fascist Italy for examples of how the upper echelons, whether political, industrial or cultural, had shown little or no spirit of solidarity with the rest of the population. The argument was that the élite, by more or less abandoning its position as the national spearhead, was guilty of the political and economic disorder. Communism, trade unionism and pacifism had been allowed to thrive in the shade of the negligent government. And, in the same breath, the government was also criticised for not being tough enough on curbing the ever more voluptuous liberalism in the shape of financial capitalism and the 'parasitic' trades. As is well known from the German case, the radical Right showed no inhibition against attacking financial tycoons and big-time stock market holders for earning fortunes at the expense of the impoverished lower classes. If the nation was to be revitalised, the line had to be drawn distinctively between economics and politics, leaving the former to the 'materialistic' ideologies and using the latter as the more effective weapon.[45] Although noticeably suffering 'economyphobia', radical conservatives were not anti-capitalist in the conventional sense of opposing capitalist modes of production or the possession of private property. The critique against capitalism was mainly directed against its speculative sides which, as they saw it, were enhanced by the recurring crises and setbacks of modern industrial society. The superior speculative forces left very little room for the common man, and the danger of alienating him and perhaps opening his ears to the siren calls of communism was not to be underestimated according to radical conservative belief.[46] In short, the ill condition of society – stemming from the contaminating 'mother bacillus of all ills', liberalism – was tied down to three forces: communism, the Social Democratic-Social Liberal government, and the unproductive capitalist industries.

If the Danish people were ever to regain its strength, here again according to Karl Bøgholm, it would take a generation. The most successful remedy, he declared, consisted of three core values which had to be drilled into the heads of future generations. They must be taught to honour the nation, pay respect to religion, and observe the importance of social consciousness: 'The national thought must be given a social shape ... and thus enter the people as national social conservatism ... that is the only way to resurrect the nation, and to combat cultural Bolshevism and the new social forms'.[47]

Taken in isolation, the solutions proposed by Bøgholm may not seem particularly radical even by the standards of his contemporaries.

As mentioned earlier, radical conservatism was not a homogenous discourse, let alone a movement. It was a heterogeneous group which showed various differences in terms of how far to take the anti-liberal position. Bøgholm's line was the most common, but it was nevertheless too far-fetched for rank-and-file conservatives because of the stress it placed on national and social issues. This, to many ardent conservatives, had the unfortunate ring of 'southern European' movements, with which they would not gladly be associated.

However, Bøgholm, and with him other radicalised conservatives and diehard nationalists, operated from the principle expressed in the common battle cry: the only way to solve our problems is by doing it the Danish way. This phrase of 'doing things the Danish way' was seen to appear almost whenever the talk was of foreign approaches to handling similar problems. The string of authoritarian dictatorships which emerged in central and southern Europe during the 1920s and 1930s were duly recognised by Danish radical conservatives, but they nearly always attempted to play it safe by assuring that 'such methods' (the oppression of political dissidents and abolition of representative assemblies) were suitable only to the temperamental Latins or the cold-blooded Germans. Still, Italy and Mussolini, and increasingly also Germany and Hitler, would mark the most important sources of inspiration. On these grounds Bøgholm's 'social national conservatism', which he later termed a 'national unity of labour', was strongly influenced by French and Italian national syndicalism.[48] The same was true of such influential radical conservatives as Ole Bjørn Kraft and his younger fellow editor of *Det nye Danmark*, Jack G. Westergaard. Their view on the necessity of creating a national unity by uprooting the sources of social dissatisfaction, and hence undermining the ground for class struggle, was ultimately identical with that of Bøgholm, only slightly more radical. Westergaard, who was also the former leader of the paramilitary young conservatives, wrote that 'I believe that our Conservatism will do for the Danes and in the Danish manner what Nazism and Fascism have done in Germany and Italy, and what are similarly done by other movements'.[49] Writing in 1934 the 'victories' achieved by Nazism and Fascism represented a 'spiritual, constitutional, economic and social renaissance at an anti-Marxist and anti-liberal national foundation'.[50] What they were effectively doing for their countries was what state conservatism should do in

Denmark; apply the view of national unity.

Kraft, whose political reputation for several reasons has never seriously been called into question in post-war Danish history,[51] was well-versed in fascism. Having written a book on the subject in 1932, he plunged himself into the abyss of political rhetoric by stating that where the liberal ideologies were undermining the country, the 'national dictatorship should be given its chance, and parliamentarism whither away'.[52] 'Being governed properly', Kraft mused, was the right of every man, and woe to that political theory which did not possess the instruments needed for undertaking such an operation. Parliamentarism and rule by parties were based on the same principle as 'cattle trading', according to Kraft, the reason being that they would perform at their very best for the sake of personal profit, but as soon as goals of a higher nature were at stake, they would start losing interest because their very political creed prevented them from understanding that the individual was subordinate to the collective. What 'real' conservatism should do was ban strife between political parties, instil a sense of patriotism and social unity in the people, demand action and activism, and leave the vital decision-making process to a handful of responsible and committed persons of excellence.

Conclusion

Although a rather summary picture of just one aspect of radical conservatism, this article has attempted to address the issue of right-wing thinking in Denmark during the 1930s. It did not develop under circumstances similar to those in many other European countries, most notably Italy and Germany. Though many of the structural problems in these countries looked identical on the surface – high unemployment, social problems and widespread dissatisfaction with the political establishment – the ideological climate in Denmark was less heated. The several small Nazi parties, the various national 'resurrectionist' movements and the Communist Party were never strong enough to pose a serious challenge to the liberal system. The radical conservatives were no match for the system either, but then they never challenged the government in the open. Radical conservatism in Denmark was, by and large, an intellectual phenomenon, which strove to discredit the legitimacy of the government, as well as the philosophical basis on which parliamentarism and democracy rested. Pluralism, understood as liberalism's uncritical acceptance of all sorts of ideas and modes of behaviour, was going to be reduced to the singular for the sake of national unity.

NOTES

1. This phrase is taken from one of the leading Danish conservative politicians of the first half of the twentieth century, Ole Bjørn Kraft. See his autobiography, *Ung Mand Undervejs: Erindringer fra Aarene 1912–1926* (København: Gyldendal, 1957), p.118. Like many conservatives of his generation born in the dying phase of the late 1890s, Kraft thought conservatism would outlive itself and become obsolete and untimely if it merely looked to the past for guidance to the future. While revering the traditional symbols of conservatism (God, King and Country), he wanted to liberate 'real' conservatism from the tight grip of backward-looking conservatism, which in his mind was little else than liberalism at a slow pace. Kraft played a leading role in the intellectual circles of the Young Conservatives and edited the main magazine of Danish 'radical conservatism', *Det nye Danmark* [The New Denmark]. The magazine ran from 1928 to 1940. In the same period in which Kraft was also a conservative MP, he published a book on fascism entitled *Fascismen: Historie, Lære, Lov* [Fascism: History, Teaching, Law] (København: Gyldendal, 1932). The book was attacked by political opponents for being pro-fascist, and within conservative ranks there were concerns that Kraft had shown his true political belief. Kraft himself, however, denied all accusations of fascistzoid leanings and stated that he was merely recording a political phenomenon which was now a major player on the international scene of politics, just like communism. In all earnest it is hard, if not virtually impossible, to find explicit statements of support for fascism in Kraft's book, but it is equally clinically free of any signs of criticism. Although this article does not concern itself with Kraft but rather with the well of ideas with which he identified, I have chosen the quotation by Kraft as an example of conservatism at conflict with itself. For conservatives to denounce the sacred past, even only partly, would be as for Marxists to abandon the class struggle and still call themselves Marxists.
2. The quotation stems from a series of articles written by Helmut Franke in the magazine *Arminus*. Franke viewed Fascism as a more updated and Latinized version of the *Preussentum* [Prussianism] which he and other nationalists considered vital for the resurrection of a strong Germany. See Stefan Breuer, *Anatomie der Konservativen Revolution* (Darmstadt: Wissenschaftliche Buchgesellschaft, 1993), p.125.
3. In this article I refer to 'Fascism' as the specific Italian form, and 'fascism' as the general concept.
4. Norberto Bobbio, *Destra e sinistra* (Rome: Donzelli Editore, 1994), p.24, refers to Alfredo Rocco's speech in the Fascist Chamber in 1934 in which he declared himself to be in favour of a 'conservative revolution'.
5. Michael Mann, *The Struggle Between Authoritarian Rightism and Democracy, 1920–1975* (Madrid: Estudio Working Paper 45, February 1993), p.6.
6. See Richard Thurlow, *Fascism in Britain: A History, 1918–1985* (Oxford: Basil Blackwell, 1987), pp.46–62.
7. R.J.B. Bosworth, 'The British Press, Conservatives and Mussolini, 1920–1934', *Journal of Contemporary History* V/2 (1970), pp.163–83, 168.
8. Arnold Leese, *Out of Step* (Guildford: The Author, 1947), p.49.
9. Hans Rogger, 'Afterthoughts', in Hans Rogger and Eugen Weber (eds.), *The European Right – A Historical Profile* (Berkeley: University of California Press, 1965), pp.575–89, considers the radical Right as a variety of conservatism: 'True, the

radicalism and populism of the Right, even when genuine, are rarely sustained into the period of power; its radicalism is more likely to be one of language, style and conduct than of social and economic program; the instincts and motivations of its followers are often conservative, born of anxiety and fear of change. All this may make it appear that a radical Right is a contradiction in terms, that the Right does, after all, have more in common with conservatives than with leftists, and that it is an extension of conservatism' (p.578).

10. Karl Mannheim, *Essays on Sociology and Social Psychology* (London: Routledge, 1953), p.166; see also Roger Griffiths, *Fellow Travellers of the Right: British Enthusiasts for Nazi Germany, 1933–39* (Oxford: Oxford University Press, 1983), pp.13–59. On the Röhm purge, Griffiths writes that there was a certain negative reaction among conservatives who were otherwise impressed with the new conditions in Germany, not least the 'handling' of communism. The killings of leading members of the Nazi Party, and perhaps more importantly of well-known arch-conservatives such as General von Schleicher and the political theorist Edgar Jung, certainly seems to have calmed the initial euphoria about Nazism, as did Dollfuss's murder shortly after. These reactions momentarily vanished only to reappear with more vigour in the wake of the *Kristallnacht* pogrom. See Griffiths, pp.331–44. The same picture is true for the Danish case. In particular, the pogroms during November 1938 left little doubt for many hitherto 'spiritual' symphatisers of Germany, for instance the famous Danish priest and dramatist Kaj Munk, that the time had come to do away with what 'respect one may have for Germany' because of their treatment of 'our half-brothers, the Jews'. See Per Stig Møller, *Munk* (København: Gyldendal, 2000), pp.232–48.

11. One should of course remember that a great number of conservatives, intellectuals and non-intellectuals alike, changed their somewhat reserved attitude towards democracy and liberalism in the light of the attacks carried out by Fascism and Nazism. One of the leading voices of the German national Right, Thomas Mann, who wrote the political treaty *Betrachtungen eines Unpolitischen* (Munich: S. Fischer Verlag AG, 1918), became gradually more pro-democratic (and also pro-Western) during the course of the Weimar Republic, starting with 'Von Deutscher Republik', his famous speech at Humboldt University in 1922. For Mann, whose process of political change was still visible in *Der Zauberberg* (Munich: S. Fischer Verlag AG, 1924), finally culminating in *Doctor Faustus* (Munich: S. Fischer Verlag AG, 1947), it was important to preserve what he considered to be the 'innermost values' of conservatism, namely virtue and scepticism. His example, among others, demonstrates the fallacy in Arno J. Mayer's assumption, that 'in ordinary times conservatives can afford to be purely practical and empirical in defense of the established order, while claiming special credit for being antidoctrinaire and above partisan politics ... In times of crisis, however, the logic of their position forces them into joining, condoning or supporting those advocating an antirevolutionary prophylaxis that is both ideological and aggressive'. Arno J. Mayer, *The Persistence of the Old Regime* (London: Croom Helm, 1981), pp.50, 55. Mann's political development from authoritarian nationalist to sceptical humanist, in both cases retaining a conservative basis, is examined by Henrik Stampe Lund, *Thomas Manns tragiske humanisme i Joseph og hans brødre*, unpublished PhD dissertation, København, 1999 (in Danish).

12. Quotation from William Ebenstein, 'The Fascist Doctrine', in William Ebenstein (ed.), *Great Political Thinkers* (California: Holt, Rinehart and Winston, 1989), p.631.

13. For a comparative presentation of the different positions within conservative parties and right-wing circles, see Panajotis Kondylis, *Konservatismus – Geschichtlicher Gehalt und Untergang* (Stuttgart: Klett-Cotta, 1986), pp.387ff. For a very instructive Scandinavian example, see Rolf Torstendahl, *Mellan nykonservatism och liberalism – Idébrytningar inom högern och bondepartierna 1918–1934* (Uppsala: Uppsala Universitetsforlag, 1969), passim.

14. Henrik S. Nissen, 'Fra mellemkrigstid til besættelsestid', in Henrik Lundbak and

Henrik Dethlefsen (eds.), *Fra mellemkrigstid til efterkrigstid* (København: Museum Tusculanum, 1998), pp.165–6.

15. Kevin Passmore, *From Liberalism to Fascism – The Right in a French Province, 1928–1939* (Cambridge: Cambridge University Press, 1997), p.xii.

16. Martin Blinkhorn (ed.), *Fascists and Conservatives – The Radical Right and the Establishment in Twentieth-Century Europe* (London: Allen and Unwin, 1990), p.3.

17. In the fascist monthly *Nationalt Folkeblad – Organ for dansk fascism*, which wanted to inform a Danish readership of the new and promising conditions in Italy, there were advertisements for tailors who could do the 'authentic' blackshirt.

18. See Henrik Lundbak, 'På sporet af en dansk fascisme', *Piranesi* (1987), pp.77–99; Søren Eigaard, 'Hele bevægelsen er endnu i sin vorden ...: Den danske fascism i mellemkrigstiden', in J. Moestrup and E. Nyholm (eds.), *Italien og Danmark – 100 års inspiration* (København: Gads Forlag, 1989), pp.315–60.

19. The conventional belief that Fascism did not have a racial discourse has been effectively countered. See for instance Daniele Carpi, *Between Mussolini and Hitler: The Jews and the Italian Authorities in France and Tunisia* (Boston: Brandeis University Press, 1994); Carlo Rosselli, 'Giustiza e Libertà, OVRA and the Origins of Mussoloni's Antisemitic Campaign', *Journal of Modern Italian Studies* 1/1 (1995), pp.22–57. Plans were drafted for introducing racial laws and a racial social policy in Abyssinia. Hence the adaptation in 1938 of anti-Semitic legislation in Italy, usually regarded as at Hitler's behest, appears less discontinuous with the stream of thinking to which Mussolini subscribed. Biological racism in the German mould was not present in Italian Fascism, at least not to the same extent. However, the drive to create an 'ethical state', as Mussolini declared, meant the exclusion of multiple minority cultures that were hence considered unworthy. The notion that Fascism was more 'humane' in relation to the question of racism is only valid when compared to the Final Solution of Nazism.

20. Eric J. Hobsbawm, *Age of Extremes – The Short Twentieth Century, 1914–1991* (London: Abacus, 1996), p.111.

21. Ulf Lindström, *Fascism in Scandinavia 1920–1940*, (Stockholm: Alquist and Wiksell International, 1985), passim.

22. The link between the First World War and the fascist parties and paramilitary squads ought to be well known. See for instance Peter H. Merkl, *Political Violence under the Swastika: 581 Early Nazis* (Princeton, NJ: Princeton University Press, 1975) and *The Making of a Storm-Trooper* (Princeton, NJ: Princeton University Press, 1980). It was in other words a common feature for the radical and fascist groups that their leadership, and many of the rank-and-file members, had done their military service and/or had active combat experience. In this context it should be noted that an estimated 30,000 ethnic Danes were conscripted during the First World War to serve in the Imperial German Army because they were legally citizens south of the Danish–German border. Some 6,000 of these men were killed. Interestingly enough, Frits Clausen, leader of the biggest Nazi party in Denmark (DNSAP), and Jens Møller, *führer* for the pro-Nazi ethnic Germans in Denmark, had both served on the German side during the war.

23. The German historian Ernst Nolte made a negative name for himself during the heated so-called *Historikerstreit* in the former West Germany in 1985–86 by stating that Nazism went to extremities out of fear of Stalinism. Without openly saying so, Nolte believes that Nazism without Stalinism would have been less lethal. His arguments were further presented in *Der Europäische Bürgerkrieg* (Berlin: Propyläen Verlag, 1987), passim.

24. Brian Girvin, *The Right in the Twentieth Century – Conservatism and Democracy* (London: Pinter Publishers, 1994), p.65.

25. See Wilhelm Christmas Møller, *Christmas Møller og Det konservative Folkeparti: Vor Klinge og vort Skjold – 1920–36*, Vol.1; *'Et stridens tegn' – 1936–48*, Vol.2, (København: Gyldendal, 1993); for an introduction in English, see Stein U. Larsen,

'Conservatives and Fascists in the Nordic Countries – Norway, Sweden, Denmark and Finland, 1918–45', in Blinkhorn (ed.) (note 16), pp.240–64.

26. Gerd-Klaus Kaltenbrunner, *Der Schwierige Konservatismus – Definitionen, Theorien, Porträts* (Berlin: Nicolai Verlagsbuchhandlung, 1975), p.26.

27. Klaus Epstein, *The Genesis of German Conservatism* (Princeton, NJ: Princeton University Press, 1966), p.12.

28. Karl Mannheim, 'Conservative Thought', in Mannheim (note 10), p.98.

29. For a good analysis of these reflections, see Martin Greiffenhagen, *Das Dilemma des Konservatismus in Deutschland* (Frankfurt am Main: Suhrkamp Verlag, 1986), pp.213–16.

30. Alfred Hirschman discusses the possibility that conservatives did not so much react to the actual changes which led to the writing of the human rights declaration and the civil rights, as to the text themselves. Thus, according to Hirschman, conservatism is an articulate defence, rather than a practical response. See Alfred Hirschman, *The Rhetoric of Reaction: Perversity, Futility, Jeopardy* (Cambridge, MA: Belknap, 1991), p.4.

31. See Hans Gerd Schumann, 'The Problem of Conservatism: Some Notes on Methodology', *Journal of Contemporary History* 13/4 (1978), pp.803–19.

32. Samuel Huntington, 'Conservatism as an Ideology', *The American Political Science Review* 51 (1957), pp.454–73, 462.

33. For a good overview of moderate and radical types of conservatism, see Jerry Z. Muller, 'Conservatism and Radical Conservatism', paper prepared for the conference on 'Radical Conservatism in Europe: Yesterday, Today, Tomorrow', Lund, 8–10 June 1995, p.25.

34. Göran Dahl, *Radical Conservatism and the Future of Politics* (London: Sage, 1999), p.2.

35. As suggested by Roberto Vivarelli, 'Interpretations of the Origins of Fascism', *The Journal of Modern History* 63/1 (1991), pp.29–44.

36. The best available work on the riveting conflicts between the radical and moderate conservatives in Sweden, which eventually caused the SNU to declare their independence, is Erik Wärenstam, *Sveriges Nationall Ungdomsförbund och Högern 1928–1934* (Stockholm: Scandinavia University Books, 1965).

37. Roger Griffin's now almost classical definition reads like this: 'Fascism is a genus of political ideology whose mythic core in its various permutations is a palingenetic form of populist ultranationalism'. Quotation from Roger Griffin, *The Nature of Fascism* (London: Routledge, 1991), p.26.

38. Ibid., p.51.

39. Of the major generic fascist movements, the Romanian Iron Guard founded by Corneliu Zedra Codreanu was the most openly religious. 'Fear of God and only of God' was Codreanu's motto. See Eugen Weber, 'Romania', in Rogger and Weber (eds.) (note 9), pp.501–75. See also Irina Livezeanu, 'Fascists and Conservatives in Romania: Two Generations of Nationalists', in Blinkhorn (ed.) (note 16), pp.218–40.

40. Arthur Moeller van den Bruck, *Das dritte Reich* (Hamburg: 1931), 3rd edn., pp.246, 264. The sentence in German reads: 'Der konservative Mensch ist jetzt notwendig Erhalter und Empörer zugleich. Er wirft die Frage auf: was ist erhaltenswert? Aber er sucht auch jetz anzuknüpfen, nicht abzubrechen – wie der revolutionäre Mensch. ... Konservativ ist, Dinge zu schaffen, die zu erhalten sich lohnt.'

41. For a detailed analysis of this party, see Henrik Lundbak, 'The Political Party *Dansk Samling* [Danish National Unity] 1936–39 – a Danish Example of Radical Conservatism', paper for the conference on 'Radical Conservatism in Europe: Yesterday, Today, Tomorrow', Lund, 8–10 June 1995.

42. Anders Vigen, 'Et Forsøg paa Orientering', *Gads Danske Magasin, 31 Aargang 1937* (København: GEC Gads Forlag, 1937), pp.129–37.

43. Ove Lundbye, 'Biologien og det moderne Verdensbillede', *Gads Danske Magasin 30 Aargang 1936* (København: GEC Gads Forlag, 1936), pp.104–16.

44. Karl Bøgholm, 'Social Konservatisme', *Det nye Danmark 1934* (København: L. Ihrich's Bogtrykkeri, 1934), pp.64–74.

45. Oswald Spengler wrote that the situation recquires an 'Endkampf zwischen Demokratie und Cäsarismus, zwischen den führenden Mächten einer diktatorischen Geldwirtschaft und dem *rein politischen* Ordnungswillen der Cäsaren', see Oswald Spengler, *Der Untergang des Abenlandes*, 2nd edn. (München: DTV, 1973), p.1144.

46. On this see Heide Gerstenberger, *Der revolutionäre Konservatismus* (Berlin: Duncker und Humblot, 1969), pp.48–64.

47. Bøgholm (note 44), pp.68, 69, 73.

48. Karl Bøgholm, 'Den korporative Stat', *Det nye Danmark 1934* (note 44), pp.137–42. Bøgholm credits Mussolini with the introduction of 'great actions' into politics: 'The Fascist social law, drafted by Bottai and Rossoni under Mussoloni's leadership, is one of the greatest achievements in post-war time. The corporative state stands as the most tremendous example of anti-Marxism ever to have been implemented. Mussolini has set the standard for social politics.'

49. Jack G. Westergaard, 'Gensvar til Harald Nielsen', *Det nye Danmark 1934* (note 44), pp.92–6.

50. Ibid., p.95.

51. That Kraft survived a German assassination attempt during the German occupation of Denmark 1940–45, was appointed Minister of Defence in the first government after the liberation, and never faltered in his attacks on communism, which as the Cold War progressed once again became a hallmark with conservatism, could help to explain why this highly controversial person has hitherto evaded a critical historical examination.

52. Ole Bjørn Kraft, 'Demokrati-Diktatur', *Det nye Danmark 1934* (note 44), pp.109–14.

2

The Dual State and Fascism

GERT SØRENSEN

The concept of the dual state was reintroduced in Italy in 1989 by the historian Franco De Felice.[1] His alignment with the Left led some revisionist intellectuals to consider such a concept almost as an invention of the Left.[2] I do not want to meddle with this typically Italian dispute. Instead, what this paper aims to do is to examine the history of the concept, and to go back to Ernst Fraenkel's *The Dual State*, published in 1941 and translated into Italian in 1983.[3]

This book is a valuable testimony on the part of its author, a German Jew who emigrated to the United States. Moreover, it is a close theoretical observation on how Hitler's regime worked – a regime characterised by the co-existence of the prerogative state (*Massnahmenstaat*) and the normative state (*Normenstaat*). However, it is not enough just to point out the co-existence of these two forms of state. It is equally important to understand the dominance of the prerogative aspect over the normative one, a fact which the growth of the German National Socialist Party and its consequent monopolisation of state violence made even more apparent.

In such a regime the holders of power did not consider themselves bound by laws, which were then substituted for an opportunist management based on sheer violence. While some groups were excluded from the national-popular community, after they had been condemned to a 'civil death'[4] (and some were actually killed), the privatisation of the state by Hitler led to a different distribution of power and of institutional protection for selected groups.

Between 30 January and 28 February 1933, all the necessary conditions for the building up of the Third Reich were established. On 30 January Hitler was elected Chancellor. On 28 February, after the *Reichstag* fire, a state of emergency was declared. This involved the suspension of some juridical guarantees, according to article 48, paragraph 2 of the Weimar Constitution, which had been approved in order to prevent acts of violence, and particularly of communist violence, intended to endanger the state. Immediately following the First World War, German Minister of Justice Schiffer admitted in the National Assembly on 3 March 1920 that article 48 allowed the president of the republic 'to spread toxic gas on whole cities, if this was … a necessary measure to restore order'. His statement (quoted by Carl Schmitt[5]) is a surprising, but surely unwanted, foreshadowing of a future which we now know all too well.

The state of emergency provided for by article 48 (and proclaimed not for the first time during the Weimar Republic), was intended simply as a temporary measure to be revoked once the danger was no longer imminent. As a means of government, it dated as far back as the Roman Republic. Beginning with this example, Carl Schmitt introduced the concept of mandatory dictatorship, limited in time and space, and therefore to be classified as a parenthesis in the normal functioning of the normative state.[6] In this particular case, the state of emergency was soon extended, so as to turn it into a permanent condition, while a wider range of measures was being adopted. The link between the state and rational law was broken and was never restored during the Nazi period. As Carl Schmitt points out in his *Politische Theologie* (1922):

> This existence of the state is accorded priority over the continued application of legal norms. The decisions of the state are freed from normative restrictions. The state becomes absolute in the literal sense of the word. In an emergency situation the state suspends the existing legal system in response to the so-called 'higher law of self-preservation'.[7]

Schmitt's doctrine was developed by SS *Oberführer* Werner Best, a consultant for the Gestapo, the feared body of Nazi repression which after 1936 was declared above and beyond any law. Not without a touch of humour, Fraenkel says that the only area not affected by the Gestapo were the driving laws.[8] In 1937, long before he was appointed *Reichbevollmächtigter* of occupied Denmark in the early 1940s, Best noted that the

> task of combatting all movements dangerous to the state implies the power of using all necessary means, provided they are not in conflict with the law. Such conflicts with the law, however, are no longer possible since all restrictions have been removed following the Decree of 28 February 1933, and the triumph of National-Socialist legal and political theory.[9]

Therefore, the state of emergency, described in this passage under the profile of the transition from a liberal state to a National Socialist one, was being seen as part of a historical process of no return.

In Carl Schmitt's words, mandatory dictatorship turns into absolute dictatorship.[10] The sovereign is the person who decides on the state of emergency, and on the continuity of the dictatorship in more permanent forms.[11] With the proclamation of the state of emergency on 28 February 1933, the Weimar Republic put the management of sovereignty in the hands of political and social forces which were not satisfied with an already formed sovereignty (such as mandatory dictatorship, for instance). In their turn, they were more and more determined to be invested with a constituent sovereignty, upon which to found a new dual state regime that best suited the Nazi idea of a guiding force. This was the beginning of a long Saint Bartholomew's night.[12]

A dual state may be said to exist 'whenever there is organisational unification of leadership, regardless of whether there is any internal differentiation in the substantive law';[13] that is, by means of exercising a power which allows it to make a wholly prerogative and draconian distinction between those individuals of German descent to be included in the very national community, and those pertaining to minority groups to be excluded from such a community and deprived of any constitutional right. It is the same Dr Best who reserves the residual juridical defence of the normative state for the 'constructive forces of the German people'.[14] In any case, such forces do not include the 600,000 German Jews, nor the working class of the German Labour Front, still 'speckled' with the ideology of class struggle.

Ernst Fraenkel overtly renounced comparative studies, even though he believed that they were extremely interesting.[15] But in any case, we might consider whether we can speak of a dual state in the case of Italian Fascism, starting from the most important aspect of the phenomenon, that is to say, the permanent state of emergency (or, at least, a long-lasting one).

In Italy, as in Germany, the political class of the post-war period was not the same as the one which, in 1915, had led the Italian nation into the First World War. Giolitti's transformism definitively failed when the great liberal statesman's fifth government fell in June 1921. However, unlike in the case of a defeated Germany, the 'red biennium' (1919–20) in Italy had no constitutional outcome. The statute (*lo statuto* of 1848) kept its function as a fundamental law of the country – even after the March on Rome and Mussolini's accession to power – and it did so until the end of the Second World War. Mussolini's first government was not the outcome of a *coup*, since he was appointed by the king. Furthermore, the *Duce*'s government was made up of non-Fascist ministers who vouched for the establishment's interests. Mussolini's appointment could not be compared to a state of emergency. As a matter of fact, the statute had nothing compared to article 48 of the Weimar constitution.[16] Therefore, apparently, the head of Fascism's purely parliamentary road to power had no illegal aspect.

Though it is 'perpetual and irrevocable', the statute has always undergone different interpretations, a fact which is amply demonstrated by the gradual introduction of parliamentarism in Italy in the second half of the nineteenth century.[17] The statute served as a reference point for political parties opposed to the democratic-parliamentary tendency as well. One need only think of the representative of the historical Right, Sidney Sonnino, who in his renowned article '*Torniamo allo Statuto*' [Back to the Statute, 1897] voiced the fear of monarchic sovereignty, provided for by article 5, shifting toward a parliamentary one – a fact which demonstrated that such a fear was widespread among classes still tied to the most genuine values of the *Risorgimento*. During the Fascist period, experts in constitutional law were convinced that the advent of the regime had not meant the end of the previous statutory order.[18] In their opinion, the regime carried out the third stage of the history of the statute, coming after the *Risorgimento* and parliamentary stages. The liberal constitution was 'perpetual and irrevocable', but it had a history *of its own* as well as a flexibility *of its own*, which allowed it always to adapt itself to a changing historical context. Liberalism, though moderate in origin, had nonetheless allowed some freedom and some pluralistic forms of representation. In this third stage – so it was assumed – a single party (the National Fascist Party, PNF), corporations and plebiscites were substituted for liberal pluralism.

However, it is hard to regard the formation of the Mussolini government in 1922 and the authoritarian shift of the 'very fascist laws' (*leggi fascistissime*) in 1925–26 as just the continuation of legality, and not as the first hints of a state of emergency which put aside the liberal state, thus highlighting the need for an analytic-theoretical vocabulary like the one used for the German case.

Despite the legal aspect of the government, it is worth noting that the new prime minister was also the head of the Fascist movement. As a matter of fact, Fascist action squads weakened the liberal state with illegal methods, resulting in the fall of the Facta government after the king, the formal holder of sovereignty, had avoided using strong arm tactics to prevent the March on Rome. As head of both the government and the Fascist movement, Mussolini embodied not only a constituted sovereignty, but also a constituent one.

The idea of marching on Rome itself was considered for the first time in August 1922, during an interview in which the *Duce* did not conceal the will of Fascism to 'become a state', a plan which, according to him, was already unfolding itself 'in an historical sense'.[19] A few months later, history had its formal, political and military outcome as well. Mussolini was well aware that the legal path to power was the one in which Fascists believed the least. The Fascists feared that their revolution might not have succeeded if they had not been able to find any alternatives to the parliamentary system, and they transformed the game of an old political class which was only anxious to normalise Fascism and allow it to be just a short break in liberal Italy's own linear history. If that had been the case, Mussolini would have been just an *instrumentum regni* in the hands of Orlando, Salandra and Giolitti.

The *Duce* did not underestimate such unfavourable perspectives. But he had his own conception of history to hold on to; a different conception, which corresponded more and more to what he thought were the intrinsic tendencies of real history. The only problem was to find the right time to carry out what had already been predicted. On 22 October, his newspaper, *Il Popolo d'Italia*, published the whole structure of the Fascist militia's high command. The militia was divided into 12 geographical regions, each presided over by an appointed military 'inspector' whose name was not concealed. Such news was a public admission of the existence of an organisation based on private violence, the counterpart to the royal army. And the institutions did not even oppose such a violation of the constitution. Therefore, Fascist action squads continued with their challenge to the traditional monopoly of the state.

Even before Fascism ascended to power, such a state actually revealed the emergency in which the liberal order existed. The situation was well understood by Umberto Guglielmotti, secretary to the Nationalist Association, a frequent visitor to the palaces of power, who was present in the Viminale Palace on the morning of 28 October. In his oral account of events, he included a remark of the utmost interest: while the Facta government was busy discussing whether to mobilise the army, in another room of the same building nationalist representatives, that included Luigi Federzoni, were given permission to contact both Mussolini, who had stayed in Milan, and the military leaders of the March, in Perugia. Guglielmotti rightly wondered when concluding his report:

> It might seem curious that, while in one room of the Viminale the council of ministers was deciding the state of siege against the Fascists, in an adjacent room the first contacts between the government and the Fascist movement were being taken – and such contacts were to be the origin, the act of birth of the new regime.[20]

There were therefore two tendencies. The first was supported by liberal politicians who, by appointing Mussolini as prime minister, legitimated the violence of Fascist action squads, hoping to get the situation back to normal after a limited period of mandatory dictatorship. The second was that supported by Mussolini himself who, starting from the temporary management of constituted and statutory sovereignty, saw the possibility of turning his mandatory dictatorship into an absolute dictatorship, thus holding complete possession of sovereignty and being allowed to perpetuate what *de facto* but not *de jure* was conceived of as a state of emergency.

The extension of Mussolini's sovereign power was thus measured against his ability to keep a permanent (or long-lasting) state of emergency alive, without anyone being a hindrance to him. Often, such ambiguous relationships between the regime and the Italian monarchy have been regarded as a 'diarchy' of parallel powers – and this was how Mussolini interpreted it as well.[21] Such an interpretation, as informative as it might be, does not point out how, within the machinery of the dual state, the monarchy adapts to the manoeuvres of the head of the government, being thus 'recycled' by him as a subordinate means of managing a state of emergency. The main problem is not to analyse the regime once its defects were clearly apparent – to Mussolini as well. It is a matter of understanding how the regime worked for over two decades. Fraenkel, in his book published in 1941, understood well the path the Nazi regime had undertaken even before the projected exterminations began.

There are many examples of the molecular suspension of the statute. Two laws (of 24 December 1925 and 31 January 1926) strengthened the executive power of the head of the government. The first gave the head of the government a constitutional position which he lacked as prime minister (*presidente del consiglio*). Mussolini was no longer the *primus inter pares* among the ministers of the government, since he was now a 'hierarchical superior of ministers'.[22] Thanks to the new law, the head of government – as Alberto Aquarone states – had become 'the main body through which the sovereignty of the state had to be expressed'.[23] In 1925 the first chief of general staff (*capo di Stato Maggiore generale*), Pietro Badoglio, was appointed as well. The law clearly stated that this new figure in the nomenclature was 'directly under the head of the government'. Since Mussolini was both the head of the government and minister of war, of the navy and of the air force, we can say, in the words of Lucio Ceva, that 'any uncertainty due to the difficult link between chief of staff, military ministers, government, parliament and crown *was removed*'.[24]

The January 1926 law gave the head of the government the power to issue laws by decree valid up to two years thereafter.[25] Alfredo Rocco, minister of justice and architect of the authoritarian shift of the regime,[26] displayed a great knowledge of legal literature in his parliamentary report on the bill. He had no doubts about the statutory legality of law by decree. The question, though, was not new to him. As a matter of fact, Rocco's opinion was not shared by every expert. At the beginning of the century, after a period of political and social tension (Milan 1898), Aldo Gamberini had already denounced the temporary legislation tendencies of previous years.[27] Rocco, in turn, came to the point where he thought it was empty work trying to base the governmental power on issuing decrees on explicit laws. Decrees, on the contrary, are justified by the 'need of the moment, which becomes the utmost reason for the government to act in the interest of the state'. Such a concept was completed by another juridicial construction:

> the *opinio iuris atque necessitatis*, with which people's juridicial consciousness accompanies such acts of extraordinary law-making by the executive power, has created an unwritten constitutional law which gives the government the power to issue such acts beyond the limits of the current legislation, as if they were laws.[28]

Thus, Mussolini made a thorough legislator of himself by acting as an absolute dictator who alone decided on states of emergency.[29]

Between November and December 1926 a series of legal measures were undertaken to 'defend' the state. Such measures followed Zamboni's attempt on Mussolini's life. The would-be assassin suffered a horrible death soon after his deed: he was lynched on the spot by Fascists. The meaning of such a violent act of spontaneous retribution was summarised well in Angelo Manaresi's parliamentary report on the bill to a special committee of the Chamber of Deputies: 'The crowd which on 31 October, in Bologna, brought about justice to the outlaw who dared lift his hand against the sacred person of the *Duce* have expressed the will of the nation. They have anticipated the work of legislators and judges. With everyone's consent, they have showed our assembly the way'.[30]

The prerogative justice of Fascist action squads (an exemplary behaviour of a pre-juridical habit of the peoples, to which Rocco also hints) was, by now, a constituent source of the law of the new regime.[31] The minister of justice, in his report on the bill to the Senate, had underlined the sacredness[32] of the *Duce*, since 'thanks to the Divine Providence, [he] was, is and will always be invulnerable'. The absolutist attitude behind the measures taken clearly demonstrated the 'determined will of the Fascist state not to grant a truce to the opponents ... and to keep the duty to repress for the state only'.[33] The sacrifice of anti-Fascist political opponents was the direct equivalent to the sacredness of the *Duce*, which was highlighted by

Manaresi as well. As a matter of fact Rocco, when presenting the bill to the Chamber some ten days before, had defended the introduction of capital punishment for attempts on the life of the king, of the queen, of the crowned prince and of the head of the government, as well as for a serious offence against the safety of the state. He did so with reference to the Enlightenment philosopher Cesare Beccaria, whose main idea was, on the contrary, to abolish capital punishment. However, according to Rocco's train of thought, Beccaria had provided for exceptions when the suspension of an individual's right to living and to being defended by the state was requested.[34]

With such juridical irrationalism, the law on Special Courts was issued. Judges for these courts were chosen from representatives of the armed forces, including the Fascist militia. Such a nomenclature went against article 71 of the statute, which stated that 'no one can be withdrawn from his or her natural judges. Therefore, no exceptional courts or committees can be set up'. Militarisation of the courts was the climax of Milan's gory deeds in 1898.[35] Twenty-eight years later, in 1926, the Fascist authorities regarded the alleged threats to the state as so imminent as to legitimise the introduction of measures considered valid only 'in time of war'.[36] Decisions passed by the Special Courts could not even be appealed against. In the beginning, Special Courts were temporary, but soon after, thanks to a number of delays, their existence was made permanent, and they were eventually made part of the 1931 Rocco criminal code.[37]

The problem of opponents was no longer either political or social (as happens in liberal and democratic regulations). Confusing domestic affairs with international ones, it was now a question of security to be solved by making an enemy of the opponent – an outlaw who was barely protected by the law.[38] This process of delegitimation of opponents was already clearly stated in Rocco's speech, the previous year, on Masonic associations. We know that Antonio Gramsci, in his sole speech to the Chamber, strongly disagreed with such a bill, fearing that his party, the PCd'I,[39] might have been definitively deprived of its legal status. Rocco, on his part, turned the whole question into a 'sheer measure of ordinary police', thus denying its political character.[40]

Alberto Aquarone regards the Great Council (*Gran Consiglio*) and the militia as the two most important Fascist institutional innovations. Mussolini himself counted on the foundation of the

Fascist militia in 1923 as if it were, 'the main deed ... which put the government on a completely different level than all the previous ones, thus making a regime of it. An armed party leads to a totalitarian regime ... Since then the old demo-liberal state could not but wait for its burial, which solemnly happened on 3 January 1925'.[41] The Matteotti case was brought to a conclusion by Mussolini's speech on 3 January, when the head of the government took on the political, moral and historical responsibility for the death of Giacomo Matteotti (although without mentioning his name). Even if the comparison is only half true, the Matteotti case has been compared to the Watergate scandal.[42] There was connivance (which Mussolini himself indirectly admitted), but, unlike in the case of American President Richard Nixon, Mussolini did not resign because he was so powerful that no one could have forced him to do so. Nixon's Watergate has somehow confirmed the power of American democracy. Mussolini's scandal, on the contrary, brought about the final annihilation of Italian liberal democracy.

Since the new body was already a result of the contingent power of Mussolini's mandatory dictatorship, which became overtly absolute after his speech on 3 January 1925, the foundation of the Great Council in December 1922 had already underlined the split with the old democratic-liberal state. In December 1928, the Great Council eventually became constitutionalised as a consequence of a new law which totally deprived Parliament of what was left of its former functions. Article 1 of this law stated that the 'Great Council of Fascism is the main body co-ordinating and integrating all the activities of the regime born out of the revolution of October 1922'. Some individuals, belonging by now to the mythology of the regime (such as the *quadrumviri* of the March on Rome), were members of the Great Council 'for an unlimited period of time'. It was now no longer a question of a mandatory dictatorship: it was a question concerning the very 'prerogatives and powers of the crown'.[43] If we compare these measures to the strengthening of the executive power (following the two laws of 24 December 1925 and of 31 January 1926 dealing with the powers and prerogatives of the head of the government), the ongoing split becomes even more apparent.

In a remarkable text, the philosopher of actualism, Giovanni Gentile, regarded the law on the Great Council in the same way he regarded the molecular transformation of the state into a regime. It is worth noting that Gentile criticised the old parliamentary system because it cancelled the 'superior discretional powers of the crown'. But instead of restoring the king to his constitutional role, Gentile emphasised the new situation born out of the Fascist revolution, as though the monarchy were already outdated:

> The Fascist state is well aware of its individuality, and possesses therefore a strong consciousness for its need to survive, as well as its potential development ... Therefore, the Fascist state opposes any idea which makes a contingent outcome of it and not a necessary principle and the original source of any value which the regime recognises. The regime has also found that the Great Council, a perennial breeding ground for its forces, born out of its instinctive revolutionary outburst, is the body which best fits its constitutional structure. Through such a body, the will of a talented man turns into a perennial and structured organisation.[44]

As Carl Schmitt had done, Gentile also regarded obscure and irrational instincts as the source of law-making. But, unlike Schmitt, Gentile appeared rather ambiguous when keeping quiet about the fact that laws of such origin cannot be separated from the general state of emergency, and the suspension of important principles of civil rights, which allowed the Fascist state to develop in a necessary and non-contingent way. Schmitt and Fraenkel, from different points of view, would have stated overtly the link between the legalisation of the Great Council and the creation of the Special Courts, as well as the politics of the civil death.

Making enemies out of political opponents, and therefore condemning them to a civil and physical death, soon became a major feature of Fascist foreign policy once this process had already reached its climax in domestic affairs with the issuing of the racial laws. Following the African and Spanish experiences, in which countless innocent civilians met a cruel death, the overt civil war taking place inside the prerogative state kept evolving during the Second World War. It is worth mentioning a letter Mussolini wrote to Hitler on 5 January 1940, where he comments on the German need for *lebensraum*:

> Russia ... is not part of Europe. Despite its vastness and its population, Russia has no power, it is weak. Most of its

population is Slavic and Asian. In the old days, the Baltics were the cohesive element. Nowadays, Jews are, and this represents it all. This is Germany's task: to protect Europe from Asia. It is not only Spengler's thesis ... The day we will have destroyed Bolshevism we will have been faithful to our two revolutions. And then it will be the turn of the great democracies. And they will not be able to survive their cancer, which is *demographic*, political and moral.

In the same letter Mussolini agreed on the German plan to gather all the Jews of conquered Poland 'in a great ghetto in Lublin'.[45] By subscribing to the *Führer*'s cruel policies, Mussolini brought the state of emergency to even more catastrophic and destructive forms.

The last example of the strategy of suspending the statute concerns the rumoured relationship between the king and the *Duce* at the time of Italy's entry into the Second World War. The war, together with the High Command of the Armed Forces, was the main point of article 5 in the statute. The person deciding on war was the holder of sovereignty. From a speech to the Senate (on 30 March 1938) it was apparent that, for Mussolini, the question was already settled: 'the war, as it happened in Africa, will be led by one single person under the king's order, that is, me'.[46] But the question was settled only in a practical way (*de facto*), since Mussolini had already been acting as an absolute dictator in making diplomatic and military decisions.

As a matter of fact, this question was not legally settled at all. In his diary, under the entry of 26 May, Ciano pointed out that the king was reluctant to appoint Mussolini as the commander-in-chief of the Italian armed forces. Three days later, on 29 May, Ciano noted that the High Command was eventually born.[47] On the same day a meeting in Palazzo Venezia was recorded. Mussolini, Chief of General Staff Pietro Badoglio, and the three chiefs of staff of the army, navy and air force were all present. Mussolini spoke well, comforted by his imminent appointment: 'today the High Command is born. Its foundation will be officially (*de iure*) announced once His Majesty the King has given me the papers appointing me with the Command of the Armed Forces'.[48] Such an appointment was confirmed with the Proclamation of 11 June 1940, when the king trusted the Fascist *Duce* with the 'command of troops on all fronts ...'.[49]

Renzo De Felice hints at an interlude of the utmost interest. General Puntoni, first aide-de-camp of the king, wrote in his diary about an interview between General Soddu, under-secretary at the war ministry, and himself. General Soddu was, Puntoni believed, inclined to let Mussolini hold both military and political power. According to what Soddu wrote on 14 May 1940, 'It would be a good solution to join the two responsibilities in one single person'. This happened thanks to the legal updating of the actual balance of power between the king and the *Duce*. Even more surprising are the words which follow, used to explain the urgency on the part of General Soddu: 'Maybe it is better that such a responsibility should not rest with the king in order to prevent him from being the rescuer of the nation in case the regime should fail'.[50] Perhaps General Puntoni really meant to prevent the king from being blamed for anything that might have gone wrong. Perhaps such words meant that the king was unable to rescue either the nation or himself, thus becoming a subordinate accomplice to Mussolini's dictatorship. By avoiding taking on his constitutional responsibility, the king gave way to the state of emergency of the Fascist dual state in its most extreme forms: war inside and outside national borders.

Instead of regarding Fascism as a failed totalitarian project, thus agreeing with Mussolini's theories regarding diarchy and parallel powers, I think it more profitable to analyse such a phenomenon as a permanent (or, at least, long-lasting) state of emergency. Since the statute maintained its validity even after 1925–26, the regime was apparently a legal institution which vouched for the co-existence of elements of a normative and a prerogative state. In conclusion, the weakening of the statute was due to the fact that there was not enough constitutional ground to transform the moderate, nineteenth century Italian liberalism into one of the mass political movements of the twentieth century. The Fascist dual state, by offering a catastrophic solution to such a passage, not only highlighted such limits, but even the fact that the modernisation process had taken different paths.

NOTES

1. Franco De Felice, 'Doppia lealtà e doppio Stato', *Studi Storici* 3 (1989). For the importance of the historiography of Franco De Felice, see F. Barbagallo, 'L'Italia repubblicana di Franco De Felice: fondamenti e categorie', *Studi Storici* 3 (1999).
2. Giovanni Sabbatucci, 'Il golpe in agguato e il doppio Stato', in G. Belardelli, L. Cafagna, E. Galli della Loggia and G. Sabbatucci, *Miti e storia dell'Italia unita* (Bologna: Il Mulino, 1999), pp.203-16.
3. Ernst Fraenkel, *The Dual State. A Contribution to the Theory of Dictatorship* (New York: Octagon, 1941, 1969); German edition, *Der Doppelstaat* (Frankfurt am Main: Europäische Verlagsanstalt, 1974); Italian edition, translated from the German edition, *Il doppio Stato. Contributo alla teoria della dittatura*, prefazione di Norberto Bobbio (Torino: Einaudi, 1983).
4. Fraenkel, *Dual State* (note 3), p.95; see also Otto Kirchheimer, 'The Legal Order of National Socialism', in *Zeitschrift für Sozialforschung*, Vol.9 (New York: 1941; reprint ed. Max Horkheimer, München: Deutscher Taschenbuch Verlag, 1980), p.406: 'Under the new system, a legal rule can have only a purely provisional character; it must be possible to change the rule without notice, and, if necessary, retroactively'. For the practical meaning of 'civil death', see also the diaries of Victor Klemperer, *Ich will Zeugnis ablegen bis zum letzten. Tagebücher 1933-1945* (Berlin: Aufbau Verlag, 1995); the author survived as a Jew in the city of Dresden.
5. Carl Schmitt, *Die Diktatur* (München and Leipzig: Duncker and Humblot, 1921), p.201.
6. Ibid., passim.
7. Carl Schmitt, *Politische Theologie* (München: Duncker and Humblot, 1922), p.13, quoted in Fraenkel, *Dual State* (note 3), p.25.
8. Fraenkel, *Dual State* (note 3), p.43.
9. Werner Best, *Deutsche Allgemeine Zeitung*, 1 July 1937, quoted in ibid., p.25.
10. Schmitt (note 5), passim.
11. Schmitt (note 7), p.1.
12. Giorgio Agamben, *Homo Sacer. Il potere sovrano e la nuda vita* (Torino: Einaudi, 1995), p.187.
13. Fraenkel, *Dual State* (note 3), p.154.
14. Werner Best, 'Neubegründung des Polizeirechts', *Jahrbuch der Akademie für deutsches Recht* (1937), p.133, quoted in ibid., pp.62, 89.
15. Ibid., p.xvi.
16. Aldo Gamberini, *I decreti d'urgenza. In teoria e in pratica* (Bologna: Zanichelli, 1903), p.26.
17. Lucio Ceva, 'Aspetti politici e giuridici dell'alto comando militare in Italia (1848-1941)', *Il Politico* 1 (1984), p.84.
18. Carlo Ghisalberti, *Storia costituzionale d'Italia. 1848-1948* (Rome and Bari: Laterza, 1974, 1981), pp.374-5.
19. Interview with Benito Mussolini, *Il Mattino*, 12 August 1922.
20. Interview with Umberto Guglielmotti, in S. Zavoli, *Nascita di una dittatura*, preface by R. De Felice (Milano: Mondadori, 1983), p.154.
21. Benito Mussolini, 'Storia di un anno. Il tempo del bastone e della carota' (1944, written after 25 July 1943), in Benito Mussolini, *Opera Omnia. XXXIV*, ed. E. Susmel and D. Susmel (Firenze: La Fenice, 1961), p.410; Alberto Aquarone, *L'organizzazione dello Stato totalitario. I–II* (Torino: Einaudi, 1965, 1978), p.291; Adrian Lyttelton, 'La dittatura fascista', in G. Sabbatucci and V. Vidotto (eds.), *Storia d'Italia. 4. Guerre e fascismo. 1914-1943* (Rome and Bari: Laterza, 1997), p.220; Salvatore Lupo, 'La decisione politica nella storia d'Italia', *Meridiana. Rivista di storia e scienze sociali* 29 (1997), p.41.
22. Ceva (note 17), p.108.

23. Aquarone (note 21), pp.75, 395–6, reproduces the text of the law, 24 December 1925 (n.2263, *Attribuzioni e prerogative del Capo del Governo*).
24. Ceva (note 17), pp.108–9, Ceva's italics (n.866, the law of 8 May 1925).
25. Aquarone (note 21), pp.399–400, reproduces the text of the law, 31 January (n.100, *Sulla facoltà del potere esecutivo di emanare norme giuridiche*).
26. Emilio Gentile, *Il mito dello Stato nuovo dall'antigiolittismo al fascismo* (Rome and Bari: Laterza, 1982), p.167.
27. Gamberini (note 16), p.23.
28. Alfredo Rocco, 'Legge sulla facoltà del potere esecutivo di emanare norme giuridiche. Relazione sul disegno di legge', presented in the Camera dei Deputati, 26 May 1925, reprinted in Alfredo Rocco, *La trasformazione dello Stato. Dallo Stato liberale allo Stato fascista* (Rome: La Voce, 1927), p.152.
29. On the dictator as a legislator and the transition from the mandatory dictatorship to the absolute dictatorship, see Schmitt (note 5), p.129.
30. Angelo Manaresi, 'Relazione della Commissione speciale nominata dal presidente sul disegno di legge sui Provvedimenti per la difesa dello Stato', *Atti Parlamentari. Camera. Legislatura XXVII. Sessione 1924–26. n.1100–A (documenti – disegni di legge e relazioni)*, 9 November 1926, p.2.
31. Schmitt (note 5), p.142, points at the irrationalistic origin of constituent power (Sieyès' *le pouvoir constituant*).
32. Emilio Gentile, *Il culto del Littorio. La sacralizzazione della politica nell'Italia fascista* (Rome and Bari: Laterza, 1993).
33. Alfredo Rocco, 'Provvedimenti per la Difesa dello Stato', presented in the Senate, 20 November 1926, reprinted in Rocco (note 28), pp.123–4.
34. Alfredo Rocco, 'Provvedimenti per la Difesa dello Stato', presented in the Camera dei deputati, 9 November 1926, reprinted in Rocco (note 28), pp.99–120; see C. Beccaria, *Dei delitti e delle pene*, preface by S. Rodotà, 1764, ed. A. Burgio (Milano: Feltrinelli, 1997), ch.XXVIII.
35. Romano Canosa e Amedeo Santosuosso, *Magistrati, anarchici e socialisti. Alla fine dell'ottocento in Italia* (Milano: Feltrinelli, 1981), pp.100–4.
36. Aquarone (note 21), p.429, reproduces the text of the law, 25 November 1926 (n.2008, *Provvedimenti per la difesa dello Stato*, art. 7).
37. Ibid., p.102.
38. Schmitt (note 5), p.176.
39. Antonio Gramsci, 'Origini e scopi della legge sulle associazioni segrete', pronounced in the Camera dei deputati, 16 May 1925, *L'Unità*, 23 May 1925, reprinted in Antonio Gramsci, *La costruzione del partito comunista. 1923–1926*, ed. E. Fubini (Torino: Einaudi, 1971, 1974), p.75.
40. Alfredo Rocco, 'Sulle associazioni segrete', pronounced in the Camera dei deputati, 16 May 1925 (not without polemicising with Gramsci), reprinted in Rocco (note 28), p.39.
41. Benito Mussolini, prefazione a Partito Nazionale Fascista, *Il Gran Consiglio nei primi cinque anni dell'era fascista* (Rome and Milano: Libreria del Littorio, 1927), p.xi, in Aquarone (note 21), p.17.
42. Martin Clark, *Modern Italy. 1871–1982* (London and New York: Longman, 1984, 1990), p.224.
43. Aquarone (note 21), pp.493–5, reproduces he text of the law, 9 December 1928 (n.2693, *Ordinamento e attribuzioni del Gran Consiglio del Fascismo*).
44. Giovanni Gentile, 'La legge del Gran Consiglio', *Educazione fascista* 9 (1928), pp.513–17, reprinted in Aquarone (note 21), pp.496–500.
45. Benito Mussolini, letter to Hitler, 5 January 1940, *I documenti diplomatici italiani*, Nona serie: 1939–43, Vol.III (Rome: Istituto Poligrafico e Zecca dello Stato, Libreria dello Stato, 1959), pp.21–2.
46. Mussolini, in the Senate, 30 March 1938, quoted in Emilio Faldella, *L'Italia e la*

Seconda Guerra Mondiale. Revisione di Guidizi (Bologna: Cappelli, 1967), p.61; see also Ceva (note 17), p.116.

47. Galeazzo Ciano, *Diary. 1939–1943*, ed. M. Muggeridge (London and Toronto: William Heinemann, 1950, 1960), pp.254–5, 256.
48. *I documenti diplomatici italiani*, Nona serie: 1939–43, Vol.IV (Rome: 1960), p.496.
49. Renzo De Felice, *Mussolini il duce. Lo Stato totalitario. 1936–1940* (Torino: Einaudi, 1981), p.809. The proclamation of 11 June 1940 was published in *Relazioni Internazionali*, 15 June 1940.
50. P. Puntoni, *Parla Vittorio Emanuele III* (Milano: A. Palazzi, 1958), pp.11–12, quoted in De Felice (note 49), pp.808–9; see also Ceva (note 17), p.116.

3

The Strategy of Fascist Italy: A Premise

LUCIO CEVA

If strategy means the use of a nation's armed forces to accomplish goals set by the political leader, then there can be no doubt that Fascist Italy possessed both characteristics: a political leader with goals and a military leader who would accomplish them. The fact that the same person was holding these two functions is a Fascist Italian peculiarity: on a *de facto* basis we can say this held true ever since October 1922. If the juridical figure of the political leader was still linked theoretically to the ancient model of the President of the Council of Ministers, and if this figure was not yet in charge of the armed forces, the role played by Mussolini in the Corfu expedition (August-September 1923) clearly shows who the actual decision maker was, both political and military.

On a *de jure* and *de facto* basis the tyranny was granted its juridical status in 1925–26. Then, the Head of the Government, Mussolini, became minister of the three armed forces; Royal Decree Law number 68 of 6 February 1927 granted him the power to decide on plans of campaign. The chief of staff could only make suggestions and act as a consultant.[1] If we ask ourselves what the nature of the political goals of the sole decision-maker was, we can state that they always had an aggressive character. In other words, they could only be accomplished by means of aggression, or at least by means of military occupations when the opponents decided not to fight. This held true for defence policy as well, since such an attitude was a perfect way of masking other aggressive projects.

As for the ways to accomplish these goals, they can effectively be grouped into four categories, although their characteristics easily intertwine and overlap:

- use of the Italian armed forces;
- actual, threatened or feared use of other countries' forces by means of foreign policy (alliances, alignments of convenience and so on);
- belief in the non-belligerent status of the chosen opponent;
- the bluff.

During the five different wars fought by the regime over the course of the Fascist period in Italy (the 'reconquest' of Libya, Ethiopia, Spain, Albania and, in 1940, intervention in the Second World War), reliance on Italian military force was almost total, at least in the case of four out of the five conflicts (the reconquest of Libya, and the wars in Ethiopia, Spain and Albania). This proved to be a common feature, even if marked by different characteristics.

The reconquest of Libya, begun by liberal Italy, was carried out while the other nations were not much interested in it. Some colonial powers were even satisfied with it, since it served as an example of the imposition of power which was useful to them. Accidental and superficial criticism of the Italian way of dealing with the reconquering of Libya (the use of chemical weapons and deportations, and the slaughtering of enemies), concerned only parts of public opinion and not governments charged with foreign policy responsibilites. The Ethiopian enterprise, meanwhile, is known to have two sides: the war aspect at first concerned the campaign against the Negus's armies (1935–36), but was swiftly followed by the fight against the indomitable rebellion (1936–41). Without discussing the war's technical and military dimensions, we may say that Italy confronted both events relying only on its own military force.

In the controversy with the League of Nations and, above all, Great Britain, Mussolini mixed military bluff with political blackmail. The British unwillingness to fight (despite the positive forecast of Britain's military chiefs about the eventual outcome of a Mediterranean conflict) depended upon broader political and strategic considerations, along with the hope of bringing Italy back into line with its Stresa commitments. Such reasons were made explicit in British diplomatic policy toward Italy, and also in confidential documents which were acquired by Italian military intelligence. All this confirmed Mussolini's political perceptions.[2] In other words, the British non-belligerent attitude was born out of the fear of threats on the part of Germany (and maybe Japan). Throughout this period, the components of this fascist cocktail never changed, even though the quantities varied. Examples of this were the alignment with Germany in January 1936, and the exploitation of the fear of democratic nations as a result of the German occupation of the Rhineland in March 1936. This event coincided with the Fascist victories over the Ethiopian army. It remains doubtful whether the Italian military bluff in the Mediterranean and Libya caused serious effects. Maybe the only temporary British concern was of the possibility that a 'mad dog' act by Mussolini could really affect the political calculations on which British forbearance was based.[3]

In the Spanish Civil War (1936–39), Italian military intervention was of considerable consequence, despite the Guadalajara affair and Mussolini's gradual subordination to Franco. Italian aid to Spain did not produce the hoped-for effect, but in the end it brought about victory. The democratic powers were prevented from intervening for two reasons. First, Britain (and France) were barely interested in maintaining the Spanish Republic's integrity. Second, Britain was so concerned about a potential escalation of the conflict that it even tolerated Italian submarine attacks against British ships. The British government feared that military intervention in the Mediterranean – as in the case of the Ethiopian crisis – would start a bigger conflict. British tolerance was encouraged by Mussolini's attitude. He seemed to be strongly supporting Germany with an overtly pro-Nazi policy (as epitomised by his proclamation of the Axis, adherence to the Anti-Comintern pact, visit to Germany in September 1937, acceptance of the *Anschluss*, and so on). On the other hand, he seemed to be trying to keep the balance of the *status quo* of the Mediterranean area by concluding the Gentleman's Agreement of 2 January 1937 and the Easter pact of 1938.

The last episode in which Italian military force alone took part was the occupation of Albania (April 1939), at which point the alliance with Germany was close to being signed (22 May 1939), and the second stage of the Czechoslovakian affair (15 March 1939) had brought about the break between Germany and the Western democratic nations. As for Italian intervention in June 1940, a series of factors must be taken into account. They are connected mostly with the inner character of the political and moral structure of the head of the Fascist government. Apart from periods of non-action and temporary changes of mind, the common feature of the *Duce*'s ambition is clearly characterised by his constant reiteration of the 'mutilated victory' myth. This theory was used by Fascism long before the March on Rome, and it was used again in the Fascist foreign policy programme after Mussolini had seized power (characterised, for instance, by the *Duce*'s speech of 16 November 1922, when he uttered the famous phrase '*do ut des*', 'treaties are not forever'). The same myth, used at the time of the Corfu crisis (1923) and in 1924 during general Cappello's secret mission to Germany, was more or less trumpeted continually until June 1940. Since Italy, in 1918, was one of the victorious if unsatisfied powers (hence the term 'mutilated victory'), hatred for the victorious and satisfied powers (Great Britain and France) was a natural consequence. So, too, was Mussolini's eventual alignment with a revisionist, National Socialist, Germany. However, long before Hitler's rise to power, and the breakdown in the European balance of power, Fascism was relying on Germany, and on the possibility of a European war.

These are the entries in the Dino Grandi (Foreign Minister, 1929–32) diary for 6 June, 24 June and 18 August 1930, and for 3 April 1931, in which Mussolini declares:

> We must wage war on France; but war must be prepared with diplomacy, weapons and the proper spirit ... Germany and Italy will, some day, be allied ... If we want the ultimate goal of our diplomatic action (Italian–German alliance) to be successful, it must be presented not as *a policy out of necessity* on our part – and this was, unfortunately, the case at the times of the Triple Alliance – but as *a policy out of our willingness* ... We shall be on Germany's side ...

The words of general Pietro Gazzera, War Minister at this time, are no less meaningful. After his talks with Mussolini of 11 June 1929, 30 May and 23 December 1930, and 22 July 1932, he wrote:

> Germany is unarmed. No negotiations for co-operation against France (Capello in 1924). In case of war, maybe Germany would be [on our side] against France, but now is unarmed ... We have the power to decide for war ... when [French] troops leave the Rhine on July 1st, we'll see what will happen in Germany. *It's a turning point* ... We must take into account a war against France and Yugoslavia within four or six years ... We

have already taken two steps toward Berlin, i.e. Budapest and
Vienna. We shall take the last one. But we must *give* unto
Germany, and not *be given*. We must be ... towing, not be towed
... We'll be at war between 1935 and 1936 ... Within four or five
years Germany will be ready to wage war on France ...[4]

After 1933, and in spite of Mussolini's occasional changes of mind
(as a consequence of the Dolfuss crisis in 1934 and Stresa), the pro-
German attitude was more and more constant and overt. On the
other hand, though, Mussolini was putting off German offers of a
military alliance. This might have been mainly due to Italy's trying to
gain space to undermine the Anglo–French coalition.[5]

A very important feature of this aggressive characteristic was the
attitude of Mussolini during the autumn 1938 crisis which gave way
to the unexpected, and temporary, Munich compromise. Hitler had
visited Rome in early May of that year. He fully intended to strike
against Czechoslovakia, and he had clear views about Fascist Italy, as
he confided to his aide, Colonel Rudolf Schmidt, a few days before his
visit. In short, Hitler argued, either Mussolini was satisfied with what
he had had up to now (in which case Czechoslovakia would be
postponed and the *Führer* would return from Rome with an 'empty
case'), or he did genuinely want his '*Imperium*' in Africa, which he
would not secure unless the Germans helped him. But, if he wanted
Berlin's aid, he would need to meet Hitler's requests, in which case the
German dictator would go back 'with Czechoslovakia in the bag'.[6]

The *Führer* was right. Even though Rome only hinted at
Czechoslovakia, and kept postponing the German proposal for a
military alliance, from the following August onwards Mussolini was
constantly, and overtly, supporting Germany's claims on
Czechoslovakia by assuring, both on a private and on a public basis,
that Italy would be on the Reich's side when the European war broke
out.[7] Now, since Chamberlain's offer of 28 September was
unexpected, and since Hitler on that very day rather surprisingly
accepted the (feigned) mediation of Mussolini, we may wonder
which tactic the *Duce* was relying on for his military intervention. It
must have been a mixture of two of the above-mentioned premises:
the belief in the non-belligerent, even decadent characteristics of the
democratic countries, and the exploitation of German power.
However, an Italian military intervention was never seriously taken
into consideration.[8]

Mussolini's reluctance to consider a military solution (Alberto Pariani, Domenico Cavagnari and Giuseppe Valle, respectively the army, navy and air chiefs, were summoned to Munich on 29 September, and then ordered not to come) seemed to last until January 1939 when, on the occasion of Chamberlain's and Halifax's visit to Rome, Ciano wrote in his diary:

> German rearmament is a burden to them [the English]. They would give everything they own to be able to see the future. Their determination has led me to favour a triple military alliance. It could get us what we want most. The English don't want to fight. They are withdrawing slowly, but they really don't want to fight.[9]

Did this attitude change between 1939 and 1940? What factors led to Mussolini's and Ciano's conclusion of the Pact of Steel on 22 May 1939, to the declaration of 'non-belligerency' on 7 September 1939, and then to Italian intervention on 10 June 1940?

With regard to foreign policy, it is worth noting the prolonging and the worsening of the ill-mannered treatment Hitler reserved for Mussolini in the most critical moments:

- he informed him of the *Anschluss* when it had already begun (12 March 1938);
- five months later, Hitler was not willing to tell Mussolini about how, and when, he would strike Czechoslovakia, when Mussolini insisted upon having news of it while letting Italy and the world know about his strong support for German military decisions;
- most of all, Hitler told Mussolini about the final *mainmise* on Prague (15–16 March 1939) when it had already been completed, thus destroying the Czechoslovakia that had been a product of Mussolini's public efforts at Munich (28 September 1938) and Vienna (3 November 1938).[10]

Even though all this worried Mussolini, he decided not to change his policies 'because we are not whores'. Therefore, he agreed to sign the Pact of Steel provided that he had Albania, and that Hitler assured him Germany had no interests in Croatia. The pact contained general provisos on mutual consultation (articles 1 and 2), which nonetheless did not provide against military intervention carried out in an automatic manner (article 3). The pact, however, did not contain any of the Fascist *desiderata*. No hints at postponing the war until 1942. No hints at 'crossing one's t's with regard to the mutual relations since the Germans are moving ... from a plan for power to a plan for imposition'.[11] This does not mean that Italy gave up its aggressive intentions in the short term. In a letter to Hitler of 30 May 1939, Mussolini reasserted Italy's need to postpone the eventual conflict, while at the same time urging his German counterpart that preparations for the war should begin in earnest. In the meantime, the intrigues with Croatian separatism to 'relocate' Yugoslavia went on, as well as proposals to Spain for a division of the French empire (Morocco to Spain, Tunisia and Algeria to Italy).[12]

As for domestic policy, there were worries among those sectors of Italy where Mussolini's domination was based on compromise: the crown and part of the armed forces, the Roman Catholic church, bourgeois public opinion and the industrial and financial côté. The negative feeling toward Germany on the part of the king, of some senior officers and of the middle-classes was reinforced by the feeling that Axis policy was only functioning on a one-way basis: Germany was the central power in Europe, while Italy was left with the Albanian scraps. Mussolini, helped by Achille Starace (the Fascist Party secretary, 1932–39), worsened the malcontent through little acts of arrogance which he defined as 'powerful blows to the stomach of the middle-class'. In other words, the institution of the *passo romano*, and the 'racial legislation' (accepted by the king, albeit with disgruntlement). These innovations were celebrated in Mussolini's 'semi-secret' speech of 25 October 1938 to the National Council of the Fascist Party.[13] The speech was followed by a document of 4 February 1939 announcing to the Grand Council that the 'march to the Ocean' (or, in other words, the total conquest of the Mediterranean area) was the ultimate goal of Italian foreign policy.[14]

At this point worries arose about the condition of Italian armaments and weaponry. Apart from unheeded warnings by Badoglio in January 1938,[15] how is it that the poor condition of the Fascist military apparatus was noticed only in the spring of 1939, and in particular during the crisis in August-September 1939 which led to the 'non belligerency' declaration? There were some who had noticed the risk run in September 1938. The limited mobilisation which the regime then cancelled following the Munich compromise had made it clear that the Italian army was in a pitiful state, and especially so after the campaigns in Ethiopia and Spain. The discontent and the worries had increased with the beginning of the mobilisation of the few trained troops needed for the Albanian invasion the following April.[16] On the other hand, the British had made it clear that they were about to intervene (mandatory conscription, rearmament, admonitions to Germany, 'guarantees' to Greece and Romania, a pact with Turkey). This, and Roosevelt's attitude, had, however, only slightly affected Mussolini, who was still convinced that the democracies had no real will to fight. Even when the possibility of war became more and more concrete, Mussolini still hoped that Italy could play an outward role. It was at this point that the 'non belligerency' policy came into play. In the winter of 1939–40 it was accompanied by Mussolini's fear of a German revenge for the September 'desertion', and by an Italian lack of confidence in Germany's eventual victory (even if this attitude was contradicted by private, bombastic declarations of confidence).[17] If this was not the case, it is difficult to understand why Mussolini, on 10 December 1939, ordered General Edoardo Monti to reinforce the German border with concrete and iron (which were both lacking at the time).[18] As a matter of fact, Mussolini himself, in a letter to Hitler dated 4 January 1940, wrote that he doubted Germany had any chance of winning the war.[19] All the same Mussolini went to the Brenner meeting of 18 March 1940 to confirm his support for Germany, and to reassert his intention to enter the war when he felt ready. As he told Ciano:

> I'll do as Bertoldo did. He accepted his sentence to death provided that they let him choose the tree to which he would be hanged. It goes without saying that he never found such a tree. I'll accept entering the war, but I'll be the one to choose when. I'll decide, and *much will depend on the outcome of the war* (my italics).[20]

Not 'much' but, on the contrary, everything depended on the outcome of the war (or, at least, on Mussolini's perception of it). After the peripheral German victory over Norway, the turning point occurred between 14 and 30 May 1940: the defeat of French troops in the Ardennes,[21] the Belgian capitulation, and the British withdrawal toward the English Channel. Mussolini then sent Hitler a letter stating that Italy would enter the war on 5 June (later postponed until 10 June at Hitler's personal request).[22] Maybe Mussolini – who realised how the imperialist war was, finally, crowning the path he chose on 28 October 1922 – thought that the

German victories were his last chance to appear as a victorious leader, thus reaching the climax of his political career.

The non-belligerency of the previous months had helped Mussolini to take his time, and to hide his aggressive policy toward the Balkan countries. When Ciano, on 13 August 1939, came back from Salzburg angered and disappointed by the German mistrust toward Italy, Mussolini welcomed him with soothing considerations about 'honour', and with his declaration that he wanted 'his share in Croatia and Dalmatia'.[23] Therefore, Badoglio and Pariani were ordered to prepare operations against Yugoslavia and Greece. The plot with Croatian separatism had been going on over the winter and the spring.[24] On 29 May 1940, when the news of Germany's western victories was spreading, Ciano used the following 'polite' words to the Yugoslavian ambassador, Cristich: 'When Italy entered the war against France and England, it would do it through the front door, rather than through the servants' back entrance'.[25]

The same meaning was to be found in the 'very secret' memorandum of 31 March 1940, which Mussolini sent to nine key Italian personalities (the king, Ciano, Badoglio, the three chiefs of staff, as well as to Teruzzi, Muti and Soddu), and which set out his general battle plan: Italy would be on the defensive apart from in eastern Africa toward Gibuti and Kenya, at sea, and perhaps in Yugoslavia.[26] This document must be seen as more than an official outline of a battle plan. It should be considered chiefly as the first step taken by the *Duce* in deprivng the king of his power over the armed forces.[27]

Things only changed with the memorandum of 29 May 1940 (followed by the letter to Hitler of 30 May):

> I think the situation [of the army] is not ideal. Nonetheless, it is satisfactory. As a matter of fact, a delay of two weeks or a month would not be an improvement, and Germany could think we have entered the war when the risk is very small ... And this could be a burden on us when peace comes.[28]

Indeed, Badoglio recalled that in a conversation allegedly on 26 May 1940, Mussolini stated, 'I need a few thousand dead to take part in peace talks as a real belligerent'.[29] The situation seemed to justify a total reliance on German power, even greater than that of September 1938.

It is worth trying to understand the true reason why Mussolini expended such significant sums between 1935 and 1940 (116 bn lire)[30] in order to provide Italy with a modern fleet, a large air force (even though its aircraft were antiquated after 1937–38) and new weapons.[31] It was due to the Fascist inclination to compromise, and to the need to be deferential to the only powers which could have overthrown Mussolini. That is, the armed forces, the ruling dynasty and the industrial élite. Of course, wars and expeditions actually based on Italian military force had been very expensive, even if the weapons from the 1915–18 war were enough to overcome the Libyan *mugiahidin*, the Ethiopian armies and the militiamen of the Spanish Republic (although on that occasion troops were aided by modern aircraft). Nonetheless, Mussolini did not relinquish all hope of providing his armed forces with weapons suitable enough to enable them to challenge much stronger opponents. But, in doing this, Fascism – despite its totalitarian mask – had to be careful not to hurt the vested interests of the three military services, and of the war industries. From 1923 onwards a complex machinery for 'civilian mobilisation' had given the nation a strong, and complicated bureacracy that allowed Italian industry to provide its armed forces only with what it wanted, and according to the conditions it favoured. So, the three military services could develop independently. Moreover, the new cumbersome 'civilian mobilisation' organisation allowed many of Italy's unemployed to get a job.

This explains why the army had been satisfied for so long with the 'number = power' thesis, instead of electing to increase power through mobility. The same holds true for the preference accorded, in autumn 1938, to a total, last minute (and more profitable) renewal of the artillery, instead of a gradual improvement of the existing weaponry. This choice met with the approval of the industrial sector owing to a substantial advance payment of around 15 per cent of the total cost.[32]

The same considerations are valid for the increase in air force strength, which had no real military value. Starting from 1927, the choice of new aircraft was no longer made by the most appropriate scientific body – the air force's own engineers – but by new bodies appointed by the minister on the basis of personal interests.[33] Meanwhile, the navy was a case on its own. Its development in the years 1920–30 in terms of cruisers, small craft and battleships had seen a decrease in the level of safety and quality, even though they were faster craft (theoretically, at least). But, most of all (and Italy is alleged to be the only nation to have done so), industries were allowed to practise the huge tolerance (1 per cent) on the weight of ordnance which, as a matter of fact, nullified the military power of the navy. This is why, during three years of war in the Mediterranean, no enemy ship was hit by Italian high-calibre shells.[34]

It is pointless to debate whether Mussolini, in 1940, had to pass off as 'false' to the king a war which he desired to be real, as MacGregor Knox argues, or if he opted, according to Renzo De Felice, for an outward show of military intervention based on his political interests.[35] By now, no real aggressive intervention was possible. This was not due to the actual poverty of the nation, but, rather, to personal interests and corruption over the whole Fascist period. Most probably, had the German victories been understood as non-definitive, there would have been no Italian intervention. Fascist policy – and of course its military consequences – had undergone different, opportunistic shifts. Very often, although not always, it had been an attempt to gain the favour of public opinion on a day-to-day basis. At its heart the lethal combination of revisionism with racism in the later 1930s was bound to lead to an alliance with Nazi Germany. Therefore, the conclusion of June 1940 was no real surprise at all.[36] It can only be said that Mussolini was a prisoner of his personal coherence, and that he gave up the nation to comply with his brutal proclivities and connivance. After June 1940 his private anti-German outbursts represented his ever growing awareness that Italy was to expect one of two possible outcomes of the war: either being defeated or being put aside.[37]

Moreover, the *Duce* and his military chiefs were to blame because they did not understand (or because they understood too late) that taking advantage of the victories of one's allies was not so simple. They could not hope to get something without obtaining at least an external and temporary victory. And they should have known that a totally defensive policy could not have helped them achieve this. A more rational use of the Italian military apparatus could not have led to victory. At the very least, though, it might have won Italy greater respect from its opponents. What is more, a wiser political and military leader would have prevented so many dramatic events which heaped discredit on the nation, such as the disastrous war against Greece. These are minor matters though. The fact remains that the *Duce* had led Italy into a war which it could never have won. Mussolini was desperately seeking an ally who had the same moral and ideological characteristics as Fascism. Luckily, neither Fascism nor Nazism won the war.

NOTES

1. Fortunato Minniti, 'Profilo dell'iniziativa strategica italiana dalla non belligeranza alla guerra parallela', *Storia Contemporanea* 6 (1987), pp.1123–34; Lucio Ceva, 'Aspetti politici e giuridici dell'Alto Comando in Italia (1848–1941)', *Il Politico* 1 (1984), pp.110–15, and 'Pianificazione militare e politica estera dell'Italia fascista 1923–1940', *Italia Contemporanea* 220–221 (2000), pp.281–92.

2. See Arthur Marder, 'The Royal Navy and the Ethiopian Crisis of 1935–36', *The American Historical Review* 5 (1970), pp.1337 (n.30), 1334, 1339 (n.34), 1344 (n.39); Ministero degli Affari Esteri (ed.), *Documenti Diplomatici Italiani (DDI)* Series VIII, Vol.2, No.166, p.149; Manfred Funke, *Sanzioni e cannoni. Hitler, Mussolini e il conflitto etiopico* (Bari: Laterza, 1972; 1st edn. 1970); Jens Petersen, *Hitler e Mussolini. La difficile alleanza* (Bari: Laterza, 1975; 1st edn. 1973); Renato Mori, *Mussolini e la conquista dell'Etiopia* (Firenze: Lemonnier, 1978), p.100ff and passim; Robert Mallett, 'The Italian Naval High Command and the Mediterranean Crisis, January–October 1935', *The Journal of Strategic Studies* 4 (1999), pp.77–102; Brian R. Sullivan, 'The Impatient Cat: Assessments of Military Power in Fascist Italy, 1936–1940', in W. Murray and A. Millett (eds.) *Calculations. Net Assessment and the Coming of World War II* (New York: Free Press, 1992), pp.97–133; Brian R. Sullivan, 'More than meets the eye: The Ethiopian War and the Origins of the Second World War', in G. Martel (ed.), *The Origins of the Second World War Reconsidered, Second Edition: A. J. P. Taylor and the Historians* (London and New York: Routledge, 1999), pp.178–203.

3. Fortunato Minniti, *Fino alla guerra. Strategie e conflitto nella politica di potenza di Mussolini 1923–1940* (Napoli: ESI, 2000), pp.123–40.

4. 'Diario Grandi' and 'Carte Gàzzera', quoted in B. MacGregor Knox, 'The Fascist Regime. Its Foreign Policy and its Wars: An 'Anti-Anti-Fascist' Orthodoxy?', *Contemporary European History* 3 (1995), pp.347–65. My warmest thanks to MacGregor Knox for copies of these documents.

5. Brian R. Sullivan, *'Where One Man, and Only One Man, led'. Italy's Path from Non-Alignment to non Belligerancy to War 1937–1940*, forthcoming. Once more my hearty thanks to Brian R. Sullivan for his valuable uninterrupted advice.

6. *Documents on German Foreign Policy (DGFP)*, Series D, Vol.II, No.132 (London: HMSO, 1950), pp.238–9.

7. G. Bruce Strang, 'War and Peace: Mussolini's Road to Munich', *Diplomacy and Statecraft* 3 (1999); G. Ciano, *Diario 1937–1943* (Milano: Rizzoli, 1980), 6, 22, 23, 25–28, 31 May, 3 June, 19, 20, 24, 29 August, 2–28 September 1938; Williamson Murray, *The Change in the European Balance of Power 1938–1939. The Path to Ruin* (Princeton NJ: Princeton University Press, 1984).

8. Minniti (note 3), pp.169–72.

9. Ciano (note 7), 12 January 1939.

10. 'Arbitrato di Vienna' (Czechoslovakia–Hungary).

11. Ciano (note 7), 15–22 March, 6–7 May 1939.

12. Ibid., 9–21 March, 5 April, 2 May, 14 June 1939.

13. All this was called 'Cultural Fascist Revolution' by Renzo De Felice, *Mussolini il duce*, Vol.2, *Lo stato totalitario 1936–1940* (Torino: Einaudi, 1981), pp.100–5, 537.

14. Benito Mussolini, *Opera Omnia* (Firenze and Roma: La Fenice, 1951–80) Vol.47, pp.151–7; see also William Deakin, *The Brutal Friendship. Mussolini, Hitler and the Fall of Italian Fascism* (New York: Harper and Row, 1962), pp.5–6; B. MacGregor Knox, *Mussolini Unleashed 1939–1941* (Cambridge: Cambridge University Press, 1982), p.40.

15. See Lucio Ceva, 'Un intervento di Badoglio e il mancato rinnovamento delle artiglierie italiane', *Il Risorgimento* (Milano) 2 (1976); Ciano (note 7), 29 April, 2 May 1939.

16. Ciano (note 7), 4, 8, 29 April 1939.

17. Ibid., 2, 4, 7, 9 September, 7, 9, 25 October, 9, 21 December 1939; 1, 5, 11, 22, 23 January, 1, 7–9, 26, 28–29 February, 4, 8, 10–12, 23, 26, 28, 31 March, 2, 6, 9–11, 20, 28 April, 3, 10, 13, 18, 21 May 1940.
18. Knox (note 14), pp.61, 315 (n.78); see also letter from Ciano to Dino Alfieri, 6 October 1941, in Ciano, L'Europa verso la catastrofe (Milano: Mondadori, 1948), p.677.
19. Ministero degli Affari Esteri (note 2), Series IX, Vol.3, No.33, pp.19–22.
20. Ciano (note 7), 16 March 1940.
21. Francesco Pricolo, La regia aeronautica nella seconda guerra mondiale (Milano: Longanesi, 1971), pp.194–5.
22. Ministero degli Affari Esteri (note 2), Series IX, Vol.4, No.646, p.500, and No.680, pp.519–21.
23. Ciano (note 7), 13 August 1939.
24. Ciano (note 7), 12 October 1939; 21 January, 9 April, 3, 10 May 1940. See also Brian R. Sullivan, 'The Balkans: Or What Is Past, or Passing, or to Come', in W. Murray (ed.), The Emerging Strategic Environement. Challenges of the Twenty First Century (London and Westport, CT, 1999).
25. Quoted in Knox (note 14), p.102 (from German documents).
26. Minniti (note 3), pp.211–14, 103–5.
27. Lucio Ceva, 'Vertici politici e militari nel 1940–1943. Interrogativi e temi d'indagine', Il Politico 4 (1981), p.692.
28. Ufficio Storico dello S.M. Esercito (USSME), La preparazione del conflitto e l'avanzata fino a Sidi el Barrani (Roma: Tip. Regionale, 1955), encl.13.
29. Pietro Badoglio, L'Italia nella seconda guerra mondiale (Milano: Mondadori, 1946), p.37.
30. 77 bn of this amount for Ethiopia, Spain and Albania. See Brian R. Sullivan, 'The Italian Armed Forces 1918–1940', in A.R. Millett and W. Murray (eds.), Military Effectiveness, Vol.II, The Interwar Period (Boston: Allen & Unwin, 1988), p.171.
31. Lucio Ceva, 'L'evoluzione dei materiali bellici in Italia', in E. Di Nolfo, R.H. Rainero and B. Vigezzi (eds.), L'Italia e la politica di potenza in Europa (1938–1940) (Milano: Marzorati, 1985).
32. Fortunato Minniti, 'Due anni di attività del Fabbriguerra per la produzione bellica', Storia contemporanea 4 (1975); 'Aspetti organizzativi del controllo della produzione bellica in Italia (1923–1943)', Clio 4 (1977); 'Aspetti territoriali e politici del controllo della produzione bellica in Italia', Clio 1 (1979); 'Le materie prime nella produzione bellica in Italia (1935–1943)' (parts I and II), Storia contemporanea 1 and 2 (1986). Lucio Ceva, 'Grande Industria e guerra', in Commissione italiana di storia militare (ed.), L'Italia in guerra, il primo anno 1940 (Roma 1990), pp.33–53; entry on Carlo Favagrossa, Dizionario biografico degli Italiani (Roma: Istituto dell'Enciclopedia Italiana, 1996); 'Prime riflessioni sulla guerra italiana. Interpretazioni, testimonianze e apologie 1945–1946', Italia Contemporanea 213 (1998); Lucio Ceva and Andrea Curami, 'Industria bellica e stato nell'imperialismo fascista degli anni '30', Nuova Antologia 2167 (1988).
33. See Italo Balbo, Sette anni di politica aeronautica (Milano: Mondadori, 1935), pp.22–5; Lucio Ceva, 'Le guerre degli anni Trenta. L'aeronautica italo-fascista nella guerra civile spagnola (1936–1939)', forthcoming.
34. Lucio Ceva, 'Gli ultimi anni dell'Ansaldo privata', Nuova Antologia 2212 (1999), pp.103–15; 'La gestione Cavallero 1929–1933', in G. De Rosa (ed.), Storia dell'Ansaldo, Vol.VI (Roma and Bari: Laterza, 1999), pp.30–5; Erminio Bagnasco, Le armi delle navi italiane nella seconda guerra mondiale (Parma: Albertelli, 1978).
35. Knox (note 14); 'L'ultima guerra dell'Italia fascista', in Bruna Micheletti and Pier Paolo Poggio (eds.), L'italia in guerra 1940–43 (Brescia: Annali della Fondazione 'Luigi Micheletti', 1990–91); Minniti (note 1), pp.1171, 1173–86; Minniti (note 3), pp.224–33 and passim.

36. See the masterly analysis of Mario Donosti (Luciolli), *Mussolini e l'Europa. La politica estera fascista* (Roma: Leonardo, 1945) pp.79, 103, 212–13, 226 and passim.
37. Ciano (note 7), 6 September, 8, 12 October 1940; 27 April, 3, 13, 31 May, 6, 10, 13, 29, 30 June, 1, 6–7, 13, 20 July, 25–27 September, 4, 6, 10, 13, 15 October, 3, 6 November, 20 December 1941; 6, 12–13, 25 January, 20 February, 11, 24 March, 1, 11, 19, 24 April, 21, 24 July, 29 August, 6 November 1942; 20, 22 January, 5, 8 February 1943.

4

Mussolini, Franco and the Spanish Civil War: An Afterthought

MORTEN HEIBERG

Today we have acquired some knowledge about Fascist Italy's intervention in the Spanish Civil War. This is due mostly to the American historian John Coverdale, who, 25 years ago, published his pioneering study *Italian Intervention in the Spanish Civil War.*[1] This book has influenced a generation of historians interested in the international aspects of the Spanish conflict. Particularly interesting is Renzo De Felice's 1981 study of the political aspects of the Italian intervention in the civil war.[2] Now, with more documents available from Italian and Spanish archives, perhaps the time has come to consider these and other works on Italian intervention in Spain. On the basis of fresh documents, this article briefly analyses two key aspects of this critical historical event. That is to say, it focuses on the Italian decision to send combat 'volunteers' to Spain, and on the so-called 'fascistisation' of Spain; in other words, on Italian attempts to make Nationalist Spain a fascist state. Both aspects are important for our understanding of the motives behind Italian intervention.

Italian Military Intervention (Autumn 1936)

The main argument of Coverdale's well-grounded study is that Mussolini's policy toward Spain was based on traditional political and strategic considerations, rather than on ideological reasons. Through armed intervention Mussolini – Coverdale maintains – tried to prevent the balance in the western Mediterranean area from being altered. In short, Mussolini tried to avoid an alliance between a left-wing France and Republican Spain. Such an alliance might have helped the French to manage their imperial territories in northern Africa, and to use Spanish bases in case of armed conflict against Italy. It was a defensive policy which according to Coverdale resembled traditional pre-Fascist Italian foreign policy.[3]

Over the last 15 years, historians have begun to question Coverdale's book. After Italy's military archives were partially opened to the public in the 1990s, his military and strategic considerations have been put to the test. Important official military studies, and some contributions by Lucio Ceva, have underlined some of the limitations in Coverdale's work. And it was Ismael Saz and Paul Preston who actually questioned the American historian's reconstruction of Mussolini's sudden decision to support Franco in July 1936.[4]

As for the reasons behind Italian foreign policy, Coverdale's arguments have been seldom questioned – and, when questioned, such questioning was rarely based on archival research. De Felice agreed with Coverdale's argument, and used it as a basis for one of the chapters of his biography on Mussolini. This may have induced many historians to consider it as trustworthy. Accordingly, Gianluca Andrè noted in 1986: 'Coverdale's argument, which De Felice has adopted after filtering it, is convincing'.[5] De Felice, Andrè and, more recently, the military historians Alberto Rovighi and Filippo Stefani maintain that in late October or at the beginning of November 1936 Mussolini began to consider the possibility of large-scale Italian military intervention. The so-called 'shift' in Italian policy is alleged to have been born out of the changed military situation. The Nationalists were disadvantaged because they failed to capture Madrid, and because the Russians were supporting the Republic militarily. Many historians have agreed on this fact. As an American scholar has recently pointed out, the Italian decision should thus be regarded as a *counter-escalation*, that is, a reaction against the Soviet decision to stir up the conflict by sending troops and weapons to Spain to support the Republic.[6] In addition, Rovighi and Stefani also point out that Italy watched with some concern the fast-growing German military presence in Spain.[7]

Brian Sullivan is one of the few historians who has actually pointed out that these arguments, albeit substantially correct, perhaps fail to interpret the Italian intervention in relation to the overall strategy of Fascist foreign policy, which was experiencing a dramatic change in this period:

Without rejecting entirely this explanation of Mussolini's increasing aid to the Nationalists, it undervalues other strategic, foreign policy, and political issues influencing his policy toward Spain. By the early fall of 1936, arguments over Italian involvement in the Spanish conflict had divided Mussolini's military advisers. In part, these arguments reflected fundamental disagreements over the wisdom of a major shift in Italian foreign policy toward cooperation with Germany against Britain and France, a policy openly favoured by Ciano and increasingly attractive to his father-in-law. By late August, Mussolini already had begun to coordinate with Hitler their aid to the Nationalists. The increases in Italian involvement in Spain strongly indicate an increasingly pro-German, anti-French foreign policy and the growing possibility of an eventual alliance with the Germans against the West.[8]

Combined research in Italian and Spanish archives cannot but confirm this assumption. Fresh documents actually cause us to think that Mussolini might have already planned massive intervention in September 1936. An Italian note of 27 September reads that it was actually the trustee of the Spanish rebels in Rome, Antonio Magaz, who, 'in the name of the government of Burgos',[9] urged the Italian government to send voluntary troops to Spain led by General Ezio Garibaldi. According to a secret political report by Magaz, at least 20,000 volunteers were expected to leave. Another Italian note reads that Garibaldi accepted leadership of the expeditionary force only if the *Duce* himself appointed him. A report saying that the *Servizio Informazioni Militari* (SIM, Military Intelligence Service) should 'be ascertaining' the requests of the Spanish government, was endorsed by the following handwritten, unsigned remark: 'the news is valid and the expedition will be allowed'. Magaz maintains that Garibaldi accepted the task of organising the expedition during a meeting with Mussolini. Nonetheless, on 1 October Garibaldi was notified that 'due to the current situation, it is advisable that the expedition should not be organised'. Four days later, Magaz reported to his Spanish companions that 'though the Garibaldi expedition has already been planned, it must be delayed due to unpredicted difficulties'. On 9 October, Magaz announced that, 'if General Franco thinks the Garibaldi expedition is necessary, it will be reconsidered'. The following day, in order to avoid Russian and British opprobrium,

Franco recommended that the expedition should not be organised. A telegram of 23 September from the Italian consul in Tangier, Pier Filippo De Rossi, to the Italian foreign minister, Ciano, shows that Franco already knew about the Garibaldi expedition. De Rossi revealed that Franco did not want to start negotiations unless the Fascist government approved the plan. Mussolini read the telegram. Therefore, it is unthinkable that the subsequent approval and dropping of the plan, which both Magaz and Italian documents mention, took place without Mussolini's direct participation. It might be that Mussolini approved of the expedition in late September only later to reject it. In so doing, he may have tried to avoid complications in Spanish and European politics.[10]

With the purpose of providing support for his thesis that a significant increase of Italian intervention had a sudden and improvised nature to it, De Felice has pointed out that until December Franco never asked Mussolini to send troops, and that the decision was taken without consulting Franco.[11] But, the question was more complex. According to Italian documents, in September Magaz is alleged to have acted in the name of 'the government of Burgos'. Nevertheless, we cannot be certain that it was Franco who pressed for Italian intervention. It is certain, however, that on 20 September, a Spanish diplomat quoted Franco as saying that Mussolini 'had promised' him strong support.[12] This pressure dated back to the days during which the leadership of the Nationalist zone still had to be decided. After his election, Franco's ideas might have changed radically. It is likely that the *Generalísimo* was of the opinion that his domestic leadership could be endangered, at this point, by a heavy foreign presence in what amounted to a Nationalist uprising. Perhaps this appears a more credible explanation than the alleged fear of the immediate British intervention he mentioned in the telegram of 10 October. Franco might also have changed his mind, as it was in those particular days that he slowed down the pace of the war to buy more time to secure his own political position. Instead of taking Madrid, ending the war, and having to deal with numerous political enemies, he chose to conquer Toledo in late September, an easy but prestigious victory. Seen in the light of this much-discussed thesis, put forward by Paul Preston, the potential influx of Italian soldiers might have endangered his plan.[13]

It appears that the first plans for Italian intervention in the conflict dated back to 22–23 September, if not before. With regard to Italy's motive for entering the conflict at this point, it is important to stress that in September the possibilities for ending the war quickly were much greater than in November-December, at which point the military situation appeared much more compromised. One might also have doubts about the nature of the alleged '*svolta*', or shift in Italian foreign policy, in November. The intervention plans of November-December were essentially the same as those of September: divisions of Italian combat troops to be sent to Spain under the command of an Italian general. It does not seem that the *Duce* was unwillingly dragged into the conflict. The sources analysed above, rather, give the impression that Mussolini, to some extent pushed by the inner cabinet members at the *Palazzo Chigi*, the Italian foreign ministry, was waiting for the right moment to have his share of the battle in Spain. Probably, it was fear of political complications that blocked the initial project of sending 20,000 men to Spain under Garibaldi's leadership. Perhaps, as suggested by Magaz, it was Cavagnari, or other important military advisers, who influenced Mussolini towards a more prudent position:

> no difficulties were foreseen in the Ministry of Foreign Affairs. However, a few days later, without any new clouds appearing on the international sky, which was already quite dark, they told me that due to international complications the expedition had been called off. Why not think that the Ministry of the Navy ['*La Marina*'], who was to be responsible for the important sea transport, also on this occasion feared international complications?[14]

Magaz's version, in this respect, seems credible, as such ministerial disagreements increased after Italy's rapprochement with Germany.

Was the Garibaldi plan a way of countering the increasing Russian military presence in Spain? The exact date of the increase in Russian military aid has been much debated. In August, the Soviet involvement was, undoubtedly, negligible. In my view, the increase of the Soviet commitment is more likely to have occurred some time after the creation of the Largo Caballero Cabinet on 4 September. Fresh Soviet sources, provided by the two Spanish historians Elorza and Bizcarrondo, indicate that in early September the decision was still that of not interfering unnecessarily in the conflict. Only increased fascist aid could make the Russians alter their position.[15] Elorza and Bizcarrondo argue that the decision to create the

International Brigades was not made until 18 September, around the time of the Garibaldi plan.[16] This indicates a certain parallelism in the Italian and Soviet assessments on the need to intervene in Spain. The Russian accusations against the fascist aggressors in the Non-Intervention Committee in London, which met for the first time on 9 September, might have prompted Mussolini and his inner cabinet toward more radical measures. Still, the bulletins from the Italian *chargé d'affaires* in Moscow, Vincenzo Berardis, in August and September all stress that behind the hardening of the Soviet position, Russian foreign policy was driven by the desire to reach agreements with Paris and London, and to avoid conflict with Italy (*'non inimicarsi l'Italia'*).[17] Nonetheless, it is difficult to say what value Mussolini might have attached to Berardis's reports.

Probably, one should also consider Mussolini's increasing determination to challenge London and Paris over the Spanish question. On 5 September, Mussolini informed Grandi that he 'should not even concede the minimum requests put forward by Great Britain (and France)'.[18] Mussolini was furious, as he had observed 'anti-Italian' trends in British policy: George V had avoided visiting Italy on his tour of the Mediterranean, and the Italian language had been suppressed at Malta, just as Britain had agreed on an anti-Italian protocol with Egypt.[19] In Robert Mallett's view, Mussolini's reasons for writing to Grandi 'were clearly not governed by a mere desire for spiteful reciprocity. On the contrary, the *Duce* seemed determined to use the excuse that London now threatened to encircle Italy as a means of thwarting Anglo-French attempts at blocking Italo-German aid to the Nationalist armies in Spain'.[20]

Apart from the excuse provided by British 'anti-Italian' trends, there was probably also an anti-communist motive to Mussolini's reasoning. Mussolini's disgust at the Republic in Spain can only have increased after the creation of a cabinet headed by the socialist leader Largo Caballero, the 'Spanish Lenin'. It is likely, at this point, that Mussolini was convinced of the prophetic nature of the unpublished aphorisms on Republican Spain he had written back in 1931. In them he had predicted that the Spanish Republic, like liberal republics in general, would inevitably lead to communism. Perhaps, Caballero's entrance on the political scene convinced Mussolini that the moment for concrete action had come.

Having said that, it is important to stress that anti-communism might also have been a perfect disguise for expanding Italian influence in the western Mediterranean. In the autumn of 1936, Ciano mentioned the strategic objectives of Fascist policy in the western Mediterranean: Ceuta and the Balearic Islands. He also referred to Spain as an 'extension of the Axis toward the Atlantic Ocean'.[21] Mussolini, too, was optimistic: 'The Balearics are in our hands', he declared to the *Gran Consiglio* on 18 December.[22] Perhaps MacGregor Knox has a point, when he claims that in autumn 1936, 'Mussolini, Ciano and the Germans, to mask the expansionism of the Axis, raised the anti-Bolshevist flag'.[23]

In sum, Italy was willing to send troops to Spain as early as September. This means that the Fascist government approved of the intervention in a context totally different from that of November-December, when the military situation worsened. The final intervention was, apparently, a mere re-thinking of an existing plan. Mussolini did not approve of intervention simply out of fear of Soviet aid to the Republic. Neither does the 'defensive', 'traditional' and 'anti-French' foreign policy line, suggested by Coverdale and De Felice, seem a fully satisfying explanation. Research by an increasing number of scholars seems more accurate in interpreting Fascist foreign policy and military strategy toward Spain as much more aggressive than pre-Fascist Liberal foreign policy. Reliable English sources quoted by Paul Preston state that in May 1937, after the Italian defeat at Guadalajara, Mussolini was inclined officially to declare war on the Spanish Republic, thinking it the only way to enforce his military presence.

Fascistisation

Perhaps Mussolini's own declarations on 'fascistisation' are a good starting point for the second part of this discussion. In 1932, Mussolini put his revolutionary ideas forward in a speech addressed to a fanatical crowd in Milan:

> I tell you, immense crowds, that the twentieth century is going to be the century of Fascism, it is going to be the century of Italian power, it is going to be the century in which Italy returns for the third time to become the leader of human civilisation ... In ten years, one may say without wanting to act as prophets that Europe will be changed ... In ten years Europe will be fascist or fascistised! The antithesis in which the contemporary

civilisation is writhing can only be resolved in one way, with the doctrine and wisdom of Rome.[24]

Accordingly, we might ask if Mussolini had any concrete plans to make Spain fascist. In the revised Italian edition of his study (which includes a wider range of documents), Coverdale claimed:

> Fascist ideological aims were more negative than positive. Mussolini was more concerned with the triumph of the revolution of the Spanish Left than with promoting fascism in Spain. Apart from the events which followed the 1937 Farinacci expedition, nothing was made to convince Spanish Nationalists to follow the fascist model ... [The intervention] demonstrates that the traditional characteristics of Spanish foreign politics – based on prestige and force – and the negative ideological aim to avoid the defeat of the political forces with which [Mussolini] had got involved proved stronger than the will to promote fascism ...[25]

Coverdale also maintains that Franco united the various political factions of the Nationalist movement without consulting his supporters, Germany and Italy. De Felice fully agreed on this point. He even went as far as to state that, 'it cannot be proved that, during the first period of war, the Italian attitude was influenced by short-term plans to make a fascist dictatorship of Spain'.[26]

De Felice is probably right when he claims that Mussolini knew it would be difficult to impose fascism in Spain, provided that by this De Felice meant a fascist regime identical to the Italian one. One might argue, though, that De Felice hereby ignores an important aspect of Mussolini's foreign policy, namely that he actively promoted fascism in different countries, and that he was fully aware that this *'fascismo d'esportazione'* always had to adapt to the politics, culture and religion of those countries. He thought that an aggressive foreign policy might have helped to influence the political parties of the Right and the regimes of other nations, so that they might have institutions similar to Italian Fascism. As Saz has pointed out, Mussolini was convinced that it was possible for such regimes to achieve an external appearance, and, in time, move from this 'container' to the 'content', namely fascism.[27]

We may start with the case of Ernesto Giménez Caballero, to whose missions not many historians have paid attention. Caballero was a talented Spanish writer, and an aide to the *Comitati d'Azione per la Universalità di Roma* (CAUR – Action Committees for the Universality of Rome) in Spain. On 27 September 1936, he requested an audience with Mussolini to 'get back to Spain, fight for the triumph of Spanish fascism which I foresaw ten years ago ... Long live the *Duce*. Long live Roman Spain'. He did meet Mussolini on 7 October in Palazzo Venezia, where he met him again on the following day. We do not know what they talked about, but the events which followed make us think that the role of fascism in Franco's Spain was at stake. And maybe Mussolini gave Giménez Caballero special instructions. They met again on 22 January 1937. Before analysing this meeting, it is important to stress what happened between January 1937 and 19 April 1937, the day that saw the decree on the unification of the Spanish political parties. Through the Italian press attaché in Salamanca, Guglielmo Danzi, who was in reality a secret agent with direct access to the *Generalísimo*, Mussolini urged that Franco should unite the different political parties into a single one. On 18 April, Danzi wrote to Rome: 'Tonight I met General Franco at the Headquarters and together we planned the union of the parties into a single one led by General Franco'. Giménez Caballero and Franco's brother-in-law, Serrano Suñer (the *éminence grise* of the new regime) are alleged to have written the Spanish text of the decree.

On April 24 Giménez Caballero wrote to Mussolini to inform him that he had carried out the mission he had personally appointed him to 'on January 22 at 7 pm'. Such a mission implied 'to work hard trusting in the final triumph of fascism'. Moreover, Caballero had to urge that Franco should unite the different parties along the guidelines of Italian Fascism. Proud to have written most of the text of the decree and of Franco's speech, Caballero informed Mussolini that he had not only 'reported' his task to Franco, but also 'carried it out'. In a letter of 19 April, the ambassador Roberto Cantalupo, back in Rome, pointed out that the pro-Falangist version of Franco's speech was new. He also wrote that, as he had previously stated, Franco had probably 'been ordered to report' to Mussolini, who had imposed his 'political battle plan' on him. As a matter of fact, we cannot really say that Franco was ordered to report. Nonetheless, we can argue that the *Unificación* took place mainly because Franco needed to control the different political parties, including the original *Falange*. Still, we should not underestimate Mussolini's determination to 'fascistise' Spain by playing an important role in the foundation of the new state.[28] Spanish interest in following Rome's suggestions (*'le linee segnate dal Duce'*) and in installing a fascistic regime (*'tipo fascista'*) is furthermore confirmed by numerous documents published by the Italian foreign ministry in 1993–94.[29]

Projects to create a 'Roman Spain' – as Caballero called it – continued throughout the summer of 1937. On 10 June, Caballero informed the *Duce* that he was back in Rome pretending to visit his family. As a matter of fact, he wrote to Mussolini, 'I have to talk to you, sir, in secret. Salamanca need not know of our meeting'.[30] He met Mussolini two days later, but no one knows what they discussed. According to the way Mussolini was treating the Spanish ambassador in Rome, we may suppose that he was using Caballero to urge that Franco should form a new government on the anniversary of the rebellion.[31] On 4 August 1937, Franco signed the *Falange* statutes and he was granted full powers. When Mussolini was informed that Franco had taken his advice, he wrote, 'one party, one militia, one syndicate. These are the foundations of the great Spain of tomorrow'.[32] Therefore, the Danzi, Farinacci and Caballero missions were clearly the means through which Mussolini pressed for Franco's introduction of a fascist-like political system. Yet De Felice considered the mission by Roberto Farinacci (who in a conversation with Franco in the beginning of March 1937 urged for the creation of a 'Spanish National Party') an exception promoted exclusively by the Italian Fascist Party, the PNF.[33] In my view, this mission was merely one of a series of intiatives to fascistise Spain promoted by Mussolini and the *Palazzo Chigi*. It thus seems increasingly difficult to maintain, as De Felice and Coverdale have done, that Mussolini's attitude was exclusively based on a sort of 'hands-off policy'. True, after the embarrassing Italian defeat at Guadalajara in March 1937, Mussolini could no longer treat Franco as a mere subordinate, as he now depended on the *Generalísimo*'s support if he wanted a quick victory that could wipe out the *'brutta figura'* his troops had cut. Still, this fact does not seem to have stopped him from trying energetically to secure a fascistisation of the New Spain through both secret and open initiatives.

Franco created the new Spanish government in January 1938. The Italians pressured for some pro-Italian members of the government to be appointed, among these, Serrano Suñer (secretary of state). Moreover, documents point out that many Nationalists found the co-operation with Italy convenient, since Spain lacked actual models and solutions to build a new society. It is well-known that the *Fuero del Trabajo*, a statute-like document for the rights of the working-class similar to the Italian *Carta del Lavoro*, followed Italian models. The very name *Fuero* was introduced to substitute the *Carta* just before the document was approved.[34] Italian Fascism seemingly influenced the Spanish school system as well. Another memorandum pointed out that the Spanish minister of education 'has shown the desire to exalt Italian education. A number of requests have been approved: the presence of Italian technical staff, teaching of Italian in Spanish schools, University training programmes for teachers, Italian staff teaching in Spanish universities ...'. Two hundred Spanish primary school teachers attended programmes on Fascist educational systems. Representatives of the *Falange* were sent to Italy to study the Italian Fascist administrative system.[35] Italian initiatives were not aimed solely to justify the support given to an authoritarian and conservative regime. They confirm as well Mussolini's determimation that Spain should follow Italian political directives and should introduce a fascist system. Under this specific point of view, Mussolini's foreign policy toward Spain was both ambitious and coherent.

If it is plausible to speak of Italian attempts to fascistise Spain, we still have to discover the reasons behind them. It is a very complex question, so all we can do here is to focus on some main characteristics. In the first place, Mussolini's view of the world was one concerned with a struggle between communism and fascism. As a matter of fact, he considered other forms of government as anachronistic. This is proved by his private writings (among which, many interesting 1931 aphorisms on Spain). Mussolini was convinced that only a fascist-like regime could grant Spain political stability. This, he thought, could prevent Spain from being the stronghold of anti-fascism and from being torn by class struggles. Under this point of view, ideology plays a very important role. Furthermore, perhaps Mussolini thought that exporting Fascism – which he thought of as a sort of personal 'trademark' – might have given him more prestige, both in Italy and abroad.

Above all, to 'fascistise' Spain was by far the surest way to subordinate it to Rome. This is proved by Mussolini's several attempts to influence the choice of Spain's new regime. For instance, he recommended that Franco should not allow for a return of the monarchy. As for foreign policy, Mussolini wanted Spain to remain a satellite state of Italy, something which must be seen in relation to

Mussolini's overall Mediterranean ambitions. As a matter of fact, Franco had often reassured the *Duce* about Spain's subordination to Italy – even though Franco defended Nationalist Spain's independence and imperialist ambitions. In 1939 Franco told Ciano that he was waiting for Mussolini to give him instructions. Although Ciano's diary may not be entirely credible on this point, Spain subserviently subscribed to the Anti-Comintern Pact and left the League of Nations.

Attempts to make Spain 'Roman' failed. Franco adopted the external forms of fascism, but the desired passage from the 'container' to the 'content' was never really accomplished. This was partly due to the fact that the *unificación* was a *de jure* unification, and not a real one, since the different political factions kept fighting each other. It is also important to note that the Spanish *Falange* was made up of poorly educated and poorly trained individuals. In 1939, Spain might have become more fascistised, but the *Falange* lacked skilled bureaucrats and this also slowed down the process. As Javier Tusell and Genoveva García Queipo de Llano have pointed out, Franco was, to a certain degree, forced to rely on traditional forces and on the army to build the new state.[36] The outbreak of the Second World War subsequently prevented Franco from going to Rome to meet the *Duce*. According to Franco, this trip would have been the first important stage of his political training. Mussolini was then facing many serious military problems. Therefore, he could not be the protector of anyone, least of all of Nationalist Spain. More importantly, Mussolini began to regard Franco as a possible rival in grabbing the French colonies in northern Africa. Their friendship was by then *'una amistad fallida'*, and their imperialist ambitions now depended entirely on Hitler.[37] In 1943, when giving the cabinet the news of Mussolini's arrest, Franco burst into tears. He was certainly more concerned that he might suffer the same destiny than he was feeling sorry for a faraway companion. But in the sometimes strange world of international relations his inferior position in the Axis hierarchy saved him from being shot, or from having to commit suicide in the bunker like his fellow tyrants, Mussolini and Hitler.

NOTES

1. John F. Coverdale, *Italian Intervention in the Spanish Civil War* (Princeton: Princeton University Press, 1975); revised Italian edition: *I fascisti italiani alla Guerra di Spagna* (Rome and Bari: Laterza, 1977).

2. Renzo De Felice, 'La politica fascista nelle sabbie mobili spagnole', ch.4 in Renzo De Felice, *Mussolini il Duce. Lo stato totalitario* (Torino: Einaudi, 1981), pp.331–466.

3. Coverdale, *I fascisti italiani* (note 1), pp.70–1.

4. Paul Preston, 'Mussolini's Spanish Adventure: From Limited Risk to War', in Paul Preston and Ann Mackenzie (eds.), *The Republic Besieged: Civil War in Spain 1936–1939* (Edinburgh: Edinburgh University Press, 1996), pp.21–51; Paul Preston, 'Italy and Spain in Civil War and World War 1936–43', in Sebastian Balfour and Paul Preston (eds.), *Spain and the Great Powers in the 20th Century* (London and New York: Routledge, 1999), pp.151–84; Ismael Saz, *Mussolini contra la II República: hostilidad, conspiraciones, intervención 1931–1936* (Valencia: Institut Alfons el Magnamim, 1986); Lucio Ceva, 'Conseguenze politico-militari dell'intervento italiano nella guerra di Spagna', in Gigliola Sacerdoti Mariano, Arturo Colombo and Antonio Pasinato (eds.), *La guerra civile spagnola tra politica e letteratura* (Firenze: Shakespeare, 1995), pp.215–29; Lucio Ceva, 'Ripensare Guadalajara', *Italia Contemporanea* 192 (1993), pp.475–86; Lucio Ceva, 'L'ultima vittoria del Fascismo. Spagna 1938–1939', *Italia Contemporanea* 196 (1994), pp.519–35. Official military studies: Ferdinando Pedriali, *Guerra di Spagna e aviazione italiana* (Rome: Aeronautica Militare-Ufficio Storico, 1992); Alberto Rovighi and Filippo Stefani, *La partecipazione italiana alla guerra civile spagnola*, 4 volumes (Rome: Ufficio Storico dello Stato Maggiore dell'Esercito, 1992–93).

5. Gianluca Andrè, 'L'intervento in Spagna e la politca estera fascista', in Ismael Saz (ed.), *Italia e la guerra civil española* (Rome: Centro de estudios históricos, 1986), p.12.

6. Stanley G. Payne, *Fascism in Spain 1923–1977* (Madison: University of Wisconsin Press, Madison, 1999), p.206.

7. Rovighi and Stefani (note 4), Vol.1, *testo*, p.143; Andrè (note 5), p.14; De Felice (note 2), pp.381, 385.

8. Brian R. Sullivan, 'Fascist Italy's Military Involvement in the Spanish Civil War', *Journal of Military History* 59 (1995), p.703.

9. As the telegram is from before 1 October 1936, the expression 'governo di Burgos' must be a poor translation of the Spanish 'Junta de Burgos', because the first government had not been appointed yet.

10. De Rossi, telegram to Ciano, 23 September 1936, *Documenti Diplomatici Italiani* (DDI) (Rome: Istituto Poligrafo e Zecca dello Stato/Libreria di Stato, 1952–), Series 8, Vol.V, pp.105–8; Magaz, 'relazione riservata', 17 October 1936, Archivo Renovado (AR), Leggio (l.) 1459, expediente (e.) 3, Archivo General del Ministerio de Asuntos Exteriores (AGMAE), Madrid; 'appunto' (with handwritten note by De Peppo), 27 September 1936, Gabinetto del Ministro 1923–43 (GAB) 50, Archivio Storico-Diplomatico del Ministero degli Affari Esteri (ASDMAE), Rome; 'appunto', 26 September 1936 (with unsigned note), GAB 50, ASDMAE; Magaz, telegram to Duque de Almazan, 5 October 1936 and 9 October 1936, AR, l.1455, e.1, AGMAE; Duque de Almazan, telegram to Magaz, 10 October 1936, GAB 50, ASDMAE.

11. De Felice (note 2), p.385.

12. Duque de Almazan, telegram to Magaz, 20 September 1936, AR, l.1455, e.1, AGMAE.

13. Preston, 'Italy and Spain' (note 4).

14. Magaz, handwritten report, 17 October 1937, AR, l.1459, e.3, AGMAE.

15. Antonio Elorza and Marta Bizcarrondo, *Queridos camaradas. La internacional Comunista y España 1919–1939* (Barcelona: Planeta, 1999), p.460.

16. Ibid., p.461.

17. Reports by Berardis: 6, 8, 13, 20 and 27 August, DDI (note 10), Series 8, Vol.IV, pp.760–2, 774, 798–800, 848–9, 884–6; 3, 9, 17 and 28 September, DDI (note 10), Series 8, Vol.V, pp.9–10, 85.

18. Quoted in Robert Mallett, *The Italian Navy and Fascist Expansionism 1935–1940* (London: Frank Cass, 1998), pp.64, 87.
19. Ibid., p.64.
20. Ibid., p.64.
21. MacGregor Knox, 'Il fascismo e la politica estera', in R.J. Bosworth and S. Romano, *La politica estera italiana, 1860–1995* (Bologna: Il Mulino 1991), p.326.
22. Giuseppe Bottai, *Diario 1935–1944* (Milano: Rizzoli, 1997), entry for 19 November 1936.
23. Knox (note 21), p.326.
24. Mussolini quoted in Ismael Saz, 'El Franquismo. ¿Régimen autoritario o dictatura fascista?', in Javier Tusell, Susana Sueiro, José Maria Marín and Marina Casanova, *El régimen de Franco* (Madrid: UNED, 1993), Vol.1, p.200.
25. Coverdale, *I fascisti italiani* (note 1), p.366.
26. De Felice (note 2), pp.358–60.
27. Saz (note 24), pp.194, 200. For De Felice's reluctance to recognise any ideological similarities between the various 'fascist' regimes, see Renzo De Felice, *Fascismo* (Milano: Luni editrice, 1998).
28. Ministero dell'Interno, telegram to Segreteria Particolare del Capo di Governo/Esteri, n.61574, 27 September 1936, GAB 70, ASDMAE; Segreteria Particolare, letter to Caballero, 5 October 1936, GAB 70, ASDMAE; Segreteria Particolare, letter to Caballero, 8 October 1936, GAB 70, ASDMAE; Caballero, letter to Mussolini, 8 January 1937, GAB 70, ASDMAE; Caballero, letter to Mussolini (written on the paper of the Italian embassy in Salamanca), 22 April 1937, Ufficio Spagna (US) 10, ASDMAE; Italian embassy in Salamanca, 'telespresso' to Ministero degli Affari Esteri, 23 April 1937, seen by Mussolini, US 10, ASDMAE; Cantalupo, letter to Pietromarchi, 19 April 1937, US 10, ASDMAE; Enrique Selva, *Ernesto Giménez Caballero. Entre la Vanguardia y el fascismo* (Valencia: Pre-Textos 1999), pp.272–82.
29. Pedrazzi, telegram to Ciano, 8 September 1937; De Rossi, telegram to Ciano 23 September 1937; Pedrazzi, telegram to Ciano 5 October 1937; Pedrazzi, telegram to Ciano 18 October 1937; and not least Anfuso, telegram to Ciano, 4 November 1937; all printed in DDI (note 10), Series 8, Vol.V, pp.32–6, 105–6, 166–76, 269–72, 387–8.
30. Caballero, letter to Mussolini, 10 June 1937, GAB 70, ASDMAE (on the reverse of this document it is written that Caballero was received by Mussolini on 12 May 1937).
31. Conde García, letter to Franco, 15 July 1937, AR, l.1459, e.9, AGMAE.
32. Mussolini, telegram to Viola, 9 August 1937, Autografi del Duce, GAB 24, AGMAE.
33. De Felice (note 2), p.380.
34. Payne (note 6), pp.297–9; Paul Preston, *Franco* (London: Fontana Books, 1993), pp.288–9, 302.
35. Ciano, telegram to Ministero di Cultura Popolare, 22 January 1938, US 2, ASDMAE; Gabinetto dell'Interno, telegram to Ministero degli Affari Esteri, n.3121, 8 August 1938, US 2, ASDMAE; Viola, telegram to Ministero degli Affari esteri, 'spese viaggio e soggiorno nel regno di 200 maestri spagnuoli', n.3393, 5 November 1938, US 2, ASDMAE.
36. Javier Tusell and Genoveva García Queipo de Llano, *Franco y Mussolini. La politica española durante la segunda guerra mundial* (Barcelona: Planeta, 1985), p.61.
37. Ibid., pp.271–89. Preston, 'Italy and Spain' (note 4), pp.174–6.

5

'The war that we prefer':
The Reclamation of the Pontine
Marshes and Fascist Expansion

STEEN BO FRANDSEN

South of Rome the plain of Agro Pontino stretches along the Tyrrhenian Coast with the steep Monti Lepini forming a natural barrier to the east. Today, the province of Latina makes a rather dynamic impression with its modern towns and heavily trafficked roads. Canals and straight lines dominate the open land, with its small farms and the plastic-covered fields of specialised agricultural production. Even if the signs of uncontrolled building activities are impossible to ignore, this area presents itself as a highly organised and planned region.

For almost two thousand years, though, Agro Pontino was one of the largest marshes, and one of the most feared malaria infested zones, on the Italian peninsula. Its vicinity to Rome made it one of the most notorious wastelands too. Among the fraternity of classical authors it was frequently mentioned, and ever since the Romans several tragic attempts had been undertaken in order to win back this potentially fertile area. After Italian unification, dozens of laws were passed by parliament on this matter, but they never resulted in effective action. Not only administrative and technological insufficiencies denied success, but the omnipresent threat of malaria ended all the offensives in the Agro Pontino. It was only from the beginning of the twentieth century that medical progress, combined with important developments in engineering, altered the prospects for the area.

Consequently it was a long overdue project that awaited the Fascists as they came to power. However, hardly any action was taken during the first decade of Mussolini's rule, and it was only in the

1930s that the Pontine Marshes came to occupy a prominent position in the politics of the government. During the *Ventennio* it developed into one of the most renowned regions, becoming the most 'fascist' landscape on the peninsula: the warlike attack on the swamps and, subsequently, the disciplined organisation of a new society according to Fascist principles were impressive examples of what Fascism claimed to be. No other Italian region could claim a similar position in the official propaganda that turned the resurrected Agro Pontino into a model for the future. Internationally, it was listed together with the Zuidersee and the Tennessee Valley as the most impressive public works of the day.

Where the Romans, the Popes and the liberal politicians had failed, Fascism needed only a few years to turn the poisoned area into a potentially model agrarian society. Admirers of Mussolini in Italy and abroad never ceased to celebrate this spectacular triumph. Disciplined, well-organised and brilliantly masterminded by the *Duce* himself as the commander-in-chief, the working brigades had brought this large-scale attempt to dry up the marshes to a triumphant conclusion. The victorious battle against nature was extensively exploited by propaganda, and new media such as film and radio were protagonists in a widely successful attempt to present Fascism as the ideology of a new Italy, and Mussolini as its genius. In years when the democracies were struggling with all sorts of economic, social and political problems, Mussolini launched a huge programme for rebuilding his country. Located close to Rome, and therefore easy to reach for journalists, foreign visitors and for the *Duce* himself, the Agro Pontino became the positive symbol of Fascism.

Mussolini did not invent this intervention himself as Fascist propaganda tried to convince the world. Most of the planning had been done before he took over power, but the realisation was to be inseparably associated with the figure of the *Duce*. There can be no doubt about his decisive role during the whole process. He took all the important decisions, and his frequent visits to the area during the first years of his rule contributed to underlining its importance. Even if the decision to build new towns in Agro Pontino was against his original intentions, he went on to become an enthusiastic founder. Finally he turned the newly reclaimed area into a new province.

This project embraced a number of important aspects of Fascism. Among them were the demographic considerations about birth rates, genetics and the moving of large populations from one part of the country to another. It was reckoned to have a positive influence on unemployment, and it was claimed to be the fulfilment of the old slogan of *terra ai contadini* from the war. The organisation of the new land represented a decisive step in the agricultural ideology of *ruralizzazione*, containing the ideas of *autarchia* and the vision of a solid society of fertile peasant-soldiers, well organised in hierarchic structures and free of all depravations and the immoralities of modern city-life. Building up a new healthy society according to Fascist values also supported the idea of the mobilisation of the masses, in order to keep the population activated in a sort of continuous revolution. Finally, one should notice the *tabula rasa* perspective of having an empty area without history and tradition – especially in a country like Italy.

The successful realisation of the huge project in a short time, and the almost mythic founding of a new society, gave the reclamation of the Pontine Marshes a positive reputation after the collapse of Fascism. There seemed to be no room for critique or revisionism *vis-à-vis* such a large-scale work of civilisation. Although Fascist speculations about the value of the area proved to be totally unrealistic – it was only in the 1960s that the expectations began to be fulfilled – the civilising aspect is probably responsible for the fact that the activities of the regime in this specific area were seldom considered for their military or colonialist implications. Still, the project demonstrated the presence of foreign politics even within an apparently exclusive domestic project. This becomes clear from political speeches, from the press and from the documentary films made about the activity in the countryside just outside the capital.

The modern province of Latina, with its expanding cities and its industries, its heavily trafficked roads and the ever growing number of tourists on its beaches, has obviously not followed the path of development laid out by the agricultural ideologists of fascist *ruralizzazione*.[1] But the traces of the old Agro Pontino are not lost, and there remain elements enough for a reading of monuments and landscapes along the lines of the original Fascist project. Before proceeding in this direction the role of *romanità* – the Fascist cult of antiquity – should briefly be considered. Here, we find some important ideological elements of importance to the foreign policy of the regime, although understanding the Roman connection is also necessary for the reading of the Pontine Marshes. Roman ideology had a strong impact on several aspects of Fascism, but one of the most important was the idea of constructing an empire. In the realisation of this grand plan the Pontine Marshes took a prominent position.

Fascism and the Myth of Rome

Mussolini discovered Rome relatively late in his career, even if he said – on the occasion of receiving Roman citizenship in 1924 – that Rome had always been on his mind since his youth. Being himself a *romagnolo* from Predappio in the hills south of Forlì, he spent an important period of his life in Milan. Italy's self-proclaimed *Capitale Morale* remained the point of departure, and Fascism would continue to be largely a phenomenon of northern Italy until the March on Rome of 28 October 1922. In April that year Mussolini wrote in *Popolo d'Italia*: '*Roma è il nostro punto di partenza e di riferimento: è il nostro simbolo, o se si vuole, il nostro Mito*'.[2]

The choice of Rome for the role of capital in the Italian nation-state had been heavily influenced by the weight of the mythological idea of the eternal city. But even if the decision was inevitable, it still had its critics. Liberal democrats argued that its long tradition of universalism, despotism and oppression disqualified Rome as the capital of a liberal democracy, while Catholics found the decision an intolerable insult to the Pope. Liberal Italy never succeeded in reconciling the paradox of having a national capital with an outspoken universalist tradition. No solution was found to the problem of *coabitazione* with the Pope, with whom the liberals remained on bad terms. National ideology had never regarded antiquity as a suitable point of reference, even if the Roman past was always echoed in the idea of uniting the peninsula. The mainstream of Italian nationalism was orientated towards the Middle Ages as the glorious moment of the past: it was the medieval city states that were idealised, rather than the Roman Empire.

It was unavoidable, however, that antiquity gained a prominent position after the conquest of Rome in 1870. Excavations began immediately after the arrival of the Italian army. Later, an archaeological itinerary was constructed in order to facilitate visits to some of the most famous Roman monuments. Throughout the history of liberal Italy however, antiquity remained part of a highly élitist culture. Sometimes symbolic parallels were too obvious. Liberal politicians would not hesitate to draw upon the Roman tradition to defend their imperialist projects in Africa. All the same antiquity did not figure as a prominent part of state ideology: it did not provide the justification for the new state, and the liberals were not presenting themselves as the Romans of the nineteenth century.

Fascism took a different approach to these questions. Arguably Mussolini was the last political leader to take historical continuity seriously in his propaganda, and it is impossible to read his *Third Rome* without a historic perspective. Fascism claimed to take up old Roman traditions. Mussolini denounced liberal democracy, *plutocrazia*, as a foreign and 'un-Italian' import, and he was often portrayed as a tribune of the people, or a *condottiere*, to underline the tradition of populist leaders and men of action, before he finally became the *Duce*.

Mussolini's interest in Rome grew stronger during 1920 and 1921 as his nationalistic fervour turned into an imperialistic project. He declared that, 'Our imperialism is Roman, Latin and Mediterranean. The Italian people must be, of necessity, expansionist'.[3] He demanded colonies, and claimed the Mediterranean as *mare nostrum*, as it had been to the Romans. In this particular context, Mussolini's choice of Roman ideology was a brilliant move. It postulated a historical right by referring to Roman times, but it also promised a solution to the problems of the Italian capital. If the nation state was to be surpassed by an empire, the problems of continuity not only vanished, but this very continuity, this tradition, was the justification for Mussolini's programme. Rome would become the centre of a recreated empire, of a new, a third and Fascist civilisation. The *Third Rome* – very soon the Fascists monopolised this terminology to such a degree that it has almost been forgotten that the liberals used it too – re-established continuity and took up the tradition of classical Rome. The period from 1870 to 1922 was virtually ignored and, as Fascist power became indisputable, Mussolini was in a position to conclude the *conciliazione* with the Pope. The Italian capital was no longer in conflict with the universal tradition. The *Third Rome* became inseparable from the idea of an empire and of *romanità*. The creation of a worthy capital and a scenography of power, characterised by a new monumentalisation of the city, particularly preoccupied Mussolini in his first 15 years in power. In this perspective, the use and abuse of antiquity became a means to promote and diffuse the idea of the continuity and the historical tradition of an empire.

If liberal Italy had had its problems with having a national capital with a universal tradition, of combining modern democracy with the Caesarism of the Romans, and the national ideology with that of Roman imperialism, Mussolini solved all these problems by accepting the universal role of Rome, the dictatorship, and by idealising an Italian imperialist mission beyond the scope of the nation-state. At least in this respect Fascism provided a homogeneous and self-evident ideology.

The 'Myth of Rome' was omnipresent. It left its mark on the urban projects of the capital, it had its role in linguistic politics, in the symbols of Fascism, in monuments, in rhetoric, in architecture and in the cult of Mussolini as a modern Augustus. It provided an argument – even if a doubtful and problematic one – for an imperialist expansion, which was presented as the historical mission of the Italian people. The 'Myth of Rome' was also present in the reclamation of the Pontine Marshes, the Agro Pontino.

Here, the Fascists worked on Roman ground, and they never forgot to remind everyone about it. The Via Appia, the most famous of all Roman roads, crossed the plain. Earlier works in the area had made it possible to re-establish its old route, but it was only with the Fascist reclamation that this major infrastructural construction won back its prominent position in the landscape. Since the Romans, the Agro Pontino had been a neglected and extremely disreputable area. In vain Pliny the Elder had appealed to his contemporaries to do something about the humiliating growth of the marshes so close to the capital, but neither the Romans nor anybody else had ever been able to control this piece of nature.

Mussolini was explicitly referring to the Romans as the work of reclamation began. It was one of the aims of Fascism to re-educate the Italians and make them as tough and victorious as the Romans. This could not be achieved in one day, but Mussolini was always impatient. He could not await the appearance of this new Italian race. Already during the works in Agro Pontino a stage was reached where the Fascists surpassed their idealised ancestors. Pliny's famous words were put at the front of the new provincial *Palazzo del Governo* in Littoria,[4] where they reminded Italians about the Roman dimension to this landscape, and made it clear for all to see that Fascism had finally done what Pliny had demanded.

In Italy, where not only Marinetti and his fellow futurists found the weight of history and tradition intolerable, Agro Pontino emerged as a fascinating *tabula rasa*, as virgin soil. With the sole exception of the Via Appia there were no traces left of a history that had to be recorded or respected. This was quite different from the difficulties that met planners and politicians in the centre of Rome. It was very much like conquering land in Africa, or in some other space beyond civilisation. Here, in the Agro Pontino, Fascism conquered a new land for Italy. In 1934 Mussolini decided to transform it into a new province, the 93rd Italian province, bearing the symbolic name of Littoria – like its newly founded capital. The symbolic denomination underlined the crucial role that this new province was expected to have in the Fascist state.

The War that we Prefer

'*È questa la guerra che noi preferiamo*', Mussolini proclaimed in his speech at the inauguration of the new town of Littoria on 18 December 1932.[5] It went on to become one of the most popular maxims of the *Duce*, and a sort of headline for the gigantic work of pulling the marshes out of two and half millennia of neglect. And this way of waging war with tractors, threshing machines and thousands of peasants, with the digging of canals instead of trenches and fighting mosquitos instead of enemy soldiers, perfectly suited the dictator in his ambition to present himself as the promoter of a new and stronger Italy. The world outside also became impressed with this activity, and the reclamation of the marshes developed into a symbol of peace and prosperity.

'*È qui che abbiamo condotto e condurremo delle vere e proprie operazioni di guerra. È questa la guerra che noi preferiamo*', Mussolini said, adding, '*Ma occorre che tutti ci lascino intenti al nostro lavoro*'.[6] Here, the applause of the thousands gathered in the square of the new town interrupted his speech. Mussolini realised that his audience had understood, and omitted the following sentence: '*se non ci vuole che noi applichiamo in altri campi, quella stessa energia, quello stesso metodo, quello stesso spirito*'.[7] This warning clearly pointed toward the military and aggressive dimension that never disappeared from Mussolini's rhetoric. The reclamation of the Agro Pontino was a work of peace, but it was accompanied by metaphors of war. This '*guerra che noi preferiamo*' was closely connected to Fascist plans for expansion and imperialism.

The unfolding of the Fascist organisation of the Agro Pontino did not follow any masterplan; in fact, the total lack of regional planning was often criticised. Similar to many other developments during the *Ventennio*, it was characterised by those typically spontaneous and impulsive decisions that were an inseperable part of Mussolini's political style. Still the works in the reclaimed fields did fall into a general pattern: that of building up an ideal society based on the principles of *ruralizzazione*, *autarchia* and a corporate and hierarchic structure of society. This pattern was to be exported to the future colonies; the Agro Pontino became the training ground.

Mussolini always stressed the future role of the peasants. He was proud of being one himself, and he was the first Italian political leader to take the world of the peasants seriously. No liberal politician had ever taken active part in the harvest and seated himself among the farm workers. He wanted to stop the peasants moving to the cities; partly due to a strong agrarian romanticism and a disgust for the mentality of the city proletariat, and partly because he wanted the peasants to form the stable backbone of society. Their values would be an important ingredient in the future state, just as they had been in antiquity. But the peasants were also much more fertile than the rest of the population. As fertility and demography became fixed ideas with the *Duce* from the late 1920s onwards, the ideology of a *ruralizzazione* developed. Agro Pontino opened up possibilities for realising this agrarian society.

The fertility of the peasants was an important argument, but Fascism also expected them to form the core of the armies of the future. In the trenches, Mussolini had experienced the superior quality and morale of soldiers from peasant backgrounds. As the project of colonising the Agro Pontino took shape, Fascism picked up another Roman tradition. Although the land was not divided into the same rigid pattern as Roman newland, it was organised into small plots, each with a farmhouse, that would be the home of a colonising family (up to 17 persons). The organisation of the land was delegated to the veteran's organisation, the *Opera Nazionale dei Combattenti*. Once more following Roman tradition, Mussolini wanted the veterans of the Great War to settle in the new land. These brave men – the real aristocracy of the Italian state as Mussolini called them –

would turn the wasteland into cornfields, and raise a new generation of peasant warriors. During the first phase the settlers were chosen by application. Later, Agro Pontino turned into a place where local Fascist authorities in the Romagna and in Veneto exported politically or socially problematic families. Very often these deported newcomers had no agrarian background at all, and their lack of experience (combined with an obvious absence of enthusiasm) soon became a threat to the success of the whole project.

Moving peasants from northern Italy to Agro Pontino was a large-scale example of Fascist demographic policy. In the province of Littoria hardly any locals were settled, and in this respect the fifth province of Lazio remains estranged from the rest of the region. In fact, an alien community was implanted much the same way as happened in the colonies. Loyalty toward the regime was more pronounced, especially in and around Littoria, where the most convinced Fascists were settled. If the results of the land reclamation were frustrating during the first years, the newly installed peasant population lived up to expectations with respect to fertility. The province conquered the leading position in the birth rate statistics.[8]

In the 1930s, Agro Pontino became one of the main theatres for the so-called *Battaglia del grano*, which was one of the links between the politics of *ruralizzazione* and the idea of *autarchia*. This once more moved attention away from the city culture and out into the open fields, where a new aesthetic of cornfields and open landscapes was presented to the Italians. The stereotypes of Italy should no longer be limited to the Cupola of Brunelleschi in Florence, the Campo of Siena, the Castel Sant'Angelo of Rome, the San Marco of Venice or some of the other famous illustrations of the city culture of the peninsula. The noble art of threshing was demonstrated in the *piazzas* of Rome, and a cornfield was arranged in the centre of Bologna. The rhetoric of war dominated: it was a battle, the *Duce* had set up a general staff, and the peasants were an army of *veliti*, fighting another decisive battle for Italy. Mussolini himself could not be a passive spectator, and regularly participated in the harvest in the wheat fields.[9]

The province of Littoria was populated and structured very much the same way as would be the case in a newly conquered colony. The construction of small service-centres (*borghi*) and of cities that were not supposed to be called cities at all, underlined this dimension of the work. The large-scale moving of peasants and their housing, and the creation of a hierarchical structure in the countryside, could be interpreted as a peaceful and progressive project. But in Fascist rhetoric, peace and war were always two sides of the same coin. In Littoria a monument reminding one of an antique *rostra* was raised to symbolise it: one side celebrated the battle of Monte Grappa, the other was dedicated to the battle against the Pontine Marshes. The small *borghis* that are spread around the countryside still bear the exotic names of the long forgotten battlefields of Bainsizza, Podgora, Carso, Isonzo, Sabotino and the Piave. The names were chosen to keep the memory of war alive among the peasants, who were, of course, supposed to be ready for future battles.

Beyond any doubt Fascism succeeded in creating a new agrarian landscape in the Agro Pontino, although the expected results only turned up decades after the fall of the regime, and although the territory owed its prosperity only in part to an agrarian economy. It is interesting that the Agro Pontino almost exclusively contributed to a positive image of Fascism – that of the *guerra che noi preferiamo*. During Fascism it became the symbol of an effective political leadership, and thereafter it remained one of the positive deeds of a no longer admired regime.

There remains plenty of evidence that testifies to the special position Fascism accredited to the province of Littoria. The name of the province and of the provincial capital in itself demonstrates the close affinity with the party, Littoria being of course synonymous with Fascism. Mussolini would visit this real Fascist town more often than most other Italian places. In the 1940s the Fascist Party was erecting the largest provincial party headquarter outside Rome (a huge building in the form of an 'M'), and even in the *Stadio dei Marmi* in Rome the figure symbolising Littoria has a conspicuous position and holds the *fasces*, whereas all the other allegoric statues of provincial capitals encircling the stadium only hold requisites of different sports. No other province could be said to be Fascist in the same degree as Littoria. A number of provinces had been created by Mussolini, but only Littoria had been created in an area which Fascism had conquered for Italy. Also, in this sense, one must understand the connection between reclamation and colonial expansion. The Agro Pontino was a new land very much in the same sense as Ethiopia. Only Fascism had brought 'civilisation' to these malaria-ridden areas that used to be wasteland.

Agro Pontino and the African War

Monuments and symbols in the provincial capital were – similar to the new names of the *borghi* – generally dedicated to the memory of the recent war.[10] Later on the emphasis was changing. In the third, and best preserved, of the five Pontine new towns, Pontinia, the congruence between the founding of the town and the African war is clearly demonstrated. Here, the few visitors find themselves confronted with three texts on the front of the rustique Palazzo Comunale. One is written around the top of the tower quoting the final passage of Mussolini's speech at the inauguration of the province of Littoria; one of those sentences that most clearly stresses the double-sidedness of the activity: '*È l'aratro che traccia il solco, ma è la spada che lo difende. E il vomere e la lama sono entrambi di acciaio temperato, come la fede dei nostri cuori*'.[11] The second inscription is written on a travertine plate placed on the wall beside the entrance. It contains a condemnation of the 52 countries behind the so-called *assedio economico* – the international sanctions against Italy imposed during the Ethiopian war – and their ingratitude toward the people that offered civilisation to the rest of the world.[12] The last one, placed above the balcony, is the birth-certificate of the city. It links its foundation directly to the African war:

> *Il XVIII dicembre l'anno XIV E.F. XXXI giorno dell'assedio economico Pontinia III città fondata nell'agro redento inizia la sua vita consacrando la vittoria dell'Italia fascista sulla ribelle mortifera palude mentre le legioni di Roma sorrette dalla volontà indomabile del popolo Italiano conquistando alla patria nel continente africano con la spada con l'aratro ed il piccone una nuova provincia.*

Mussolini himself mentioned the war in Africa in his inauguration speech in Pontinia, which he gave on the 18 December 1935,[13] and *Il Popolo d'Italia*, in its extensive report from the day of Fascist celebration and success in the Pontine Marshes, underlined the connection between the two wars:

> *La nascita di Pontinia, infine, nell'ora stessa in cui il tricolore sventola sulle conquistate terre del Tigrai e della Somalia, viene a chiarire, se ancora fosse necessario, le necessità umane, indifferibili e imperative, e quelle storiche e militari, da cui è*

*stata generata la nostra impresa africana: quelle stesse necessità
che ci hanno indotti precisamente a riscattare e utilizzare, con
uno sforzo eroico, ogni zolla del territorio nazionale e dare pane
e lavoro a migliaia e migliaia di famiglie.*[14]

Building up the new province of Littoria was the conquest of a
new colony. It also represented the Fascist victory over nature, and
not least the realisation of a project that not even the mighty Romans
had been able to complete. From here, new legions would be
prepared to cross *mare nostrum* and continue the work abroad.

The inscriptions from Pontinia only constitute one of several
examples of the continuous presence of Mussolini and Fascism in the
modern province of Latina. Today they are mostly ignored, and even
though the connection between the reclamation of the Agro Pontino
and Fascism's imperialist efforts in Africa is clearly demonstrated, its
meaning is hardly understood. How the Italians dealt with Fascism
after the fall of Mussolini still offers lots of fascinating questions.
This aspect can easily be studied in the former marshes south of
Rome. Another location, where the Pontine Marshes and the African
war are present, takes us finally to Rome, to a monument that is still
very much intact and not only a very obvious example of how the
Fascists used the Roman tradition, but also a celebration of Fascism
and of the foundation of the new empire – and last but not least a fine
example of how Italians have tried to 'historise' Fascism. *Foro
Mussolini* – today known as *Foro Italico* – is the setting created for
the Olympic Games of 1940 and for the education of the *Balillas*.
Behind the obelisk – a *carrarese* monolith with the well-preserved
inscription '*Mvssolini Dvx*' – lies a large rectangular *piazza* with
mosaics. It was inaugurated to celebrate the first anniversary of the
proclamation of the Empire in 1937, and it was carefully restored
before the finals of the football World Cup in 1990, where even some
of the most directly propagandist mosaics underwent a thorough
restoration; a couple of them were even reconstructed. The black and
white mosaics are quite similar to those Roman mosaics found during
the excavations in *Ostia Antica* in the 1930s. Some of the motives are
obviously inspired from antiquity and others are dedicated to
different sports. But, then, there are also 'M's and 'DVCE'
inscriptions. In the middle of it all the scene is suddenly taken over
by tanks, airplanes, guns, *balillas* and a truck with *squadristi* with

grafitti 'A Noi' or a flag with 'me ne frego' written on it. An Ethiopian warrior pays tribute to an Italian soldier, and the text informs the reader that on 9 May 1936 Italy finally got its empire.

Two rows of marble stones flank the *piazza*, and each stone bears an inscription that recalls an important date in the history of Fascism. Together, they establish a chronology containing the glorious moments of the *Ventennio*. The visitor can literally stroll along the course of history, starting with the entry into the First World War and moving on to the creation of the Fascist state, the founding of the new cities in Agro Pontino,[15] the war in Ethiopia and, on the seventeenth stone, to the proclamation of the empire. On the eighteenth stone suddenly appears the inscription: 'Fine del regime Fascista'. The following two marble blocks record the abolition of the monarchy, and the introduction of the republican constitution in 1948. After Fascism the monument was not destroyed, but rather these additions succeeded in turning the story upside down.

NOTES

1. Mussolini himself took the first step in this direction by allowing the construction of cities in the Agro Pontino.
2. 'Rome is our point of departure and our point of reference: it is our symbol, or if one wishes, our myth', *Popolo d'Italia*, 21 April 1922.
3. Speech at the second adunata fascista, 29 maggio 1920, quoted in Angelo del Boca, 'L'impero', in Mario Isnenghi (ed.), *I luoghi della memoria* (Rome and Bari: Laterza, 1996), pp.415–37, here p.417.
4. After the collapse of Fascism, Littoria had its name changed to the more neutral Latina.
5. 'La nascita di Littoria', in Benito Mussolini, *Opera Omnia di Benito Mussolini*, eds. Eduardo Susmel and Duilio Susmel, 36 volumes (Firenze: La Fenice, 1963–73), pp.184–5.
6. 'It is here that we have undertaken and will undertake real military operations. This is the war that we prefer. But it is important that people allow us to work'.
7. Riccardo Mariani, *Fascismo e 'città nuove'* (Milano: Feltrinelli, 1976), pp.87–8.
8. Carl Ipsen, *Dictating Demography. The problem of population in Fascist Italy* (Cambridge: Cambridge University Press, 1996).
9. Some of these aspects are treated in Simonetta Falasca-Zamponi, *Fascist Spectacle. The Aesthetics of Power in Mussolini's Italy* (Berkeley, CA, and London: University of California Press, 1997).
10. In front of the elementary school of Latina both sides of a stone is used for commemorating on the one side the battle of Mount Grappa and on the other the 'battle' of the Pontine Marshes.
11. 'L'aratro e la spada', 18 December 1934, in Mussolini (note 5), Vol.XXVI, pp.401–2.
12. '*18 novembre 1935 XIV A ricordo dell'assedio perchè resti documentata nei secoli l'enorme ingiustizia consumata contro l'Italia alla quale tanta deve la civilizzazione di*

tutti i continenti'. Similar inscriptions were placed in townhalls all over Italy, and they still can be seen in a few remote places, such as Licenza (Lazio) and Gesualdo (Campania).

13. 'Inaugurazione di Pontinia', 18 December 1935, in Mussolini (note 5), Vol.XXVIII, pp.202–3.

14. 'Il Duce comincia con il gesto del seminatore la vita del nuovo comune di Pontinia', *Il Popolo d'Italia* 313, 19 December 1935.

15. Interestingly all the new towns outside the province of Littoria are not mentioned, but neither is the town of Sabaudia, which was the second of the foundations in the Agro Pontino. Sabaudia was – as her name tells – not connected with the party or Mussolini, but with the royal dynasty of the Savoia.

6

The Papacy in Two World Wars: Benedict XV and Pius XII Compared

JOHN F. POLLARD

Introduction

The publication in 1999 of John Cornwell's book, *Hitler's Pope*, has refocused attention on the role of the papacy during the Second World War.[1] The role of the papacy in the First World War is much less well known, yet it could be argued that many of the problems and challenges facing Pius XII between 1939 and 1945 had already been experienced, albeit in a minor key, by Benedict XV between 1914 and 1918. Indeed, until recently virtually the only thing for which Benedict's short pontificate has been remembered is his 'Peace Note' of August 1917, by means of which he hoped to bring the warring powers to the negotiating table. By contrast, despite the controversy that has surrounded the wartime role of Pius XII since the publication of Hochhuth's play *Der Stellvertreter* in 1964, his 'Five Peace Points' of December 1940 have been almost completely forgotten.

This article will examine the similarities and differences between Pius's response to total war and that of Benedict. In particular, it will consider the influences of Benedict's experience of the First World War on Pius's conduct of Vatican policy during the Second. It will also assess the impact made by the intervening experience of the rise of fascist regimes in Italy and Germany, and the double polarisation of Europe in the 1930s – between the democracies and the fascist dictatorships, on the one hand, and between the Soviets and the rest on the other – on Pius XII's policies during the Second World War.

Neutrality and its Problems

Modern warfare was bound to pose serious problems for an international organisation with absolutely universalistic claims like the Roman Catholic Church. Pius IX had first raised the alarm about the threat which war between nations could pose to the unity and loyalty of European Catholics, when he denounced the armed struggle between the Italian nationalists and the Habsburg Empire in 1848, and disassociated himself and the army of the Papal States from it. In his allocution of that April he argued that he could not declare war on Austria because he represented, 'Him who is the author of peace and the lover of concord and who seeks after and embraces all races, peoples and nations with an equal devotion of paternal love'.[2] And this was precisely the kind of language that was to characterise papal utterances during both world wars.

The Franco–Prussian War of 1870–71 realised Pius IX's worst fears when a great Catholic power, the Second French Empire, was humiliatingly defeated, torn by civil strife and then left in the hands of republican forces which would eventually pursue an anti-clerical vendetta against the Church in France. The creation of the German Empire in 1871 constituted another defeat for Catholicism, with the subjection of the Catholic South German states to Protestant Prussia, and later Bismarck's unleashing of the *Kulturkampf*. Closer to home, the Franco–Prussian War led to the withdrawal of the French garrison from Rome, and the occupation of the city by Italian troops who finally put an end to the temporal power of the popes.

The First World War threatened to repeat this experience, but on a larger scale. Millions of French and Belgian Catholics, and substantial Catholic minorities in the British Empire, were pitted against their co-religionists in Germany and Austria-Hungary, and after May 1915, Austro-Hungarian Catholics would be fighting Italian Catholics as well. The conclave in which Cardinal Giacomo della Chiesa was elected pope as Benedict XV, in August-September 1914, was deeply affected by the war, while one cardinal-elector, the Frenchman Billot, learned of the deaths of two of his nephews on the Western Front,[3] another, Piffi, Archbishop of Vienna, received news of the terrible battle of Lemberg between Habsburg and Russian forces.[4] Before the doors of the conclave were reopened, the cardinal-electors had received addresses from leading French Catholics, with a reply from their German counterparts, about culpability for the outbreak of war.[5]

Much the same situation, of course, prevailed in the Second World War, though there were some obvious and significant differences in terms of the alignment of Italy and the fate of the Catholics in Poland and other central European countries conquered by Nazi Germany. All of this made the Vatican's necessary policy of impartiality and neutrality very hard to sustain in either conflict. The anti-German activities of an outstandingly patriotic churchman like Cardinal Mercier of Belgium, which created enormous difficulties for the diplomacy pursued by Benedict XV and his secretary of state, Cardinal Pietro Gasparri, exemplified this problem in its most acute form.[6] No such rival to the authority of the reigning pontiff appeared in the Second World War.

The Vatican's neutral stand in the First World War was regarded with suspicion from the beginning. The Papacy's traditional closeness to the Habsburg Empire, the last Catholic great power in Europe, which was seen by Vatican diplomats as the bastion against the Orthodox, Slav threat posed by the Russian Empire, suggested that papal diplomacy inclined toward the Central Powers. The fact that the Vatican was still involved in church–state disputes with both France and Italy, and that the British Empire was an officially Protestant power, seemed to provide the ultimate proof, as did knowledge that German Catholics provided the Vatican's principal means of financial support. The latter argument has been rehearsed more recently by the Serbo-American historian Dragan Zivojinovic.[7] So Benedict ended up being stigmatised as 'Le pape Boche' in France, and this was the general perception in *Entente* countries, even if there were accusations from time to time in the German press that he was 'Der Französische Papst'.[8]

Pius XII had similar problems. His long experience as nuncio in Germany from 1917 to 1930, his known admiration and affection for the country and the presence of German religious figures, including the controversial Mother Pascalina Lehnert, in his entourage, all seemed to suggest that he was pro-German. Yet there is ample evidence from a variety of sources that the Nazi leadership, despite Pacelli's eagerness to conclude the *Reichskonkordat* in 1933, was suspicious and hostile toward him, and toward the Catholic Church in general.[9]

If total war cut across the allegiances of Catholics, it also created serious, practical problems for the functioning of the Papacy as the headquarters of a worldwide religion. In particular, the Vatican's capacity to communicate with the various parts of the Church, especially in Europe, and especially in those countries under German occupation (and especially during the Second World War), were seriously obstructed. The Vatican's lack of independent statehood in the First World War meant that once Italy intervened in May 1915 on the side of the *Entente* powers, the ambassadors to the Holy See of Germany and Austria-Hungary were obliged to withdraw from Rome to neutral Switzerland, significantly complicating the problem of communicating with their governments.[10] In any case, as David Alvarez has demonstrated so clearly, in both wars Italian Intelligence's cracking of the rather primitive Vatican codes meant such communication as the Vatican had with its nunciatures and with other governments was far from secure.[11] The continuing predominance of Italians among the Vatican's representatives abroad, diplomatic and non-diplomatic, caused problems in both wars; in Germany and Austria-Hungary in the First, and in parts of the British Empire, especially the Middle East, in the Second.[12]

The success of Pius XI's negotiations with Mussolini for a settlement of the 'Roman Question', which led to the Lateran Pacts of 1929, meant that in strictly legal and financial terms the Vatican was much more independent between 1939 and 1945 than it had been during the First World War. The sovereign, independent and neutral status given to Vatican City by the 1929 settlement made it possible for the Holy See to accommodate the embassies of Belgium, Britain, France, Poland and Yugoslavia inside its territory after Mussolini declared war upon those countries; conversely, when the Allies liberated Rome in June 1944, the German ambassador von Weizsäcker was able to take refuge inside the walls of the Vatican.[13] Benedict faced considerable financial difficulties after the outbreak of war, when the flow of Peter's Pence from Belgium, France and, to a lesser extent, Germany, diminished, and this was exacerbated by the scope of the humanitarian and relief operations upon which he embarked.[14] But as in the Second World War, the Vatican was able to make up the losses from the old world by the generosity of the new: archival evidence shows that it was precisely at this time that increased offerings from American Catholics became the mainstay of Vatican finances.[15] This was also true, although to a lesser extent, of the situation during the Second World War for, by then, Bernardino Nogara's very wise investment of the financial compensation paid to the Papacy in 1929, and above all his transfer of the bulk of the Vatican's gold reserves to America in 1940, made it possible to survive the effects of Italian inflation and the increasing burdens of Pius XII's own humanitarian efforts.[16]

Even if there were times, most especially during the German occupation of Rome between September 1943 and June 1944, when the independence and neutrality of the Vatican seemed to be very fragile, there is no doubt that it afforded Pius XII and his collaborators a rather more secure base from which to conduct their humanitarian efforts and peace diplomacy than that available to Benedict XV. One example of the greater difficulties Benedict faced during the First World War is that Monsignor Eugenio Pacelli, the future Pius XII, like a number of other leading ecclesiastics in the Vatican, was actually called to arms in 1915, and only the intervention of Baron Carlo Monti, the unofficial intermediary between Benedict and the Italian government, was able to obtain his exemption.[17]

Vatican 'War Aims'

While the relief of human suffering and the conclusion of peace were undoubtedly major objectives of papal policy during the two world wars, the Vatican had other important 'war aims', so to speak, as well. One vital aim for both popes was the preservation of the *status quo ante bellum*, though more in Benedict's case than that of Pius. And again, for Benedict, the only exception to this general rule was the Holy See's desire to strengthen its position *vis-à-vis* Italy and thus enable it to obtain a resolution of the 50 year-old dispute with the Italian state on its terms.[18] What Benedict essentially sought was the retention of the balance of power in Europe which would permit the shaky Habsburg Empire to survive, but prevent either Germany or Russia from extending their influence. Russia was seen as constituting an especial threat to Catholic influence in the Balkans and further afield. Uppermost in the minds of Benedict and Gasparri was the fear that Russia would finally destroy the tottering Ottoman Empire, seize Constantinople and erect there a sort of Orthodox 'Vatican on the Bosphorus' to rival theirs on the Tiber, with all the consequences that would have for the prestige and influence of the Roman Catholic Church.[19] Such was the intensity of this fear that, as Roberto Morozzo della Rocca has demonstrated, the Vatican strayed so far from its policy of neutrality that Gasparri embarked on an extraordinary initiative, in

April 1916, to persuade the general staffs of the Central Powers to take steps to halt the Russian advance on Constantinople.[20]

While Pius XII faced no particular diplomatic problems with Fascist Italy, other than its adherence to the Rome–Berlin Axis and the consequences both domestic and foreign of that alliance, Russia remained a major threat to the Catholic Church, this time in strictly ideological rather than religious terms, because of its militant atheism rather than its championing of Orthodoxy. All the pragmatic attempts of both Benedict XV, and his successor Pius XI, to reach some sort of accommodation with Moscow, which would have permitted the survival of the Catholic Church in the Soviet Union, failed.[21] The persecution of the Church in Russia, and in the Baltic states after the Molotov–Ribbentrop Pact, indicated the fate which awaited Roman Catholics were the Soviet Union to prevail over Nazi Germany and achieve hegemony in eastern Europe. As nuncio in Munich, Pacelli had himself witnessed Bolshevism at work in 1919.[22] The Hobson's choice of either Nazi or Soviet victory was thus the great agonising dilemma facing 'Papa' Pacelli after June 1941, and one whose implications would affect both the direction of his peace policy and his attitude toward war crimes.

Papa Pacelli wished to return not so much to the *status quo ante bellum*, but, rather, to that which existed in Europe before the *Anschluss* in March 1938. Thus, the Vatican's wartime policy was fundamentally conditioned by the consequences of the rise and expansion of Nazi Germany. Despite Benedict's deep reservations about the Versailles peace settlement in general, and the principle of national self-determination in particular, he and his secretary of state had embraced the 'successor states' to which the principle gave rise; indeed, the expansion of Vatican diplomacy and its prestige after the First World War owed much to the establishment of relations with these states.[23] So the restoration of Catholic Austria and a partially Catholic Czechoslovakia, as well as the resurrection of Catholic Poland and the freeing of Catholic Hungary, France and Belgium were all essential aims of Pacelli's wartime diplomacy. It is important, therefore, to grasp that the implication of the title of Cornwell's biography of Pacelli, *Hitler's Pope*, is thoroughly misleading. It is clear that Pius XII was in no way sympathetic either to Hitler or to Nazism; that he desired a Germany free of both is proved by his incredible courage in agreeing to act as a channel of communication between the Allied powers and those German generals plotting to overthrow their *Führer* in 1940.[24] The Germany which Pacelli wanted to save would thus be freed of the Nazi tyranny at home, and be able to oppose the communist one abroad. Unfortunately for Pius, that was not a realistic prospect.

Papal Peace Diplomacy

The parallels between the peace-making efforts of Benedict XV and Pius XII are no mere coincidence. As first under-secretary of state in the Vatican from 1912 onwards, and then nuncio in Munich from 1917, the young Pacelli was intimately involved in Benedict's peace diplomacy, and most especially the famous 'Peace Note' of August 1917, for which his despatch to Germany in May was meant to prepare the way.[25] Indeed, given his apprenticeship under Benedict XV and Cardinal Gasparri, it can be argued that he was the heir to the tradition of papal diplomacy established by Leo XIII and his secretary of state, Cardinal Rampolla, in which Benedict and Gasparri had been trained in the last two decades of the nineteenth century. Leo's diplomacy had been active, interventionist and open to making peace efforts – mediation in disputes between Germany and Spain being the obvious example of this – whereas that of his immediate successor, Pius X, and his secretary of state, Cardinal Merry del Val, had been distinctly passive. The latter did little, for example, to try to prevent the outbreak of the First World War. Furthermore, the essence of Cardinal Rampolla's diplomacy had been to balance Germany, a Prussian, Protestant power, with Catholic, cosmopolitan Austria. Faced by the rise of Nazi Germany in the 1930s, Pius XI, Pacelli's master when he was secretary of state, had tried to continue a variant of this policy by encouraging Italian leadership of a 'third force', a Catholic bloc, including Austria and Hungary, between Nazi Germany and the Soviet Union. But the emergence of the Rome–Berlin Axis after 1936 put paid to this hope.[26]

Like Benedict, Pius XII sought both to avert war and to encourage peace efforts after it had started. Again like Benedict, he devoted particular attention to Italy, using maximum pressure to dissuade Mussolini from entering the war in 1940 and assisting efforts to negotiate an Italian exit from the war as early as October 1942.[27] In his pursuit of peace diplomacy, Pius XII enjoyed a number of advantages over his predecessor. Papal diplomatic influence was much stronger and more widespread in 1939 than it had been at the beginning of the First World War, and by the end of the Second World War the Vatican had relations with all the major belligerents except the Soviet Union. That was perhaps the great irony of the papacy's experience of total war: though it deeply deplored wars and sought to bring them to an end, at the end of the day it was a great beneficiary of war, in terms of prestige and influence. The First World War, thanks to Benedict's activist peace diplomacy and also his humanitarian efforts, rescued the papacy from the relative isolation to which the diplomacy of Pius X and Merry Del Val had condemned it. Both Britain and, to a lesser extent, France were anxious to establish diplomatic relations with the Vatican in order to counter the influence of the Central Powers, and, hopefully, win the moral support of the papacy for the *Entente* cause.[28]

Pius XII was in a much stronger position than Benedict from even before his election in 1939. Benedict had not only inherited a diplomatically isolated papacy, but he was also personally almost entirely unknown to the world before he came to the papal throne, whereas Pius XII was quite well known before his election: as Cardinal secretary of state he had been at the centre of affairs in the Vatican for nine years and, moreover, had visited North and South America and was personally known to President Franklin D. Roosevelt. Thanks to the growth in the numbers of American Catholics, and their consequent pre-eminent position among the financial supporters of the Vatican's activities, Pius XI and Pacelli had been able to strengthen both their financial and political links with the US from about 1936 onwards. This paid off in 1939 when Francis Spellman, Archbishop of New York, brokered a deal whereby a 'personal representative' of the US president was accredited to the papal court in late 1939.[29] This unprecedented situation markedly distinguishes the wartime experience of Benedict from that of Pius. Benedict quickly recognised the pivotal role of the US in world affairs, especially after its entry into the war in April 1917, but he had been quite unsuccessful in his attempt to win President Woodrow Wilson's support for his peace efforts. Pius XII, on the other hand, had what one could almost describe as a 'special relationship' with the United States, even though this did not prevent serious difficulties arising between the Vatican and the Allies from time to time.[30] The relationship was to stand Vatican diplomacy, and especially its efforts on behalf of defeated Italy after 1943, in good stead.[31]

Yet, despite all of these efforts, Pius XII's peace diplomacy was no more successful than that of Benedict. His 'Five Peace Points' plan of 1940,[32] which, it has to be said, was a much more vague formula for peace-making than Benedict's 'Peace Note', has hardly been remembered, even though it evoked much greater support in the belligerent countries, especially those of the Allies, than Benedict's 'Peace Note' of 1917. Whereas Benedict's 'Peace Note' was even denounced from the pulpits of French Catholic churches,[33] ironically, Pius XII's proposals received the support in Britain of both the Archbishops of Canterbury and York and of the Moderator of the Free Church Federal Council, and was praised by a *Times* editorial.[34]

Atrocities, War Crimes and the Holocaust

Given the enormity of the Holocaust, and the extent of other war crimes in the Second World War, it is extremely difficult to establish a moral equivalent with atrocities during the First World War. Yet it can be argued that Benedict XV faced moral dilemmas over how to react to reports of alleged atrocities and war crimes which were not entirely dissimilar from those facing Pius XII. As in the Second World War, so in the First the papacy was approached by belligerents on both sides anxious to elicit the moral condemnation of the pope for what they judged to be 'war crimes' allegedly committed by the others. In particular, the British, French and Belgians demanded that Benedict condemn German violation of Belgium's neutrality and atrocities subsequently committed there, including the sacking of Louvain and the shootings of civilians.[35] The Germans countered by accusing Belgian civilians of breaking the rules of war by forcibly resisting the occupation of their country.[36] Another major complaint was against the enforced labour, and even deportation, of civilian populations in Belgium and northern France by the Germans.[37] The Vatican's response to these demands was to point out the complaints from the Germans about the behaviour of *Entente* armies: in particular, Russian troops' treatment of Jews and Catholics in occupied Poland.[38] By the end of the war, the Vatican's archives were bulging with 'white', 'grey', 'green' and 'orange' books produced by the belligerents on both sides detailing alleged atrocities perpetrated by the enemy, along with carefully argued ripostes to them.

Though called upon explicitly to act as a final court of war morality, Benedict was very unwilling to get involved in these disputes and the Vatican's Congregation of Extraordinary Ecclesiastical Affairs, the consultative organ of the Secretariat of State, pronounced the opinion that condemnations of alleged atrocities would hamper the Pope's humanitarian work and hinder his peace efforts, leading Gasparri to declare that 'the Holy See preferred the good of suffering humanity'.[39] Pius XII, who was secretary of the Congregation when this opinion was given, seems to have allowed its policy to guide him as pope during the Second World War. This is one way to explain his alleged 'silences', or at best very vaguely worded protests, against the Holocaust and other mass killings.

Like Benedict, Pius XII faced the problem that the specific naming of atrocities committed by one side would have to have been accompanied by condemnation of those of the other. Thus, in the Second World War, had Pius XII condemned Nazi crimes against the Jews and Poles, and those of the Croats against the Serbs and gypsies, then he would also have had to condemn Soviet ones, such as the deportations of ethnic and national minorities like the Volga Germans, Tartars, Chechen-Ingushi and so on, not to mention the Allied bombing of Dresden. That would not have pleased the Allies.[40]

The real difference between the situation which faced Benedict and that to which Pius XII had to respond, was the fact that the Second World War was a racial war, indeed a war of racial extermination, whereas the First was essentially a conflict between nations. Nevertheless, the influence of the racial theorists of the nineteenth century, with their idea of racial struggle, was already discernible in the attitude of the Germans towards the Belgians and in the general staff's demands for *Lebensraum* in eastern Europe. Certainly, Benedict sensed the racial undertones of the struggle taking place between 1914 and 1918, and denounced them in his encyclical *Ad Beatissimi* of November 1914, when he wrote, 'Race hatred has reached its climax'.[41] Pius XII was rarely so explicit, if only because one of the belligerents, Germany, was publicly pursuing a racial policy. His predecessor, Pius XI, had condemned both the Marxist ideology of class war, and the practice of class extermination by Stalin. He had also condemned the politics of race in both Germany and Italy: in the former case in his encyclical *Mit Brennender Sorge* of 1937, and, in the latter, in a public audience after the announcement of the introduction of the Racial Laws in September 1938.[42] And in his 'hidden encyclical' *Humani Generis Unitas*, Pius XI had planned to denounce so-called 'scientific' racialism *tout court* in 1939.[43] That this encyclical never saw the light of day is undoubtedly attributable to Pius XII's intervention after his election following Papa Ratti's death in February of that year. The 'diplomatic pope' was not prepared to confront racialism head on.

It can also be argued that there was nothing remotely on the scale of the Holocaust, or other racial extermination programmes such as those against the gypsies, the Serbs or the Poles, facing Benedict and the papacy in the First World War. That is true. But genocide was by no means a product of the Second World War. The papacy faced the attempted genocide by Turks of the Armenian population of the Ottoman Empire: it has been estimated that over one million Armenians died between 1914 and 1918, either killed outright by the Turks, or as a result of maltreatment, or from starvation and disease.[44] Benedict made strenuous and public efforts to stop it, earning himself the erection of a statue in his honour in Istanbul after his death.[45]

Unlike Benedict, Pius XII also had to face the real dilemma that a condemnation of Nazi or Soviet atrocities might make matters worse by provoking further atrocities, and even reprisals against the Church. This is the very convincing argument of Father Blet, one of the leading apologists for Pius XII.[46] But the major factor inhibiting the papacy from operating as a tribunal of final moral authority, in both wars, was the fundamental problem of needing to avoid alienating the loyalties of countless Catholics on both sides. This concern is clearly evident in the public utterances and diplomatic correspondence of both popes.

Conclusion

Like the Second World War, the First World War was a total war in that it involved the total, or near total, mobilisation by the warring powers of their resources. While it may not have been quite so highly ideologically charged as the Second, it involved a strong sense, on the *Entente* side at least, of fighting a *moral* struggle, and for the Central Powers of a struggle for 'civilisation'. The First World War also brought into play new weapons and methods of warfare which Benedict found abhorrent (such as submarine warfare, especially against civilian passenger ships and merchant vessels, and aerial bombardment and the shelling of cities), and against whose use by both sides he publicly protested.[47] But, by the outbreak of the Second World War, despite the Geneva Convention, the vulnerability of civilians was accepted and tolerated, and racial extermination, *as a war aim*, was pursued by a major belligerent. In these changed circumstances, which were essentially the result of the rise of National Socialism, Pius XII could not completely rely on his experience of the Vatican's handling of the First World War in his reactions to the Second.

The differences in the papacy's reaction to the First and Second World Wars may also stem from the different careers and personalities of the two popes. Benedict, as well as having had a curial and diplomatic career of 24 years, had the very formative pastoral experience of seven years as Archbishop of Bologna. Pacelli's was a wholly curial and diplomatic career; he had had no pastoral experience to speak of. Whereas Benedict was volatile, impatient and immensely compassionate, Pius XII presents the picture of a rather cold, calculating and emotionally isolated man. One cannot imagine Benedict standing by and allowing the Holocaust to happen without making strident public protests: even less Pius XI, who publicly condemned the introduction of the racial laws into Fascist Italy in 1938.

The two popes' wartime aims were essentially the same, to bring about peace and to extend as far as possible humanitarian aid to suffering peoples. In addition, their ultimate concern was the survival of the institution which they represented, the papacy, and the defence of the reality on which it rested, the loyalty of Catholics to the Pope. They almost inevitably failed in the first aim and achieved a degree of success with second. In the circumstances, they were remarkably successful in achieving the third. Both wars threatened the essential unity of the Catholic Church: there was talk of the dangers of schism within the Church in the First World War and in the Second. If these two popes were successful in avoiding this danger then it is quite simply because neither pope ever put Catholic loyalties to the test by publicly condemning their various governments for crimes they had committed, or were alleged to have committed.

NOTES

I am grateful to my colleague Dr Theo Schulte for reading an early draft and making many helpful suggestions.

1. J. Cornwell, *Hitler's Pope: The Secret History of Pius XII* (London and New York: Penguin, 1999).
2. As quoted in E.E.Y. Hales, *Pio Nono* (London: Eyre and Spottiswoode, 1956), p.77.
3. C. Zizola, *11 Conclave: Storia e segreto* (Rome: Garzanti, 1993), p.196.

4. Ibid., p.192.
5. M. Liebman, 'Journal secret d'un conclave', *Revue Nouvelle* 19/XXXVIII (1963), p.37.
6. J. F. Pollard, *The Unknown Pope: Benedict XV (1914–1922) and the Pursuit of Peace* (London: Cassell, 1999), p.95.
7. D.R. Zivojinovic, *The United States and the Vatican Policies, 1914–1918* (Boulder, CO: Colorado Associated University Press, 1978), pp.12–13.
8. Pollard (note 5), p.94.
9. See for example, D. Alvarez and R. Graham, SJ, *Nothing Sacred. Nazi Espionage against the Vatican, 1939–1945* (London: Frank Cass, 1997), pp.xi–xii, 59–60.
10. Pollard (note 5), pp.98–100.
11. D. Alvarez, 'Vatican Communications Security, 1914–1918', *Intelligence and National Security* 7/4 (1992), pp.443–53; Alvarez and Graham (note 9), Ch.5.
12. Pollard (note 5), p.73; A. Rhodes, *The Vatican in the Age of the Dictators, 1922–1945* (London: Hodder and Stoughton, 1973), pp.278–82.
13. See O. Chadwick, *Britain and the Vatican during the Second World War* (Cambridge: Cambridge University Press, 1986), Ch.5 and p.261.
14. It has been estimated that he spent 82 million lire on his relief efforts, Pollard (note 5), p.116. We have no comparable figures for Pius XII's war relief work, but from what is known about Vatican finances during the Second World War they must have been substantial.
15. Bishop McNicholas, Secretary of the US Bishops' Conference, letter to the Delegate, 27 September 1919, records of the Apostolic Delegation in Washington (DAUS), 284, 1, Vatican Secret Archives (ASV), where he says that the US contribution to Vatican funds for that year would be 'a little larger than usual, that is $1,500,000'.
16. Memorandum of the Apostolic Delegate, 21 September 1942, Department of Justice, Foreign Funds and Control Records, box 487, US National Archives and Records Administration (NARA) at College Park, MD, concerning the placing of Vatican funds in the US at the beginning of the war.
17. A. Scotta (ed.), *La Conciliazione Ufficiosa: Diario del Barone Carlo Monti 'incaricato d'affari' del governo italiano presso la Santa Sede (1914–1922)* (Vatican City: Libreria Editrice Vaticana, 1997), Vol.1, pp.212–13.
18. I. Garzia, *La Questione Romana durante la prima guerra mondiale* (Naples: ESI, 1981), especially pp.68, 105.
19. Pollard (note 5), pp.90–1.
20. R. Morozzo della Rocca, 'Benedetto XV e Constantinopoli', *Cristianesimo nella Storia* 17 (1996), pp.545–66.
21. H-J. Stehle, *The Eastern Politics of the Vatican* (Athens, OH: Ohio University Press, 1981), Chs.I–IV.
22. Cornwell (note 1), pp.72–9.
23. S. Stehlin, 'The Emergence of a New Vatican Diplomacy during the Great War and its Aftermath', in P.C. Kent and J.F. Pollard (eds), *Papal Diplomacy in the Modern Age* (New York: Praeger, 1994), pp.75–87.
24. See Chadwick (note 13), pp.86–98.
25. Pollard (note 5), pp.123–8; Cornwell (note 1), pp.62–9.
26. P.C. Kent, *The Pope and the Duce: The International Impact of the Lateran Agreements* (London: Macmillan, 1981), Chs.9, 10.
27. See I. Garzia, *Pio XII e l'Italia nella seconda guerra mondiale* (Brescia: La Morcelliana, 1988), Chs.1, 2, 3.
28. Pollard (note 5), pp.92–3.
29. E. Di Nolfo, *Vaticano e Stati Uniti, 1939–1952 (Dalle Carte di Myron Taylor)* (Milan: Franco Angeli Editore, 1978).
30. Quite the contrary; as Rhodes (note 12), pp.267–9, also demonstrates, the Allies were unhappy about the Vatican's passivity in the face of German atrocities, and for its part, the Vatican was appalled by the message concerning the Allied policy of

'unconditional surrender' towards the Axis which Myron Taylor, President Roosevelt's personal representative to the Pope, delivered in September 1942.

31. J.F. Pollard, 'Il Vaticano e la politica estera italiana', in R.J.B. Bosworth and S. Romano (eds.), *La politica estera italiana, 1860–1985* (Bologna: Il Mulino, 1991), pp.223–4, 224–7.

32. For the text, see P. Blet, A. Martini and B. Schneider (eds.), *Records and Documents of the Holy See Relating to the Second World War: The Holy See and the War in Europe, March 1939–August 1940*, English edition trans. G. Noel (London: Herder, 1968), pp.332–4.

33. Pollard (note 6), p.128.

34. *The Times*, 21 December 1940.

35. 'Libro tedesco sulla neutralità violata dal Belgio', Sacra Congregazione per gli Affari Ecclesiastici Straordinari, 1316, fasc.455, ASV.

36. Ibid.

37. Ibid.

38. Ibid.

39. 'Imparzialità della S. Sede', Stati Ecclesiastici, 1427, fasc.569, p.9, ASV.

40. Personal representative of the President, letter to Pius XII, Box 011, 840.4, Department of State and Foreign Relations, NARA, referring to the letter from the British minister, Francis D'Arcy Osborne, 7 November 1944, in which he says that if Myron Taylor conveyed the President's request for the Pope to condemn the deportation of 800,000 Hungarian Jews, then he was afraid that the Pope would have to condemn Soviet atrocities as well and that this would have serious political repercussions.

41. C. Carlen, IHM (ed.), *The Papal Encyclicals, 1903–1939* (Raleigh, NC: Pierian, 1990), Vol.IV, pp.144–5.

42. Rhodes (note 12), pp.213–14.

43. For the text of *Humani Generis Unitas*, see G. Passalecq and B. Suchecky, *The Hidden Encyclical of Pius XI*, intro. by Gary Wills (New York: Harcourt Brace, 1997), pp.169–277.

44. J.D. Gregory, British Legation to the Holy See, letter to the Foreign Secretary Earl Grey, 16 October 1915, Foreign Office papers, 371, 152040, Public Records Office, London; correspondence between Benedict XV and Sultan Mohamed V, Segretariato di Stato, Guerra, 1914–1918, rubrica 244, fasc.64, 1915–16, ASV.

45. A. Riccardi, 'Benedetto XV e la crisi della convivenza religiosa nell'lmpero Turco', in G. Rumi (ed.), *Benedetto XV e la Pace, 1914–1918* (Brescia: La Morcelliana, 1990), pp.83–128.

46. P. Blet et al. (note 32), pp.82–3.

47. Pollard (note 5), pp.121–2; see also Commissario del Borgo (police officer in charge of surveillance of the Vatican), letter to the Chief of Police, Direzione Generale della Pubblica Sicurezza, 1915, busta 33, Ministero dell' Interno [Ministry of the Interior], Archivio Centrale dello Stato [Central State Archives], Rome, in which he says that in a note of 6 July 1915, the Pope instructed the nuncios in Munich and Vienna to request governments there 'not to use those terrible forms of destruction and warfare not permitted by existing conventions and international law, and whose existence for warlike extermination people of Christian faith had learned with such horror'.

7

The Sentinel of the Bravo:
Italian Fascism in Mexico, 1922–35

FRANCO SAVARINO

As a Latin I see, especially in Mexico,
the people that is the sentinel of the Bravo river.
(Mario Appelius, 1929)

Mexico is, to a few, the American Russia.
(Arnaldo Cipolla, 1927)

Introduction

This article examines the relationship between Fascist Italy and
Mexico, from Mussolini's seizure of power in 1922 up to the launch
of Fascism's war of expansion in Africa in 1935. The main goal is to
assess some patterns of Fascist political and ideological activity in the
Latin American region, and the limits this little known geopolitical
front presented to the 'mother country' of fascism.

Latin America remains an area insufficiently studied within the
field of Fascist foreign policy, owing to the apparently secondary,
indeed subordinate, role that the continent allegedly played in
Mussolini's geopolitics, and to the *sui generis*, as opposed to
territorial, parameters on which Italian programmes of expansion
were developed in the area.[1] With respect to Latin America, it
remains unclear whether Fascist international politics aimed to secure
advantages through a decisive equilibrium of power, or, rather,
whether it sought an active revisionist and deliberate expansionism.[2]

Existing studies are not helpful in reaching a general overview.[3] With few exceptions research has generally analysed Italian immigration to Latin America, and in particular the fascistisation of the immigrants and anti-fascist tendencies among them. From here, academic attention exclusively focuses on the large Italian colonies in South America (Argentina, Brazil).[4] From this perspective, broader studies have also developed, to a large extent, around these themes, and underline the existence of a substantial continuity, in comparison to the previous nationalist and expansionist policies of liberal Italy.[5]

Without denying the importance of emigration, and the control over it that Mussolini's Italy had, this article offers a different argument based on the wider context of Fascist foreign policy on the South American continent. It focuses on Mexico, a country in many respects atypical, distant, enigmatic, but also a point of interest for Fascist Italy, given its important strategic position in Latin America, and its great influence over the entire area. 'Mexico', Mario Appelius warned in 1928, 'is a precious experimental field for wholly non-Anglo-Saxon Latin America'.

We will see, in fact, that the country, situated on the borders of the United States, was somehow the 'laboratory' for an ambitious Italian policy toward Latin America, in part based on economic expansion but also on political and cultural expansion. As regards Mexico, it was urgent and necessary for Italy to challenge the aggressive economic, political and cultural penetration of the United States. Moreover, it became very important for Fascism to develop a 'Latin' propaganda policy, and especially so when faced with a country, Mexico, that had undertaken the unique cultural experiment of shaping its own national identity. In Mexico, therefore, there were significant problems that helped orient the Latin American policy of Fascist Italy during the 1920s and 1930s.

Mexican Revolutionary Nationalism

In the international panorama of the 1920s Mexico was one of the states that had undergone national revolutions, such as the Turkey of Kemal Atatürk, the China of Chiang Kai-Shek, Russia and Italy. Each of those experiences must be seen as part of a tendency to search for new ways of modernising society by the underdeveloped countries of that time. This took place via the mobilisation of the masses, the middle-classes or of both.[6]

The Mexican experience is located within the most precocious phase of this revolutionary wave, having begun in 1911, at the same time as the Chinese revolution, with which it shared its nationalist and xenophobic characteristics.[7] The revolutionary process, that included a bloody civil war (1914–16), concluded toward 1919 with the consolidation of a revolutionary, if ostensibly democratic, authoritarian regime under General Álvaro Obregón. The characteristics of the new state effectively constituted something of a synthesis of previous national experiences: republican nationalism, a militant liberal secularism, and corporativism (of Catholic origins), regenerated during the revolutionary process under the influence of the international trends of the age. The revolution established a new national mythology that remodeled the cult of the country, founding it on a mass mobilisation against the old liberal ruling class, foreigners and the imperial powers. The Mexican 'cultural revolution' had an international resonance, and brought about the re-evaluation of the native, pre-Columbian past and the *mestizo* (mixed-blood) culture, against the Hispanic and Creole elements.

On the other side of the Atlantic countries were having similar experiences. In Europe, the explosion of mass nationalism during the world conflict produced revolutionary conditions that led to a general crisis of the liberal states and the consequent formation, in some countries, of authoritarian regimes, whether nationalist, socialist or fascist. Italy had narrowly avoided, between 1919 and 1922, a near civil war between nationalists and ex-soldiers on one side, and socialists on the other. The conflict had cultural implications. The experience of war had created a mass nationalism that had spread, and especially among the middle-classes, in the universities and between the former soldiers in general, and led to the establishment of a radical movement with revolutionary tendencies: 'Fascism'.[8] In 1922 a quasi legal *coup d'état* brought the Fascists, led by Benito Mussolini to power, with a nationalist-revolutionary programme.

What is important to underline here is the similarity of the Italian and Mexican political experiences. Both had revolutionary, nationalist and populist tendencies, rose in the period of the crisis of the liberal states, were pushed along by mass movements, and had strong cultural ambitions. Fascist Italy and revolutionary Mexico also created two unique state parties: the Mexican PNR (then PRM and finally PRI, founded in 1929) and the Italian PNF (founded in 1921), who adopted corporate structures and pretended to constitute a 'third way' between the 'Bolshevik' and the liberal-capitalist systems. They also had some common enemies: the liberal establishment that they overthrew (Porfirio Díaz's regime in Mexico and the Giolittian political class in Italy) and, externally, the imperialist Anglo-Saxon powers (Great Britain and the United States), against which they directed their national sense of frustration as underdeveloped and oppressed Latin countries. Such resemblances – that were not the fruit of mutual influences, but were autonomous factors – become important when studying the relationship between the two countries during the inter-war period.[9]

In this context, it is necessary to point out that considerable differences also existed. The Mexican revolution grew from within a peasant movement, even if its leaders were generally of middle-class origin. The workers' movement was of little importance, and was absorbed by the revolution. On the other hand, in Italy the Fascist revolution faced an organised proletarian movement, that had proper objectives and revolutionary ambitions.[10]

These disparities are, without doubt, valid and important from the political and social point of view. But in the cultural sense they are less remarkable, in that both movements rushed to educate the masses, were interested in remodelling the national identity and also favoured an aesthetic vanguard. In any case the Fascist regime, in its relationship with its Mexican counterpart, also had to cope with some ideological matters.

Fascism seen from afar: Mussolini's Italy and Fascist Tendencies in Mexico

The March on Rome of October 1922 also brought Fascism to the forefront in Mexico.[11] Only one month later the Italian ambassador signalled to the Italian foreign ministry that the seizure of power by the Fascists had been approved of by the Mexican government.[12] The most meaningful event was, however, the foundation, the following month, of a 'Mexican Fascist Party' (*Partido Fascista Mexicano*, PFM). This movement had a short life and a limited membership, but it is useful to examine it to understand how the regime founded by Mussolini was welcomed in Mexico.[13]

The birth of the PFM coincided with presidential elections, during which the party supported the non-official candidate Àngel Flores. The programme of the new party made reference to the middle-classes as victims of capital and the labour movement. It also advocated freedom within the workplace, and promoted the idea of small land holdings against an official tendency to create *ejidos* (collective ownership along socialist lines), within a broadly 'liberal' programme. The supreme leader of the party, Gustavo Sáenz de Sicilia, affirmed that the movement had 150,000 activists in the whole country. The party's official periodical was appropriately entitled '*El Fascista*'.[14]

It is significant that the PFM regarded the middle-class as the basis of the movement, as opposed to unionised workers. In rural areas they were landowners, whether great or small, that were attracted to the party as a means of opposing the '*agraristas*', who were in favour of a collective property system along the lines of the *ejido*.[15] This resemblance with Italian Fascism, nevertheless, was attenuated by two completely divergent elements: the PFM was not a violent movement and was openly Catholic. The government and the labour unions suspected that behind the PFM were Catholics and conservatives hostile to the revolution. Some priests, in effect, became affiliated with this 'fascism' so as to oppose official anti-clericalism; gossip also circulated that the secret head of the party was the apostolic Delegate in Mexico, Ernesto Filippi.

Moreover, the adhesion of Catholics and conservatives to the PFM was irregular and limited, and besides, the bourgeoisie attracted to 'fascism' had already been absorbed by, and become generally satisfied with, the official revolutionary movement, not having any serious reason to fight against that revolution with an alternative programme.[16] In 1923 an American journalist synthesised the ambiguities and the limitations of the PFM, comparing it to the supposed Italian model:

> Fascism in Mexico is, really, an amateurish movement ... It has no meaningful social program ... as has the government or other existing organizations. It cannot appeal to the adhesion of the middle-class. It also has no organized support among the conservatives.[17]

The Italian view of the PFM is hinted at by a comment made by the Italian ambassador in June 1923, when the movement was already disappearing:

> This party was not anything else than a bad imitation of ours, and did not possess the causes of origin and the finalities of it. It, in fact, assumed the aspect of a political movement tending to gather in the whole country old conservative and Catholic forces dispersed by the revolution, and to form, in this way, a party clearly opposed to the actual government.[18]

This distorted perspective also prevailed in Mexico from the very beginning, and as a result of the different disposition of social strengths, in a context where there seemed to be forming a solid populist coalition between the middle-class, the rural-industrial proletariat and the peasants. Only the most aware political leaders and thinkers where able to perceive the radical novelty represented by the regime of Mussolini, and that this novelty was beginning to arouse general interest.[19]

Occasional visits by Mexicans to Italy, some of them official, brought first-hand news on the development of Fascism. The Mexican Embassy, above all, kept the Italian Fascist movement under observation, and so, too, did the Mexican consulate in Genoa. The former sent regular detailed reports, some of which were solicited expressly by the government. The analyses of the birth and development of the first Fascist government made by Rafael Nieto between 1925 and 1926 were particularly incisive.[20] Nieto, in fact, thought that Fascism had been born from a meeting between a dissident socialist tide and 'the perverted revolutionary instinct' of the lower middle-class, 'compressed from above by the plutocracy and from the high bureaucratic middle-class and from below, by the proletarian class'. This combination, Nieto argued, became radicalised in the most acute moment of the post-war crisis, and could easily have diverted the initial revolutionary push of fascism in a 'violent movement of reaction against the workers' that had the support of the Italian liberal ruling class.[21]

In Mexico, the public debate on fascism was revived on several particular occasions, and especially in 1924, 1928, 1929 and 1934-35. In 1924 the murder of Italian socialist deputy Giacomo Matteotti and the arrival in Mexico of an Italian mission led to criticisms of the Mussolini regime, particularly from the labour unions of the *Confederación Regional Obrera Mexicana* (CROM) and the small Mexican Communist Party. In 1928 the country was outraged by the assassination of General Obregón, father of the revolution and recently re-elected president of the republic. The political earthquake that followed occurred in addition to the *guerrilla cristera* conducted by the Catholic farmers of the central-western part of the country against the federal army, and marked a serious conflict between the Catholic Church and the government. In this delicate situation, voices circulated of possible Italian (Fascist) help having been sent to the *guerrilleros* and the clergy. It also aroused suspicion that the Italian journalist Mario Appelius, correspondent of the Fascist newspaper *Il Popolo d'Italia* and long a resident in Mexico, had orchestrated foreign interference.

During 1928 the Italian press was denounced several times for a campaign criticising the anti-Catholic repression in Mexico. The year after, the agreement between the Church and the Italian state created a sensation in Mexico, arousing the enthusiastic approval of the Catholics and the anger of the labour organizations, freemasonry and the government. It also signalled a possible solution to the Mexican crisis, and may even have contributed toward the '*arreglos*' (June 1929) that put an end to the religious conflict in the country.

With the economic crisis of 1929 the attention of economists and the Mexican government was attracted by Fascist economic policies aimed at countering the economic downturn.[22] It seemed to many Mexican observers that Mussolini's Italy might offer some innovative economic antidote. The Fascist corporate system, internal colonisation, autarchy and the intervention of the state had been studied carefully by special Mexican missions and delegations who had been ordered to examine 'Fascism, its genesis, its organization, its development, its tendencies, its men, its work'.[23] The Italian ambassador in Mexico, Rogeri, pointed out in 1934 that even 'if Mexican revolutionary ideologies are opposite to Fascist ones, the practical realisations of the Fascist regime form a general object for study, of admiration and of imitation even by representative elements of this government'.[24]

These investigations into the Fascist phenomenon where conducted discretely by Mexican officials of the embassy and the consulates. For example, the Mexican military attaché to Rome,

Eduardo Vasconcelos noted in 1935 that:

Having discussed Italian life with many here I realise that, ultimately, Fascism is nothing more than one of many systems with state-directed economies, and that it is worth us studying it without prejudice, because such a study can be very useful, owing to the nature of this people, who are quite similar to our own.[25]

The studies of Italy undertaken by the Mexicans between 1929 and 1930 concentrated, in particular, on the inner workings of the state and the Fascist Party, and argued that these could constitute a model for the organisation of the Mexican Revolutionary Party.[26] There was a particular interest in the Fascist youth organisation, *Opera Nazionale Balilla* (ONB), and the workers organisation, the *Dopolavoro* (OND). These studies were undertaken secretly and without any public knowledge of them.

The general interest of the Mexican public toward Fascism became more widespread by 1934–35, on the occasion of the Austrian crisis – at which point Mussolini appeared as the guarantor of a European stability threatened by Hitler – and, above all, following the Italian invasion of Ethiopia. The beginning of a Fascist expansionist drive in Africa aroused anxiety in Mexico, a country that, at the time, identified Ethiopia as the victim of a Western imperialism analogous to the imperialist domination of Latin America by the United States. The word 'Ethiopia' was, at the time, spread widely within Mexico as a means of criticising the aggression of a European power toward a smaller, African one. There were also protests and workers' demonstrations against 'Fascist aggression'.[27] In fact, the Ethiopian conflict – together with the subsequent Italian intervention in Spain – marked a fundamental shift in the relationship between Italy and Mexico.

By the later 1930s the image of Fascist Italy in Mexico concomitantly polarised society as a consequence of the break-up of the international order, and the growth of various ideological threats. The government, the labour unions and the official Party increasingly adopted an anti-fascist position, while other opposition forces, inside and out of the government, came to regard fascism as a symbol of the struggle against Bolshevism and Anglo-Saxon imperialism. Intellectuals were divided, equally, between pro-fascists and anti-fascists.[28] Duly they formed political opposition groups prepared to adopt openly fascist doctrines and dogmas.[29]

Caudillos and Bolsheviks: the Mexican Image in Italy

To analyse the Italian–Mexican relationship one needs to examine not only its diplomatic and political aspects, but also the cultural contacts between the two countries. Awareness about Mexico had spread throughout Italy since the outbreak of the revolution in 1910. The spectacular fall of the regime of Porfirio Díaz, and the subsequent *coup d'état* and civil war projected a rather negative image of the country. 'Mexico' became synonymous with disorder, corruption, *caudillismo*, *guerrilla*, shootings, rapes and pillage: in short, a stereotypical caricature of Latin American political chaos.[30] The political class also used Mexico as an image representing disorder and violence: for example, on 30 May 1924, in a speech to the Italian Parliament, Giacomo Matteotti compared recent Fascist electoral violence to that that had taken place in Mexico.

At the beginning of the 1920s the political situation in Mexico could mainly be seen in two ways: the *indigenismo* and the Bolshevism of the revolution. The first aroused curiosity and produced a whole series of ambiguous reactions that oscillated between approval of the cultural awakening of an oppressed nation and disapproval of the implicitly anti-Western aspects of the Mexican cultural experiment. The second amounted to an anti-Bolshevik obsession that had spread throughout Europe since 1917. Despite the fact that the Mexican revolution pre-dated the Russian, and was most certainly not inspired by Marxism, it was believed Mexico had been contaminated by Bolshevik elements, evident in the attacks on private property, the indiscipline of the subordinate classes, anti-clericalism and the socialist rhetoric of the regime.[31]

The image of 'Bolshevik Mexico' was diffused, and particularly during 1920–22 and in 1926–29, at the same time as the civil conflict in Italy (when wide sectors of the middle-class reacted to an incumbent international 'red danger'), and on the occasion of the Mexican religious crisis. Above all, the latter brought the theme of Mexico to the foreground of the Italian public debate, particularly in the period immediately before the signing of the Lateran Pacts in 1929. In that period, Mexican president Plutarco Elías Calles

(1924–28) had often been portrayed by the religious press as a kind of Antichrist. Meanwhile the secular press viewed him as a lunatic dictator possessed by a mysterious Masonic and Bolshevik fury.[32]

The theme of agrarian reform also aroused interest in Italy. Land redistribution in Mexico – first as a restitution of that taken from the farmers, then as an endowment of public land and finally as a forced transfer (expropriation) from private landowners to landless farmers – proceeded slowly but inexorably after 1917, being one of the central aspects of the national revolution's political programme. Mexican *agrarismo* touched upon one of the weaker points of Fascist policy; namely the realisation that the regime had not undertaken agrarian reform, largely because the early Fascist movement had been incorporated into the interests of the big landowners of central Italy, from Emilia to Apulia. Faced with robust agrarian reform in Mexico, the Italian regime came to find itself in a rather embarrassing situation. The answer was merciless press criticism of land redistribution in Mexico, which, fascist newspapers alleged, precipitated a fall in agricultural production and discouraged investments and led to high quality agricultural land falling into the hands of poor quality farmers.[33]

All these images and perceptions stemmed from the trips to Mexico of Italian intellectuals, writers and journalists.[34] Some of these produced works of importance: Arnaldo Cipolla (*Montezuma contro Cristo*, 1927), Mario Appelius (*L'aquila di Chapultepec*, 1929) and Emilio Cecchi (*Messico*, 1932).[35] The first is, above all, the account of a writer interested in folklore and especially in the theme of religious conflict. The second is the report of a well known journalist of *Popolo d'Italia*, on the political and cultural aspects of Mexican life, as seen from a fascist viewpoint. The third is a study of the inner realities of Mexican culture.

Appelius's book constitutes a faithful mirror image of Mexico written for the benefit of Italian Fascism. Sent by *Il Popolo d'Italia*, Appelius had, in 1928, the official task of producing a study of the country, its economic resources, a general analysis of its culture and, above all, an analysis of the political nature of the revolutionary regime that governed it. During the ten months of his mission, Appelius saw a country that was:

> A battlefield of imperialisms and social experiments, of antagonisms of race and religious struggles, of ideological

clashes and of low personal rivalries; a country alive, alive, alive; plenty of material wealth and spiritual energies, blessed and at the same time damned by God, ... that sometimes frightens and inspires love, that always conquers the traveller and imprisons them with its charm ...![36]

In Appelius's enthusiastic description are summarised all the aspects of Mexico that attracted the attention of Fascist Italy: the struggle of a young, vital and spiritual people against imperialism (Anglo-Saxon, mercantile and decadent), to build a new destiny by developing the potential of a land rich in resources.[37] Mexico, in fact, 'shows to possess its own organic exuberance and its particular spiritual restlessness which, despite everything, are an affirmation of dynamism and denote the wish to liquidate the formidable ethnic, religious and political problems that America had inherited'.[38]

What is important here is the emphasis placed on the commonality of the cultural and geopolitical outlook; the vitality of a community fighting against Anglo-Saxon imperialism, whose Latin roots would connect it, naturally, to Rome, the lighthouse of the new civilisation created by fascism. The chief antagonist is an industrialised America beyond the Bravo river, itself the dividing line between the Latin and Anglo-Saxon world of which the Mexican people is a faithful custodian. On the other hand, there is a marked contrast with the other root of Mexican culture, the native. The Latinism of the '*littorio*' would serve in this case as an antidote, and a guideline, for avoiding the danger of a relapse in the civilisation of Central America.[39]

Appelius shows clearly that one of the principal means of penetration available for Fascist Italy in Mexico (and in Latin America) was cultural.[40] These efforts at a cultural approach nevertheless produced few concrete results. The reason was clear enough. Mexico's efforts to instill a renewed national identity among the population was based on the attempt to connect it directly to the European tradition, which diminished necessarily the importance of the native tradition so violently shaken by the Conquest. The glory of Rome was all well and good for the Italians, its presumed heirs, but the Mexicans preferred to imagine themselves as the inheritors of Aztec and Mayan civilisation, or, alternatively, as a synthesis between those civilizations and that of their Hispanic conquerors.

There were also fundamental geopolitical and economic reasons. Mexico could not afford the luxury of damaging its relationship with America in favour of a romantic 'Latin unity' that, if intended ultimately as a union with Italy, could not realistically have any political or economic basis. Mexico, in fact, had become more and more tightly bound to the economy of the United States, which absorbed almost 70 per cent of Mexican exports. Politically, the Mexican revolutionary experience was entirely autonomous in comparison to that of fascism, although there was a convergence on specific features. Moreover, the United States would not tolerate any kind of radical political change – whether 'Bolshevik' or 'fascist' – in Mexico that might threaten its national security. Thus, the Mexican government realistically had no choice but to form part of the sphere of influence of the regional superpower, and align itself with the pan-Americanism promoted by Washington.

Fascism and *Italianità*

The most direct way for Italy to penetrate Mexico was, naturally, through the local Italian population. Composed of around 7–10,000 people, the Italian-Mexican community was established in 1880 by a small migratory flood that colonised the uncultivated lands in the central regions of the country. The shortage of immigrants was owing to two factors: the presence of masses of Mexican peasants and poor labourers (that reduced the level of agricultural wages), and the chronic political instability of the country. In addition, the colonisation plans of the Italian community met with the regime's occupation of farmland. Indeed, good quality land was already in the possession of the *hacendados* (landowners), of commercial companies or peasant communities and, therefore, what remained was poor, dangerous and distant from the markets.

The only Italian colony of importance was Chipilo, a village founded by Venetians, situated not far from Puebla, at the foot of the Popocatépetl volcano. During the revolution, the farmers of Chipilo had to defend themselves several times against the assaults of rebel gangs. For these farmers the defence of the village assumed the dimensions of an epic, amounting to the reawakening of a lost national feeling.

In Mexico City the Italian colony was composed mainly of

professionals, artists and intellectuals: a relatively wealthy middle-class that had integrated without difficulty into Mexican society, thanks to their common Latin background. During the revolution, Italians living in the capital city had suffered very few inconveniences compared to those living in the provinces. The outbreak of the First World War awakened within the Italian community emotional feeling for the motherland. Some Italian-Mexican youngsters even departed as volunteers for the front. The eventual victory in 1918 generated great excitement and a hope for the future of the proletarian Italy from which so many had had to depart.

In the post-war period, news on the economic difficulties and near civil war that raged in the motherland remained a distant echo in Mexico. In 1922, therefore, the advent of Fascism passed almost unnoticed among native Italians living in Mexico. Rather, a change in their outlook occurred following the 1924 mission and the arrival of the first *fuoriusciti* (Italian anti-Fascist exiles).

On 23 August the ship *Italia* arrived at the port of Veracruz, disembarking a key group of Italians. The *Italia* carried a sample of Italian industrial products together with a large group of businessmen, journalists, artists and political representatives – 700 persons in all – led by the extraordinary ambassador, Giovanni Giuriati.[41]

The Italian group was immediately taken with the political turmoil in Mexico that followed the Matteotti scandal, whose body had been discovered a week earlier in Rome. The Mexican left-wing press criticised the visit by the representatives of the Fascist government.[42] The Mexican Communist Party invited activists and workers to protest against the undesirable foreign guests. In the port of Veracruz there also appeared countless red and black ribbons. President Obregón, fearing incidents, telegraphed the military commander of Veracruz to keep a close eye on the situation,[43] and to notify Giuriati that the Italians would not be allowed to wear black shirts on Mexican territory.

The disappointment of the Italian delegation was partly relieved by the success of the visits paid to the ship: more than 10,000 boarded the *Italia* on the first day. Italians then boarded a train with a strong military escort, and headed for Mexico City. Here, the government received the delegation rather coldly. The Italians had, however, the time to strengthen relations with the Italian community that had by and large mobilised to welcome their fellow countrymen with reception committees. Before returning, Giuriati visited Chipilo, where a triumphal reception awaited him. Italian farmers, in fact, celebrated the arrival of their compatriots, showering them with flowers and playing the national anthem and Fascist songs very loudly. They were offered, in exchange, a rock from Mount Grappa and the assurance that, from now on, they could be sure that Fascist Italy would no longer abandon its lost children in the world.[44]

As a corollary of the visit of 1924 an important change occurred at the Italian embassy. Count Nani Mocenigo, in charge since 1919, was replaced by Baron Giovanni Di Giura; he, in turn, was replaced by Gino Macchioro Vivalba a few months later.[45] Both were career diplomats, committed nationalists and, later, Fascists. Di Giura and Macchioro represented the transition from the pre-Fascist diplomacy of Contarini to that of Fascism; that is, active and ideological. The change was completed between 1925 and 1927. The consuls all stuck to the new course, especially that of Puebla Carlo Mastretta, on which the village of Chipilo depended. In addition, the new commercial attaché, Umberto Fabbri, acted as the personal informant of Mussolini.

Around the Italian Legation there soon grew a grouping that succeeded in mobilising a large part of the Italian community by way of the Dante Alighieri Society, the Italian Committee of Assistance and, above all, the *fascio*. The Mexican *fascio* was founded in 1927 thanks to the efforts of Eliseo Lodigiani, president of the ex-combatants association and an informal representative of the PNF in Mexico. Lodigiani was one of the young Italian-Mexicans who had volunteered for active service in Europe in 1915. After the armistice he joined one of the Fascist action squads and, subsequently recalled by his father, he came back to Mexico in 1920, taking charge of the family factory. With the foundation of the *fascio* in 1927, he became the *federal*, that is the representative of the PNF in Mexico. Very soon other *fasci* sprang up in other Mexican cities, all dependent on that of the capital city (they totaled nine by 1932).[46]

Most of the Italian colony joined the *fascio* of the capital city, which was considered something of a club along the lines of those run by the other more important overseas colonies. Italians would go to the *Casa d'Italia* (the House of Italy) – the seat of the *fascio* – for official ceremonies, to listen to lectures and to see Italian films.

Affiliation with the *fascio* was also a means of tightening personal relationships, and of exerting influence within the community. Around the *fascio* there took place various commemorative and ritual activities based on the patriotic calendar. There was, for example, the *appello ai caduti* (the invocation to of the fallen), which took place within a commemorative ceremony (on 4 November) for the 'war of redemption'.[47] These events tended to strengthen common identity and engendered a notion of Fascism's equalling patriotism, a notion promoted actively abroad by the representatives of the Italian government.[48]

What is more surprising is that a Mexican government, so susceptible on the matter of external interference, allowed the formation of these branches of a foreign political party on its territory. The relatively late date of the *fascio*'s foundation (1927), and the available documentation, suggests that there was some official resistance, avoided only by negotiation. All seems to point to the fact that the Mexican government consented to the foundation of sections of the PNF in exchange for an Italian guarantee that these would be limited to the small and harmless Italian-Mexican community, without trying to spread propaganda or to interfere in the internal affairs of the country.

This gentlemen's agreement seemed to work. It included a certain degree of co-operation between the Italian Legation and the Mexican Foreign Office. The former promised to avoid incidents, to check the political activities of Italians and to recommend to Rome that it moderate the tone of anti-Mexican criticism in the Fascist press. The second guaranteed the control of the activities of the Italian exiles, and to moderate the tones of anti-Fascist criticism in Mexico.

The political expatriates in Mexico were few, disparate and disorganised, tied more to ideologically similar Mexican groups than to that of their fellow countrymen. The well-known photographer Tina Modotti, for example, worked with Mexican communists without unduly upsetting the embassy. The anarchist ex-Fascist journalist, Nanni Leone Castelli, on the other hand, caused many problems and maintained contact with the anti-Fascist exiles in Paris and Argentina, as well as with the French Embassy and government.[49]

True Fascists and, for that matter, anti-Fascists, were few. There was, in reality, a limited level of politicisation within the Italian community, which saw in Fascism nothing more than a nationalist awakening that raised the prestige of the immigrants. Nationalist fervour was notable above all between the farmers of Chipilo, in touch with the motherland for the first time after years of abandonment.[50] In the capital city the *fascio* was reduced to the function of a club, through which, nevertheless, the Italian community found for the first time a meeting point and a sense of cohesion. The fascistisation of Italians was limited, therefore, to symbols, images and occasions of meeting and socialising. For the embassy the *fascio* network was useful, above all, as a means of control and of mobilising patriotism, for instance during the Ethiopian conflict.

Conclusions: Italian Fascism, Mexico and Latin America, 1922–35

The study of Fascist Italy's policy toward Latin America has been, to date, largely limited to work on immigration and on Fascist and anti-Fascist sentiments among the migrants. The scant interest in this area is also underlined by the small amount of documentation regarding Latin America published in the Italian diplomatic document collections.[51] Such indifference is due without doubt to the deeply rooted conviction that Fascism did not have ambitions in Latin America, which, to all intents and purposes, constituted a marginal area for Italian expansionism. Aldo Albonico sustains, for example, that Mussolini 'never had plans of expansion' in that continent, and that 'there was not, in comparison to Latin America, a true system of precepts, beyond rhetorical displays and the personal judgments of certain writers'.[52] Such judgments seem a little hasty and it would confuse the realism imposed by objective limitations, noticeable in diplomatic practice, with the ambition and the expansionist programmes that Italy tried to apply beyond those.

Effectively, on the basis of documentary evidence, and bearing in mind the limitations of researching only into one case (Mexico), we may argue that Fascist Italy had geopolitical ambitions on the Latin American continent.[53] These amounted partly to a continuation of the expansionist policies of liberal Italy combined with attempts to open Latin American markets to Italian commerce, while also emphasising the common cultural ties and immigration. The advent of Fascism nevertheless generated nationalist tendencies and demands for prestige from the immigrants, and introduced, especially after 1925, greater geopolitical considerations, based on the ambitions of the Mussolini regime in America, and in other parts of the world.

The available documentation makes it difficult to draw an overall picture for Latin America. What can be said is that the problems faced by Fascism and the actions it undertook, were most keenly felt within the cultural, political and commercial spheres, in which the regime attempted to counter the penetration of other powers, as well as local difficulties and resistance. In reality, these efforts were considerable. Fascist attempts at cultural expansion were expressed through numerous publications,[54] official visits, propaganda,[55] conferences and exhibitions promoting Latinism. In commercial terms the regime organised many missions and much publicity. There were also attempts to exert political influence through promoting the achievements of the regime, and offering a point of reference in fighting Bolshevism and imperialism by winning over intellectuals, politically active individuals and political leaders as well as by offering military collaboration.[56]

A summary of Fascist policy in Latin America can be found in the work of Oreste Villa, an expert on the continent, published in Italy in 1933.[57] In his long and articulate exposure, Villa denounced the absence of European influence on the continent, which had effectively opened the door to American, Asian and Russian (Bolshevik) penetration. Reviewing the potential and the problems of the continent, the author drew attention to the weakness of the governments, the poorly defined ethnic and cultural identities, a badly planned immigration policy and limited European economic investment. But above all Villa blamed Washington's pan-Americanism, which he viewed as an expression of an Anglo-Saxon monopoly capitalism that threatened to leave Latin America forever isolated from the penetration of the Latin nations of the old continent. Moreover, in Villa, as already in Appelius, Mexico appears as 'the big intransigent rampart ... the granite stone which can never clash with the United States'.[58]

Mexico, the sentinel of Latin America was, for this and for other reasons, an atypical example of Fascism's Latin American policy. The Italian-Mexican community did not represent a means of effective penetration of the country. The social-nationalist revolution of Mexico interested the Fascist government to the extent it had to make an effort to favour even this evolution toward a fascist model or, at least, prevent any Mexican shift toward a socialist or Bolshevik state. Facing insurmountable obstacles, Fascist policy was limited to monitoring the Bolshevik tendencies of the regime, the influence of Washington and Soviet activities; each used Mexico as a launch pad for the whole of Latin America.[59] Ultimately, the truly critical moment for Italian policy – the imposition of sanctions over the Ethiopian question – saw Italy totally impotent in the face of a determined Mexican position.

On the cultural level Italy failed to marry Latinism to its Italian roots, by exploiting the diffused hostility against pan Americanism. In this Fascism enjoyed more success in Spain. As a final point, the Latin American governments of the 1920s and 1930s were generally characterised by a proud and overt nationalism, and did not openly admit to European influences. Such governments mistrusted a '*littorian*' imperialism that lowered the Iberian inheritance to a secondary level in comparison to the Roman, not to speak of that native culture Fascism considered so primitive and decadent.[60]

Considerable results were achieved by Fascist propaganda aimed at Italian immigrants, which tended during the 1920s to co-ordinate activities promoted by the *fasci*, the Italian institutes and legations. But there was no hope for any positive change in the policies of the Latin American host countries. On the contrary the virtual ending of immigration from Italy during the Fascist period led to a speeding up of the integration of Italian-Americans into their countries of residence.[61] Moreover, after 1936 the Fascist alliance with Nazi Germany caused repulsion among Latin American peoples of Italian descent. The result was that

> the Italian in South America assimilated quickly with both Spanish and Portuguese races. In Argentina, where about half of the Italian stock is found, they consider themselves Argentineans [sic] and are proud of it. ... The Italians resented Mussolini's attempts to export Fascism and even more his subservience to his Nazi master.[62]

In political terms, the Latin American dictators were generally distant from the Mussolinian 'cesarist' model that Fascism represented (including the 'Bolivarian' Juan Vicente Gómez in Venezuela),[63] and there were in many cases, as Albonico suggests, conservatives too that did not want to distance the Leftist component of Fascism.[64] In the Mexican case strong men of high profile (Obregón, Calles) were politically oriented toward the Left, and highly respectful of liberal democracy. They had no propensity to imitate the experience of Italian Fascism. In turn, Italians had less trust for political movements that openly claimed to be inspired by Fascism; they were generally neither Fascist nor prepared to seize power.[65]

For the political regimes the desirable model would have been a dictatorship driven by a 'Bolivarian'-style *caudillo*, with a social-nationalist programme, a European wing with a Latin imprint, and open to the cultural (and economic) influence of Rome. None of the Latin American regimes came even close to this 'ideal'. Revolutionary Mexico was not able to meet such requirements. In short, although Italy had explored the geopolitical possibilities within the region, there was never any real prospect of an ideological propagation of the Fascist model on the American continent.[66]

NOTES

1. Studies on Fascist foreign policy rarely pay attention to Latin America. See in general on this topic, G. Carocci, *La politica estera dell'Italia fascista (1925–1928)* (Bari: Laterza, 1969); and above all, R. De Felice, *Mussolini il Duce. Gli anni del consenso. 1929–1936* (Torino: Einaudi, 1996), Ch.IV. More recent studies include, M. Knox, 'Il fascismo e la politica estera italiana', in R.J.B. Bosworth and S. Romano (eds.), *La politica estera italiana, 1880–1985*, (Bologna: Il Mulino, 1991), pp.287–330; P. Pastorelli, 'La politica estera di Mussolini', *Rivista di Studi Internazionali* 255, LXIV/3 (luglio-settembre 1997), pp.390–400; P. Pastorelli, *Dalla prima alla seconda guerra mondiale. Momenti e problemi della politica estera italiana (1914–1943)* (Milano: LED, 1998); see also E. Collotti, *Fascismo e politica di potenza. Politica estera 1922–1939* (Milano: La Nuova Italia, 2000). On Fascism's overseas organisation, see E. Gentile, 'La politica estera del Partito Fascista', *Storia Contemporanea* XXVI/6 (dicembre 1995), pp.897–956.
2. The contrasting interpretations of historians are exposed clearly in R. Mallett, 'Il dibattito internazionale sul fascismo: le implicazioni di politica estera', in Michele Abbate (ed.), *Pensiero ed azione totalitaria tra le due guerre mondiali* (Città Castellana/Orte: CEFASS, 2000), pp.25–41.
3. For a general view of Fascism's Latin American policy, see F. Savarino, 'Apuntes sobre el fascismo italiano en America Latina', *Reflejos* 9 (2000–2001), pp.100–10.
4. There are several studies on Brazil and Argentina. See among others, A. Trento, 'Il fascismo e gli emigrati in Brasile', *Latinoamerica* 9 (1988), pp.49–56; A. Trento, 'Il Brasile, gli immigrati e il fenomeno fascista', in B. Vanni (ed.), *La riscoperta delle Americhe. Lavoratori e sindacato nell'emigrazione italiana in America Latina, 1970–1970* (Milano: Teti Editore, 1994), pp.250–64; R.C. Newton, 'Ducini, Prominenti, Antifascisti. Italian Fascism and the Italo-Argentine Collectivity', *The Americas* 51/1 (luglio 1994), pp.41–66; and J.F. Bertonha, 'O antifascismo no mundo

da diaspora italiana: elementos para uma analise comparativa do caso brasileiro', *Altreitalie* 17 (gennaio-giugno 1998), pp.16–30.

5. See above all E. Gentile, 'L'emigrazione italiana in Argentina nella politica di espansione del nazionalismo e del fascismo', *Storia Contemporanea* XVII/3 (giugno 1986), pp.355–96.

6. See B. Moore, *Le origini sociali della dittatura e della democrazia* (Torino: Einaudi, 1992).

7. For a comparison of both revolutions, see J.M. Hart, *El México revolucionario* (México: Alianza, 1992).

8. From among the considerable academic works available on fascism we can highlight the works of George Mosse and Zeev Sternhell. They agree, *grosso modo*, that fascism was a 'cultural revolution', in the broader context of the changing nature of European thought at the end of the nineteenth century. G. Mosse, *The Fascist Revolution. Toward a General Theory of Fascism* (New York: Howard Fertig, 1999); Z. Sternhell, *Né destra né sinistra. L'ideologia fascista in Francia* (Milano: Baldini & Castoldi, 1997).

9. Many contemporary foreign observers noticed the resemblance of the two regimes: for example Carleton Beals compared the Mexican PNR to Mussolini's PNF; C. Beals, 'Mexico Turns to Fascist Tactics', *The Nation* 82 (28 January 1931), pp.110–12.

10. Bearing in mind the conventional metaphor of the Left-Right polarity we can state that the Mexican nationalist regime was more inclined toward the left than its Italian counterpart. Moreover, this tendency was increasing during the second half of the 1930s.

11. Italian Fascism had aroused interest in Mexico ever since 1919. Some Mexican workers' organisations warned that what had been born in Italy could constitute a serious threat to organised workers; Mussolini, the 'traitor' to the socialist cause, gave armed support to the middle-class and the landowners. Others saw in Mussolini simply an atypical symbol for the revolutionary atmosphere that characterised the European post-war period. But there were also conservatives who approved of the furious anti-communist stance of the Fascists.

12. Nani Mocenigo to Benito Mussolini, Mexico, 25 November 1922, busta 1438, Mexico, Affari Politici (AP) 1919–30, Mexico Archivio Storico del Ministero degli Affari Esteri (ASMAE).

13. For an analysis of the party's birth, see J. MacGregor, '"Orden y justicia": El Partido Fascista Mexicano 1922–1923', *Signos Históricos* 1 (junio 1999), pp.150–80.

14. C. Beals, *Mexico. An Interpretation* (New York: B.W., 1923), p.141. Sáenz de Sicilia founded another similar organization in 1936, the *Confederación de la Clase Media*, which was openly anti-communist.

15. 'The *hacendados*, were organised in the "*Sindicato de Agricultores*" to launch an offensive against the agrarian reform of the government, and frequently acted in unison with the fascists', ibid., p.141.

16. As often happened during the 1930s Mexican politics was inclined toward the left of the revolutionary spectrum, creating a sort of psychological equivalent to the 'Bolshevik danger' of the European post-war period.

17. C. Beals, 'The Mexican Fascisti', *Current History* XIX (October 1923), p.261.

18. Mocenigo to Benito Mussolini (note 12).

19. We have to bear in mind the revolutionary and modernising nature of fascism, a radical phenomenon clearly distinct from the conservative or radical Right. See for example S. Payne, *Fascism. Comparison and Definition* (Madison, WI: University of Wisconsin Press, 1980), pp.3–21; and Mosse (note 8), pp.1–44.

20. Rafael Nieto was Mexican ambassador to Sweden, where he had the opportunity to study the situation of post-war Europe closely. Thereafter he was ambassador to Italy

(1925–26). In Italy he maintained contacts with Fascist union leaders and heads of the political opposition, particularly with Filippo Turati. Before Nieto, Mexican ambassador Julio Madero – a Fascist sympathiser – claimed that Fascism had put an end to Bolshevik anarchy, thanks to the energetic action of Mussolini; Informe (Report) of Julio Madero to Secretaria de Relaciones Exteriores, Rome, 3 July 1924, Archivo Historico de la Secretaria de Relaciones Exteriores 21-26-34.

21. 'Informe del Ministro de México en Italia, Rafael Nieto', Roma, 15 March 1925, Plutarco Elias Calles (PEC) 73-55-3998-2/3, Fideicomiso Archivos Plutarco Elias Calles y Fernando Torreblanca (FAPECyFT).

22. Among Mexican economists there was a big interest in Fascist economic policies. The famous economist Díaz Dufoo greatly admired Italian economic successes, concluding, 'On the other hand this regime is founded upon the ruins of liberty!', C.D. Dufoo, *Vida y ritmo de la economía* (Mexico: Librería Navarro, 1934), p.445.

23. 'Programa que la comisión ... nombrada por el "Bloque Juventud Revolucionaria" desarrolllará en su viaje de estudio a Italia', b.2, Mexico, 1933, AP 1931–45, ASMAE.

24. Rogeri to MAE, 1 February 1934, b.3, Mexico, AP 1931–45, ASMAE. Two months later he wrote that 'in order to resolve social problems, the government and the party are deeply interested in our corporate orientation and they follow with attention our work creation schemes, are enthusiastic about our principles, and have a high consideration for Mussolinian policies', 19 April 1934, b.3, Mexico, AP 1931–45, ASMAE.

25. Report by Vasconcelos, Rome, 1935, PEC 76-32-5800, FAPECyFT.

26. Although highlighted by many historians, the 'fascist' dimension of Mexican politics between 1928 and 1934, has not been the subject of much study and has not been based on official documentary evidence.

27. In the autumn of 1935 there were various instances of protest against the Fascist war in Ethiopia. On 2 October there was a demonstration, organised by the *Frente Popular Anti-imperialista*, in front of the Italian embassy in Mexico; in another demonstration the offices of the periodical *El Correo de Italia* were destroyed.

28. Fascism divided the Mexican intelligentsia; José Vasconcelos and Gerardo Murillo became Fascist supporters, while Diego Rivera, V.L. Toledano and D.A. Siqueiros were active anti-Fascists.

29. This was the case of the famous group *Acción Revolucionaria Mexicanista*, whose members were better known as *Los Dorados* or *Camisas Doradas*, owing to the colour of their uniforms. Founded in March 1934, the 'Gilded Shirts' were organised into violent anti-communist squads. They were also inspired (even if they did not admit it openly) by the German S.A. and the Italian blackshirts; see H.G. Campbell, *La derecha radical en México, 1929–1949* (México: SEP, 1976), pp.50–61.

30. A publication of May 1922, *Italia e Messico* (Rome) carried headlines such as 'Mexican demonstrations punished by the police', 'The Mexican deeds of radiant May' and 'Mexican demonstrations', all of which referred to events in Italy. In 1919 the Italian military attaché wrote that 'the normal state of the country is, has been and will be revolutionary', Cantoni Marca to Sidney Sonnino, 2 July 1919, b.1438, Mexico, AP 1919–30, AMSAE.

31. A privileged observer of both phenomena was Count Battista Nani Mocenigo. A member of the Italian embassy in Saint Petersburg during the revolution of 1917, he had then moved to Mexico, and so could compare the two revolutionary experiences. In 1922 he noticed that 'between the two big contemporary revolutions, Mexican and Russian, there is not only a strong analogy in their meaning ... but also in the excesses of the revolutions themselves', Mocenigo to Schanzer, 9 May 1922, b.1438, Mexico, AP 1919–30, AMSAE.

32. The image of Mexican President Calles as a 'Bolshevik' originated, to a large extent, from English and American writings.

33. See the embassy report to Dino Grandi of 6 January 1931, in which Mexican agrarian reform was defined as 'a masterpiece of socialist idiocy, that has taken lands from those who worked them in order to give them to those who generally do not have the desire or the means to work them', b.1, Mexico, AP 1931–45, ASMAE.

34. The first Fascist references to Mexico were the product of the visit of the ship *Italia* in 1924; P. Belli, *Al di là dei mari* (Firenze: Vallecchi, 1925); E. Carrara, *Ventotto porti dell'America Latina tra Atlantico e Pacifico con la R. Nave 'Italia'* (Torino: Alberto Giani, 1925); M. Miserocchi, *La crociera della Nave Italia. L'America Latina attraverso il mio oblò* (Pistoia: G. Franzini, 1928); E. Rocca, *Avventura Sudamericana* (Milano: Alpes, 1926).

35. A. Cipolla, *Montezuma contro Cristo: viaggio al Messico* (Milano: Agnelli, 1927); M. Appelius, *L'Aquila di Chapultepec (Messico)* (Milano: Alpes, 1929); E. Cecchi, *Messico* (Milano and Roma: Treves, 1932). In the same years the archaeologist Guido Callegari travelled to Mexico, see his *Messico* (Milano: Vallardi, 1931).

36. Appelius (note 35), p.9.

37. In the work of Appelius there are many other themes that attracted and fascinated the authentic ideological Fascist: from the attitudes of Spartan virility and the challenge to death that they are observed in Mexican popular culture, to the 'cesarism' of the leaders of the revolution, that obviously resembled the cult of the *Duce* in Italy. Álvaro Obregón, and even the 'socialist Mason' Calles, are praised and even admired for their qualities as audacious commanders of a vital and resolute people.

38. Appelius (note 35), p.106.

39. The relationship with the prestigious past of pre-Columbian civilisations in Mexico was articulated by the same writer.

40. The 'Latinism' promoted by Italy could never really compete with the 'Hispanism' of Spain, which was more rooted in the historical-cultural sediment of the continent. They were also two distinct calls from the point of view of modernity, since Hispanism was characterised as decidedly conservative, while Latinism was potentially progressive. To Latinism was added 'Bolivarianism', that is the cult of the *libertador* Simón Bolívar. Fascist Italy promoted an active cult to Bolívar; see A. Filippi, 'Las interpretaciones cesaristas y fascistas de Bolívar en the European culture', *Latinoamérica. Anuario de Estudios Latinoamericanos* 17 (1995), pp.165–204.

41. G. Giuriati, *La crociera italiana nell'America Latina* (Roma: Istituto Cristoforo Colombo, 1925); see also *Crociera Italiana nell'America Latina. Anno 1924. Catalogo Ufficiale* (Milano: Casa Editrice di Pubblicità F. De Rio, 1924); and for the Mexican stage of the journey, *La R. Nave Italia* (México: Scuola Tipografica Salesiana, 1924); Gentile, 'L'emigrazione', pp.379–81.

42. *El Machete*, a communist periodical, was the most aggressive. The conservative press viewed the Italians as champions of the struggle against Bolshevism. Anti-Italian criticisms stopped when it published a passage from a Matteotti speech of 30 May 1924, where he compared the Fascist violence to the 'Mexican'.

43. A. Obregón to Juan A. Almazán, 11 August 1924, Mexico, Fernando Torreblanca 28–795–1/2, FAPECyFT.

44. Belli (note 34), p.297.

45. Macchioro, of Venetian origin, had begun his career in 1896, holding important posts in Africa, Brazil and Europe. In 1919 he was the Italian representative at the Paris Peace Conference before becoming ambassador to Latvia-Lithuania and Ethiopia. At the moment of the nomination to the Mexican Legation he was head of the intelligence office at the Italian foreign ministry. The successors of Macchioro – the Milanese Count Gianfranco Viganotti Giusti (1931–32); the Piedmontese Delfino Rogeri dei Conti di Villanova (1932–35) and the Turinese Count Alberto Marchetti di Muriaglio (1935–42) – were only superficially Fascist.

46. On the Mexican *fasci*, see various files in Mexico, AP 1919–30 and 1931–35, ASMAE, and the surviving editions of the magazines *Italia Nuova* and *Il Legionario*.
47. See E. Gentile, *Il culto del littorio* (Roma and Bari: Laterza, 1998).
48. On this intense propaganda effort see, for example, a statement of Macchioro's regarding the Italian community in Mexico on the occasion of the celebration of 21 April (foundation of Rome), 'The supreme reason and the principal motive to be of Fascism is the valorization of the Nation, which must be brought back to her ancient greatness and connected to the traditions of Rome', 21 April 1927, b.1440, Mexico, AP 1919–30, ASMAE.
49. Leone Castelli was the agent in Mexico of the anti-Fascist *Unione Democratica Italiana*.
50. Fascist imagery and symbolism prevailed among the farmers of Chipilo. They regularly celebrated all the main dates of the national calendar wearing the uniforms of the Militia (MVSN) and singing nationalist and Fascist hymns. The children of the village were members of the *balilla*, and they attended an Italian school, watched over by a portrait of the *Duce*.
51. In the Italian Diplomatic Documents (DDI), series 7 and 8, very few documents relate to Latin America, especially for the period 1922–34. The situation improves marginally after 1935.
52. A. Albonico, *Italia y América* (Madrid: MAPFRE, 1994), pp.165–7.
53. On the significance of Fascist Latin American politics, see Savarino (note 3), pp.100–10.
54. I have highlighted here only works referring to Mexico. A great number of books were still written on South America as a whole. There were, in addition, some specialist magazines on the subject, such as *Le Vie d'Italia e dell'America Latina* (1924–32), *Rivista d'Italia e d'America* (1923–28) and *Colombo* (1926–31).
55. We might recall the transatlantic flights of De Pinedo in 1927 and Balbo in 1930–31.
56. On the military missions, see C. Cavaglià, 'Stormi d'Italia sul mondo: America Latina e Italia fascista tra propaganda e politica estera', unpublished degree thesis, University of Turin, 1995.
57. O. Villa, *L'America Latina, problema fascista* (Rome: Nuova Europa, 1933); P. Pieri, *L'America Latina dal 1900 al 1930* (Napoli: Tipomeccanica, 1934). See also the brief speech given on Italian immigration by Gioacchino Volpe to the *Primo Convegno Nazionale per gli Studi di Politica Estera*, Milan, 15–17 October 1936, with the title 'Le relazioni politiche, economiche, spirituali tra l'Italia e L'America Latina' (Milano: Istituto di Studi Politici Internazionali, 1936).
58. Villa (note 57), p.71. On pan-Americanism Pieri specified that 'From the intrusiveness of the United States, Italy does not have anything to gain; and it has too many interests down there ... to take no interest in that matter', Pieri (note 57), p.46.
59. Mexico had had a small but active, pro-Soviet Communist Party since 1919 and maintained diplomatic relations with the USSR between 1924 and 1930. The Soviet embassy in Mexico City notoriously sustained the activity of the Komintern throughout the whole continent. On the Mexican–Soviet relationship, see D. Spenser, *El triángulo imposible. México, Rusia Soviética y Estados Unidos en los años veinte* (México: Ciesas-M.A.Porrúa, 1998).
60. According to the Fascist vision Latin America had to recognise the spiritual supremacy of Rome.
61. In the United States perspective, the possibilities for Italy in Latin America were modest in comparison to those of other European countries, 'There are the pan-Hispanic aspirations of Spain, the cultural affinity, the sentimental predisposition and melancholy rankling of France, the economic competition of England and Germany, and possibly Italy's interests in its trade and its millions of sons who have gone out to

Brazil, Uruguay and Argentina', F. Rippy, *Latin America in World Politics. An Outline Survey* (New York: Alfred A. Knopf, 1928), p.266.

62. G.H. Stuart, *Latin America and The United States* (New York: Appleton-Century-Crofts, 1966), p.77.

63. In Villa's work, Gómez is however the only dictator who merits a word of praise, Villa (note 57), pp.55–7.

64. Ironically, the two only regimes that showed signs of resemblance with Italian Fascism were the Brazil of Vargas (1937–45) and the Argentina of Perón (1946–55).

65. A 1934 Italian foreign ministry memorandum listed 'fascist' movements throughout the world. It included Argentina, Brazil, Chile, Cuba, Panama and Peru; none of them came to power. See De Felice (note 1), pp.872–919.

66. Savarino (note 3), p.107.

8

Defence of a Concept:
Raymond Aron and Totalitarianism

TRINE M. KJELDAHL

With the fall of the Berlin wall, an era heavily charged with ideological confrontations ended, and 'totalitarian' duly became one of the terms that characterised the twentieth century.[1] Totalitarianism as a scientific label seems to have survived into the new century as a term for defining present and future anti-democratic regimes, and, with this perspective in mind, it is useful to look at the concept's scope and limits. Raymond Aron's sociological and political thinking is a good place to start a critical examination of 'totalitarianism'.

During the 1930s, Aron had been among the first scholars to suggest the concept of totalitarianism. Later, Aron became one of the few that defended the theory of totalitarianism as a means of defining both Italian and German fascism. In the post-war period, Aron also termed Soviet communism totalitarian, not only until 1956 but during the whole communist period. He proposed a general use of the concept to cover the Maoist administration in China, the Khmer Rouge in Cambodia and other authoritarian and ideologically-charged regimes, although only on the basis of rigorous scientific methods as well as sound political judgement. Aron's originality is best elucidated by comparing him to other scholars of totalitarianism. This article first recalls Hannah Arendt's political philosophy and the political science approach of the Zbigniew Brzezinski school. Second, it traces the development of Aron's theory of totalitarianism, and concludes that Aron's questions concerning methodology and the ethics of science are still highly relevant when asking how we understand and explain irrational political phenomena, and what use we make of our knowledge.

The Birth of a Concept

At the beginning of the 1920s, Mussolini outlined his notion of the 'total state'. His definition identified the term as meaning a strong and authoritarian government with imperialist ambitions.[2] Later, during the 1930s, when the fascist states became anti-parliamentarian as well as externally aggressive, scholars suggested the concept of totalitarianism to describe a radical new type of regime compared to the more moderate political regimes of the past. Also, Soviet communism provided a good reason for using the concept of totalitarianism. The German-American philosopher Hannah Arendt was among the first to establish a philosophical theory of totalitarianism.[3] She argued that both Nazi rule and Stalin's regime constituted a complete break with Western-style government in the way they abolished the idea of politics as basically covering 'discussion going on among human beings as to define just political institutions'. Arendt showed that totalitarian regimes were constructed on 'arbitrary power manifestation', 'terror' and 'fear'.[4] Later, two American political scientists, Carl Friedrich and Zbigniew Brzezinski, transformed Arendt's philosophical theory into a political one that highlighted clear structural similarities between Fascism, Nazism and Stalinism by the way these regimes constituted an antithesis to Western democratic government. The concepts that they developed have since become the classic definition of totalitarian regimes. In these regimes, only 'one state ideology' prevailed; the political system was 'a single party system'; the state was controlled by 'terror police'; bureaucracy and economy were centralised; and the media consisted of systematic state propaganda.[5]

These systematically established theories of totalitarianism have since been criticised. Many historians and political scientists consider totalitarianism to be too broad, and too miscellaneous, a concept to cover political regimes which are both different in form and in ideology. And, what is more, theories of totalitarianism do not easily explain what and why specific historical processes lead to totalitarian regimes. During the 1960s, the key concepts that defined totalitarianism appeared gradually less suitable when applied to

Italian Fascism, German Nazism and Stalinism.[6] This is why Hannah Arendt chose strictly to limit the concept of totalitarianism to cover German Nazism and Stalin's terror regime of the 1930s.[7] She left out both Italian Fascism and the Soviet system after 1956. Also, the Brzezinski school began modifying their general descriptive theory due to changes in the Soviet regime during the 1960s.[8] By the beginning of the 1980s, many scholars considered totalitarianism to be a virtually useless scientific approach to the study of authoritarian forms of government.[9]

Misunderstanding Fascism

In his autobiography, Raymond Aron recalled that his political commitment after the First World War was a 'socialism' that stood for 'vague egalitarian' ideas, 'pacifism' and 'reconciliation' between Germany and France. In the early 1930s, Aron worked as a teacher in Germany, where he experienced the rise of Hitler's National Socialist regime. From this moment on, he conceived of the need for a political theory able both to act as a warning and to guide Western governments facing the threat posed by fascist regimes. He returned from his German sojourn as a liberal patriot.[10] Once back in France, Aron stressed the need to understand the radical ideological nature of fascism, including its imperialist dimension. He began to criticise the way French scholars looked at the fascist phenomenon. In France, the government's advisors were historians of diplomacy who simply produced written accounts of diplomatic events in chronological order. These historians were, in Aron's eyes, unable to establish a conceptual understanding of foreign policy events.[11] As to more concept-based social scientists, like sociologists, philosophers and economists, they did not take into account what actually took place within the various fascist states. One group of scholars[12] explained Hitler and Mussolini's behaviour as a search for recognition within the European, great power diplomatic club. Despite the fascist leaders' totalitarian and imperialist world view, these scholars deduced a rational way of thinking from within the fascist mind. They argued that negotiation with extremist regimes was possible, and that fascists could, essentially, be educated to respect international treaties.[13]

Other, more functionalist scholars, noticed an economic motive which, in their view, explained fascist behaviour. Some chose to interpret fascist states as, 'young states that strive for more global influence and a better place at the world market'. These scholars also suggested diplomatic negotiation consisting either in offering the fascist regimes a 'reasonable share in the global economy' or – more drastically – in imposing economic sanctions on them, cutting down their war industries or placing their financial sectors under international control as the means of bringing pressure to bear on them. Aron demonstrated that fascist ideas were effectively incompatible with existing Western values. In his eyes these scholars defined fascism incorrectly, and, therefore, generated ineffective policy recommendations.[14]

Hermeneutic Sociology

Aron argued that to understand fascism one should consider it as a phenomenon radically opposed to Western rationalism. He later recalled his shift of perspective by paraphrasing Michel de Montaigne:

> In our time – by the fact of fascism and national socialism before 1945 and that of communism especially after 1945 – we have encountered the *other* at our side. It was not necessary to sail to a distant and unknown country to ask oneself: how can one be Persian? It is enough to meet one's collegue, at one's side, to ask: how can he be a Hitlerian?[15]

Aron preferred the methodology of German sociologist Max Weber, known more commonly as 'historical sociology'.[16] In Weber's sociology, political acts resulted from deliberation on the nature of values. These deliberations might be irrational and ambiguous because they were part of certain world visions. It is this subjective character of political acts that the scholar must asess in such a way that even irrationality becomes comprehensible. Weber, therefore, introduced to political science the methodological problem that traditional hermeneutics had been trying to solve for centuries: how do we understand the 'other' when we are faced with multiple meanings? Weber suggested *ideal types* that only establish a methodological definition of rationality. The scholar deciphers the (ir)rationality of historical agents by observing how they put their ideas into action, or by establishing mean-goal schemes.[17] From 1933 onwards, Aron was thus able to show how the fascist world vision seemed about to be realised historically. This vision consisted of imposing tyrannous rule internally while submitting the rest of Europe to a racial hierarchy. Fascists already behaved as if their world vision had achieved 'total efficacy'.[18]

During the Second World War, Aron left a France run by the infamous Vichy regime and joined General de Gaulle in London, where he promptly established a journal that analysed the war, and in particular the political, ideological and military performance of the Italian and German military apparatus. In the resulting essays, Aron concentrated on certain key concepts. Fascist ideology constituted a complete break with national and liberal movements which, in the nineteenth century, achieved democracy and 'peoples' sovereignty'. In Germany and Italy the respective rising élites were tyrannous and violent, and aimed at the total suffocation of parliamentary government.[19] Mussolini and Hitler introduced terror police control, a single party system and a state-organised propaganda that diffused an all-encompassing fascist interpretation of history, the citizen's private life, government and international politics.[20] Aron's concepts were close to those later outlined by Arendt and the Brzezinski school. His originality lay in the way that he effectively combined a study of government with a study of international politics. When he came to analyse violent élites he used the term 'revisionist'. This term covered fascism's foreign policy orientation, an orientation that aimed not only at changing the balance of power between states, but also at strangling a constitutional-pluralist form of government that had, since 1820, been conservative as regards the international order.[21] After the war, when Aron compared fascist and Stalinist imperialism, he described the link between what he termed 'total ideology' and a 'state of war' as 'heterogeneous'. This concept referred to an international system in which a state of war reigns between fundamental values, and in which revisionists do not recognise other states' 'right to self-determination of government'.22

Secular Religion

In order to understand not only fascist doctrine but also the reasons why the German and Italian peoples obeyed their leaders, Aron made use of Weber's models of legitimacy. Totalitarianism was, for him, not simply a product of the tyrant's evilness; it also gained its historical legitimacy from the people ascribing to it a set of values.[23] Weber argued that what made political leadership possible was not the calculated interests of individuals – as many economically-oriented political scientists believed – but, rather, the systems of values to which citizens were committed. Weber established three ideal types of legitimacy that referred to categories of value systems. One kind of legitimacy lay in the idea of the justice of positivist law. Citizens believe that a rational idea lay behind the law, and that the leader essentially executed rational law. Rational legitimacy expresseed itself in bureaucratic administration and had technocratic tendencies. Another model of legitimacy was the one in which the ruled obeyed according to the 'saintly' character of traditions. Where there existed traditional legitimacy, political institutions were expressed in hierarchical orders. The last type – and most relevant for Aron's understanding of fascism – is charismatic legitimacy. In this model, the system of values emanated from an 'heroic virtue' or a 'unique personality' that entailed 'extraordinary subjugation from the ruled'.[24] Aron admitted – as did Weber – that the models of legitimacy were 'idealtypical' concepts, which only served as tools to measure real relationships between governments and citizens. The result of concrete analysis was, most often, a mixture of several types of legitimacy. The fascist dictators played on traditional values, although Aron was never in any doubt that, in real terms, the two arch demagogues, Hitler and Mussolini, with their speeches, their menacing demeanour and their promises, exercised a charismatic power over their peoples. In order to illustrate the extent to which the German and Italian peoples had both faith and confidence in their leaders, and were promised salvation in a future new order, Aron devised the concept of secular religion.[25] Despite the idiosyncrasy of the fascist world vision, the German and Italian populace behaved towards their governing bodies as if they were deities proscribing entire sets of rules in society. Charismatic legitimacy was, then, apparently compatible with modern industrialised states. It became the principal strength of the fascist dictators, and permitted the radicalisation of their movements.[26]

Explaining Fascism

Aron's theory of totalitarianism was close enough to Arendt's approach. Both scholars stressed the radical character of fascist ideology by interpreting its underlying world vision. Both scholars were committed to the idea of warning political leaders of the dangers inherent within the various fascist movements.[27] Nevertheless, Aron differed from Arendt in that he combined hermeneutics with harder scientific methods. Aron considered Arendt's rigorous theory as a valuable theoretical framework for understanding the fascist and communist regimes, but, in his view, political leaders also required a precise knowledge of how fascism and Nazism become important historical movements. Such knowledge was necessary in order to respond with an efficient policy.

The philosopher or sociologist *understands* the phenomenon as a concept. But the historian *explains* the process that leads to the given political situation. Only such a precise knowledge can pave the way for relevant and scientifically correct advice. Aron admitted that the advantage of Arendt's theory lay in its critique of functionalist theories, as well as of metaphysical explanations which strove to demonstrate a supposed inner rationality within historical processes.[28] Aron stressed, however, that the scientific process must consist of a division of labour between a committed establishment of concepts, and a positivistic methodology that reconstructed the causes that brought about totalitarian regimes.[29] Aron's liberal commitment was plainly manifest in his system of totalitarian concepts. His understanding of historiography consisted of Weber's limited methods of causal explanation.[30] The sociologist becomes the historian by stating how events are linked together, not by an inner, metaphysical or functional logic,[31] but simply by way of a chain of causes that epistemologically reveal themselves to be reactions to precedence.[32] By this choice the scholar implicitly shows that history could have taken another course had key individuals interpreted events differently, and simply made other choices.

In his analysis on the causes of totalitarianism Aron concluded that the final scientific judgement rested upon a positivist account of how political phenomena resulted from meetings between independent, causal series. A study of regimes can rely neither on pure history of ideas nor on pure sociological analysis. Aron suggested a multidisciplinary study that combined historiography, geopolitics, economics, history, sociology and philosophy. Taken together these approaches identified the evolution of ideas, and shed light on the differences between the various regimes. In Aron's view, only this kind of analysis would enable the scholar to deliver scientifically reasoned policy recommendations.

The Ideological Origins of Fascism

The fundamental question that Aron asked in his analysis of fascism was: 'what makes the charismatic legitimacy of Hitler and Mussolini possible?' In answering it, he argued that legitimacy was the result of a meeting between several independent causes. Fascism started as an idea. Aron chose the Italian sociologist Vilfredo Pareto as the thinker who most influenced the idea. Of course, Pareto drew on other thinkers, but it was, in particular, his interpretation of history that became the basic idea behind fascism. According to Aron, Pareto had a 'biological philosophy of history' that depicted a historical shift between political regimes as a 'circular movement'. Regimes succeed each other without leaving any values behind them. As Pareto saw it, at the beginning of the twentieth century democracy was about to die out and authoritarian forms of government would soon take over. Pareto combined this vision with anthropological theories that considered human beings as 'lonely, fearful and irrational'. In industrially developing societies these fearful and irrational individuals aggregated into 'amorphous masses'. And these masses could only be ruled by 'violent', strong 'élites'. Pareto considered democracies 'weak' because they were not inclined to use force. Therefore, more powerful states would take over and establish an international 'hierarchy' built on strength.[33]

In Aron's opinion, Mussolini and Hitler found much inspiration in Pareto's theory. He argued that it enabled them first to stage their respective coups d'état, second to rule, and third to wage war. The notions of violence inherent in Pareto's vision pointed to the necessity of a 'permanent revolution from above'. Forgotten, now, was the nineteenth century's revolution in its national, romantic and socialist version. The fascist revolution was arbitrary and authoritarian. Both leaders had begun destroying the pillars of the parliamentary system. Their 'spectacular terror' aimed at nothing less than proving the weaknesses of democratic government. The German and the Italian peoples had to consider the 'permanent and violent revolution' as their only way of being 'saved', and of securing a place in a new fascist Europe.[34]

The German People's Historical Experiences

Pareto's ideological vision provided a concept in which both Arendt and Aron were able to identify the essence of totalitarianism. Aron also considered Machiavelli's pragmatism, Nietzsche's nihilism, and Sorel's cult of violence as equally vital components of the ideological origins of fascist doctrine.[35] However, he also maintained that these philosophers might not have recognised their ideas in the way that Hitler and Mussolini eventually made use of them. Ideology is transformed once it becomes a part of the historical process. In Aron's analysis, the specific historical experiences of peoples were important causes that contributed to the success, or failure, of particular ideological ideas. He identified an important component of the fascist idea in the German people's 'modern consciousness'. The Germans were, he argued, inclined towards an authoritarian style of government. In the nineteenth century, German liberals were unable to unify the German provinces. They finally asked the army to accomplish national unification. Bismarck's Reich, after 1870, was the result of a revolution from above to which the whole of German civil society – industry, upper classes, peasants and working-classes – gave their consent. In 1933, Germans were captured by the idea of a strong and efficient German state. Germany's collective memory combined this modern consciousness with 'older, romanticist myths'. A German inclination for authoritarian government was also founded on a reaction against 'French rationalism', coupled with the idea of the 'German people's spiritual and physical superiority'. This was the origin of the 'Reich', a term which signified 'empire', and was opposed to the idea of a non-imperialistic nation-state.[36]

In Aron's analysis, Bismarck stood as the clever statesman who transformed the Reich into a conservative nation-state.[37] He won international acceptance by assuring his regional neighbours that he did not intend to exploit Germany's geopolitical position in order to pursue imperialist policies. His successors, in particular Hitler's

National Socialists, did not maintain such good diplomatic relations with their European neighbours. Nazism turned the German state back toward the Reich idea. The Reich seemed, to the Nazis, unaccomplished, and they could not resist the temptation of including all Germans from the North Sea to the Black Sea in a greater unified Germany.[38]

It is important to note that Aron explicitly refuted any idea that Nazi totalitarianism could be defined as a form of cultural determinism. Aron was not among those scholars who considered nationalism as the evil route to fascism, and especially German nationalism. On the contrary, he regarded the national idea as the most important source of coexistence between individuals, and he maintained that German history 'could have turned out to be different' had other political leaders emerged.[39]

The Italian Case

In Aron's analysis, the collective memory of Italians was less decisive in the origins of fascism in Italy. Aron's writings were comparatively less detailed when they concentrated on Italian fascism compared to a Nazism of which he had had direct experience between 1930 and 1933. This partly explains his less extensive analysis of Italian fascism, but only partly. Aron's treatment of the Italian case was coherent to the extent that he systematically insisted on the lack of totalitarian inclinations. In Aron's view, Italy became totalitarian not because its people was inclined toward German-style efficiency, because Italians lacked an experience of parliamentarianism. Italy's unity was also the result of a liberal revolution from above, but it differed from Germany in the fact that it did not obtain popular consent around certain myths. The Italian people's historical experience was that of competing and fragmented élites fighting for power.[40] Moreover, during the nineteenth century the Catholic Church and the aristocracy, as well as various social movements, demonstrated a certain resistance to state centrality. Mussolini was able to exploit this power vacuum. The *Duce* constructed the necessity for a strong state; he exploited the myth of a Great Roman Empire; he created a state system based on police terror, and this led to the Italian acceptance of fascism. Aron explained Mussolini's success as being based on the way he behaved. In short, the Italian dictator acted as if he were already an uncontested leader, and as if his weaker political predecessors had manifestly failed the nation at the peace talks that followed the First World War.[41]

Accidental Causes

Aron explained fascism by a whole range of succession causes which demonstrated links between events that could have turned out differently.[42] It was only when Europe experienced the horrors of the First World War that it became more susceptible to radical political ideas. Before 1914, the extreme Right and Left gathered only marginal support. European public opinion disqualified their leaders after having experienced the long and disparate war with its vast number of victims. According to a broadly-held European view, the peace of 1919 had to be proportionate to the sufferings.[43] In France, with its high number of victims, public opinion tended towards radical pacifism, socialism and the extreme Right. These radical ideas, however, were absorbed by moderate, political forces owing to France's modern republican consciousness.[44]

Among the defeated powers of 1919, the situation was different because ideological radicalism coupled with a national frustration. Aron denoted an independent cause to Germany's path to radicalism as rooted in American military intervention in 1917. In order to obtain American popular support for intervention, the United States promised to 'end all wars' and to 'create a world safe for democracy'. This propaganda induced a legal debate on classical European 'inclusive diplomacy', and it entailed a punishment of the states deemed morally responsible for the war. In American ideology, the anti-democratic states were identified as criminals. By this definition, Germany and Austria were excluded from the peace negotiations, a fact that strengthened feelings of national humiliation and revenge among Germans and Austrians.

In Aron's analysis, the economic dimension was more an accidental than a structural cause of fascism. He refuted any analysis that explained fascism as a product of a capitalist crisis. Economic causes were certainly not absent from Aron's analysis, but historically situated. It was during the 1920s that economic depression paved the way for the fascist leaders and their movements. But the crisis only partly explained the rise of Mussolini in the 1920s. It is only after the

1929 crisis that a popular fascist consensus was, in theory, established. Between 1923 and 1929, the German people forgot about Hitler. People in Germany were chiefly concerned with surviving the depression. In 1929, the millions of German unemployed generated such a widespread sense of despair that economic interest groups gave their absolute consent to Hitler, hoping that his radical nationalism would absorb social dissatisfaction and channel it into a stabilising national movement.

According to Aron economic causes were more 'accelerating' than 'adequate'.[45] The 'adequate', or most important, cause of fascism amounted to two individuals. Hitler and Mussolini were uniquely-talented demagogues who succeeded in driving already war-weary people into a dramatic, imperialist adventure. Aron argues that in the beginning of the 1930s Germans and Italians did not want war. What they wanted was security and a better position in a new fascist Europe. Tragically, they were caught up in the two leaders' elaborate game.[46] From the beginning of the 1930s, the industrial leadership and the upper-classes were also caught up in tyrannical enterprises. Ultimately, both were shocked when they discovered that the revolution from above did not signify the leadership of ruling élites, but the rule of one arbitrary power controlling the army and the police.[47] Mussolini's and Hitler's 'technique of violence' and bluffing accomplished the fascist enterprise. From 1933 onwards, Hitler took his European neighbours as hostages in a psychological war. He did not have the military hardware until the latter part of the decade, but he succeeded in playing on the fears of a Europe traumatised by war. The chain of events starting with Mussolini's spectacular intervention in Ethiopia in 1935, and ending with Hitler's *Anschluss* in March 1938, completely demoralised the democratic states and increased the Italian and German populations' 'passion for their leaders'.[48]

Aron's descriptions and explanations of the nature of fascist states in the 1930s were, at the same time, policy recommendations. Hitler's and Mussolini's *Weltanschauung* was incompatible with those of Western governments, and created a state of war from 1933. The main obstacle to an international peace agreement was the legitimacy that Hitler and Mussolini had achieved among their own peoples. Fascist regimes can be fought neither with legal arguments nor by means of economic intervention, but only by waging war. In Aron's view, the Italian and the German peoples could only be liberated from their passion for their leaders if they witnessed their humiliation in military defeat.[49]

Soviet Totalitarianism

In the light of Soviet policy in the post-war period, Aron further developed his theory of totalitarianism. Observing how Stalin 'puts his world vision into action', Aron made use of the same conceptual system that he had used to define fascism. A violent minority controlled the masses. A terror police spread fear, and state propaganda replaced the free press. The regime was a break with Western-style government. It was founded on a single party system which killed parliamentary systems.[50] Only one ideology prevailed; Marxist-Leninism served as a secular religion.[51]

Originally, Marxism was anti-religious, by virtue of the fact that it promised to liberate human beings and bring about changes in the real world. It aimed to end individual preoccupation with personal salvation. Aron argued that anti-religious Marxist-Leninism paradoxically became a religion itself. This ideology proposed a global interpretation of all aspects of the citizen's life. By stating that 'no moral thoughts are superior' to the revolution, Marxist-Leninism led to the Machiavellianism inherent in secular religions, which distinguishes them from other political movements. As with fascism, Marxist-Leninism aimed to create human beings that became instruments for the final goal, which stands at the centre of all human actions.[52]

However, Aron admits that there were essential differences between fascist ideology, which was irrational, biological and pessimistic, and Soviet ideology, which was rational, humanisticic and optimistic.[53] The reasons why a basically rational idea – Marxian socialism – had become a tyrannous enterprise could, in Aron's view, only be explained by the aid of a Weberian methodology that linked multiple and ramified causes and effects together. Soviet totalitarianism resulted from a distortion of the original idea, which took on an altogether new form once it became whirled into multiple and independent historical processes. Aron placed historical responsibility on Lenin for having transformed Marxism into an anti-Western doctrine, because Lenin 'deprives the workers of their role as rebels' and subjugates the 'socialist movement' to the control of a single party. In this ideological modification, Lenin completely abolished 'parliamentary processes'. Marxism materialised in the form of a totalitarian regime once Stalin came to power, and differences between fascism and communism were thereafter no longer ones of substance, but of degree. Whereas Lenin considered the proletariat to be incarnated within the party, Stalin reintroduced 'traditional' Russian government. In this regime, a modern tyrant reincarnated the Tsarist regime, and the party became nothing more than a 'violent minority' who indeed considered people as amorphous masses, as victims of permanent terror and propaganda.[54]

Soviet Legitimacy

As in his analysis of fascism, Aron not only explained the transformation of ideas by the fact that Stalin came to power. Stalin's power depended on the legitimacy of Marxist-Leninism, which remained the basis of his doctrine. The legitimacy of Marxist-Leninism is, in particular, caused by the First World War. Aron demonstrated that Lenin's radical ideas only had marginal support before 1914. The horrors of the long and absurd war caused public mistrust of leaders as well as a 'wish for radical, political change'. The European peoples of the interwar period therefore began to pay attention to revolutionary ideologies. Historical circumstances explained why fascism took power in Germany and Italy, and why 'red fascism' seized power in Russia. In Germany, socialism had been compromised because the people concluded that the weak Weimar social democracy was in 'agony'. In Germany, radical socialists were absorbed by the Nazi movement. In Italy, Mussolini's maneoeverings explained the socialist's impotence.[55] After the Second World War, West Germans dissociated themselves from Marxist-Leninism because they 'experience the totalitarian regime in their eastern part'.[56] In Italy and France after 1945 Marxist-Leninism continued to gain broad support.

The post war legitimacy of Marxist-Leninism, also predominant in France, explains Aron's sympathy for de Gaulle. His Gaullism was historically conditioned. Aron considered the General as the only politician with sufficient 'legitimacy'[57] to vanquish the communist idea. In Great Britain parliamentary traditions were rooted enough to restrain anti-democratic movements. In Scandinavia, the egalitarian aspects of Marxist-Leninism were formulated by trade union movements in such a way that reforming social democratic parties absorbed revolutionary aspirations.[58]

The legitimacy of Marxist-Leninism remained strong as a means of justifying the totalitarian regime. During the 1950s Aron created the concept of 'competition between two industrial societies, one favouring a single party system', the other maintaining the democratic system.[59] Here, competition entailed a new 'heterogeneity' within the international system. In 1944 Aron stressed once again the inner links between 'total ideology' and a 'state of war' which was the case in the fascist movement. Although Stalin 'only pushes walls that are about to fall' and manifests 'patience', his ideology is no less dangerous than fascism.[60]

Lenin's transformation of Marx's ideas also delivered the ideological basis for Soviet imperialism after 1945. Lenin declared that the Soviet Union must be the 'territorial bastion' of the socialist revolution. The Marxist idea of a global proletariat seizing power was, in Lenin's version, combined with a traditional international theory. Stalin later exploited the idea of the Soviet Union as a power base for world revolution in his hegemonic foreign policy. Aron also showed how the new 'state of war' in 1944 not only resulted from ideological distortion and the 'traumatic experiences of the First World War'. Soviet imperialism was also a consequence of military events in the Second World War. The United States had historical responsibility for the Cold War. The Soviet Union only became 'revisionist' as regard the international order after the United States – with the best of liberal intentions –waged a war of attrition against Germany and Japan. The Allies mixed military strategy with war propaganda, and the unlucky geopolitical result was a physical destruction of Germany which caused a direct confrontation in the middle of Europe between the United States and the Soviet Union.[61]

Explanation and Policy Recommendations

Aron's description and explanation of Soviet totalitarianism also contained his policy recommendations. Soviet doctrine was both an ideological concept and a traditional fight for hegemony. The war remained 'cold' because of a technological novelty – the atomic bomb. Nevertheless, Aron recommended the Western powers to wage the war by reasoned means. After 1949 Aron urged the French government to join the Atlantic Alliance, and, with all possible diplomatic and military means, not only seek to the defence of France but also to liberate Eastern Europe from Soviet domination. As was the case with fascism, the western post-war challenge was to accelerate the Soviet leadership's loss of prestige. In 1941 Stalin incarnated socialism, patriotism and antifascism. In 1947 Aron wanted the French government to accept Marshall Aid in order to prove to communists, inside and outside France, that the constitutional-pluralistic West was also able to assure economic growth and social welfare. As to the patriotic idea, European populations subdued by Marxist-Leninist ideology would discover that they were only part of a military empire controlled by Moscow. As regard anti-fascism, this idea would vanish when the populations realised the similarities between fascism and Soviet-style communism.[62] During the whole post war period Aron insisted on the heterogeneity of the international system. As long as Marxist-Leninism remained the ideological basis of the Soviet Union, a state of war would reign between East and West. As long as the Soviets held Eastern Europe as satellites in a totalitarian system, the war would never be over.[63] Aron recommended that the Western powers pursue a policy of strength with combined military and ideological means. He maintained that the concept of totalitarianism amply covered the Soviet regime, and refuted that the Russia of the 1960s was about to be transformed into a 'variant of social democracy'.[64] Despite *détente*, and the Helsinki process in the 1970s Aron argued that Moscow acted as a totalitarian regime and remained characterised by a single party system (lack of democracy), state ideology (lack of freedom to interpret history), a terror police network and secular religion (Marxist-Leninism as an ideology of salvation).[65] In this respect the term 'totalitarianism' was instrumental in Aron's analysis. He made use of it to 'point out the enemy',[66] and to show how the West had still not fulfilled its task.

Totalitarianism and the Philosophy of History

Totalitarianism was also a philosophical tool in Aron's historical vision. His analysis of Western history showed that there was something of an opposition between totalitarian regimes and 'free civil societies'. The expression 'civil society' refers to European peoples, their growing parliamentary consciousness and, consequently, their political performance in modern times, especially after the eighteenth century. Aron's rationalist vision of history was diametrically opposed to Pareto's philosophy. For him, people were not merely 'irrational amorphous masses' that needed 'rational' government, but were, on the contrary, ethically inclined. Civil societies necessarily develop into democracies provided that they are free, and not subjugated to totalitarian regimes.[67] Aron's historical vision identified an 'accumulated historical experience of the moral superiority of the constitutional-pluralists system'. This experience conditioned forms of government, and Western-style civil societies became profoundly committed to democracy.[68]

Aron's historical comparisons between communism and fascism also demonstrated his anthropology, and his vision of history. In the Soviet Empire, the state almost completely absorbed civil society. The populace were charactarised in terms of Pareto's concept of 'amorphous masses', being exposed to 'daily and persistent terror', and 'deprived of the possibility to transform their world into free civil societies'.[69] Aron had a rather more optimistic judgement of German and Italian fascism. In 1943, he stressed that the German and Italian peoples would soon disapprove of their leaders once they had lost the war. He built his optimistic intuition on the fact that the German and Italian fascist ideologies were too anti-Western and too limited in scope to be able, in the long run, to maintain the attention of 'old' European civil societies.[70] Fascism was never able to convert others than Germans and Italians, and would, therefore, die out with their leaders. Compared to this, Marxist-Leninism was a universal ideology, and had obtained a sufficiently strong enough moral basis to justify the existence of a totalitarian regime even after Stalin's death. Marxist-Leninism incarnated in the Soviet regime was unable to reform, and would continue to be controlled by 'violent minorities'.[71]

In the post-war period Aron maintained his view that Mussolini's and Hitler's regimes had been profoundly totalitarian, but, at the same time, he considered their impact on people as superficial. German and Italian fascism had been truly barbarous. But its return to archaic values was artificially constructed, and had only a superficial effect on the population.[72] This interpretation received much criticism from Hannah Arendt, who considered anti-Semitism as one of the basic pillars of totalitarianism. This is why she did not describe Italian fascism as totalitarian. Aron interpreted the fascist military defeat in 1945 as a fundamental change in the German and Italian historical experience. As for Italians, they would start hating their *Duce*, whose imperialist fantasies would forever be discredited. Germans would have more difficulty in forgetting their dream of strong leadership, but the idea of an imperial Reich had, now, forever vanished. Germany would convert external activities into anti-imperialistic movements; a good example being its support for European integration.[73] As regards Russia, Aron declared that it would be difficult for the post-Soviet leadership to renew their ideology, and to redefine a historical mission able to compete with the universal dimension of Marxist-Leninism.[74]

Conclusion

Aron used the concept of totalitarianism to understand the ideologies, the regimes and the international conflicts of his century. He followed Hannah Arendt, who outlined the intrinsically radical nature of totalitarian regimes. Aron's theory of totalitarianism introduced comparative political theory into the writing of history and sociology. He included the concept of secular religion as a distinctive feature of totalitarian regimes. Furthermore, Aron incorporated his theory of totalitarianism into his study of international relations. He analysed the link between totalitarian ideologies and revisionism in international relations.

Aron was in favour of a dynamic use of the concept of totalitarianism. His theory of totalitarianism was neither generally descriptive nor hypothetically deductive. It was based on Weber's hermeneutic method of understanding, combined with historical explanations of unique events. Aron's method consisted of historical comparisons between regimes, the identification of multiple and independent causes of totalitarianism, and assessments of distortions between the original intentions of principal individuals and their global historical consequences. The result is a historical, sociological study that sheds light on the differences between concept and reality. It is possible to use the concept without demanding identical causes and features in different historical regimes, and without leaving out of the study regimes that do not immediately fulfil the specific characteristics of totalitarianism. Aron includes Italian and German inter-war fascism as well as the whole period of Soviet communism in his study of totalitarianism, mainly because of the relationship between rulers and ruled in these regimes. The concept of totalitarianism can only be understood in opposition to parliamentary government, respect for human rights, free civil society and so on. Aron emphasised that totalitarianism was but one possible historical development that could occur in modern industrialised societies. It was not a kind of children's disease, something that could be cured over time, but depended on a range of historical circumstances, on political leaders, geopolitics, economics and sociological facts. Aron's theory was, therefore, both pragmatic and philosophical. His scientific ethics demanded of political theory that it made itself relevant for politicians. Weberian, contextual sociology fulfilled the criteria of relevance and the causal analysis developed concrete policy recommendations. From the 1930s, his theory of totalitarianism also aimed at establishing a liberal philosophy of history in a period of increasing mistrust in parliamentary systems.

NOTES

1. With this statement I agree with Pierre Bouretz, 'Penser au XXe siècle: la place de l'enigme totalitaire', *Esprit* 20/1 (January/February 1996), pp.122–39.
2. My translation from Raymond Aron, 'Le romantisme de la violence' (1941), in Christian Bachelier (ed.), *Chroniques de guerre* (Paris: Gallimard, 1990), pp.427–39.
3. Hannah Arendt later exposes her theory of totalitarianism in Hannah Arendt, *The Origins of Totalitarianism* (New York: Harcourt, Brace, 1951).
4. Ibid.
5. See Carl Friedrich and Zbigniew Brzezinsky, *Totalitarianism Dictatorship and Autocracy* (New York: Harper, 1956).
6. See summary of the critique in Stein Larsen, Bernt Hagtvet and Jan Peter Myklebust, *Who Were the Fascists?* (Bergen, Oslo, Tromsø: Universitetsforlaget, 1980).
7. Hannah Arendt, *The Human Condition* (New York: University of Chicago Press, 1959).
8. Zbigniew Brzezinsky, 'Soviet Politics: from the Future to the Past', in P. Cocks, R.-V. Daniels and N. Whittier Heer (ed.), *The Dynamics of Soviet Politics* (Cambridge: Harvard University Press, 1976).
9. For an example see the conclusions in Larsen, Hagtvet and Myklebust (note 6).
10. Raymond Aron, *Mémoires. 50 ans de réflexion politique* (Paris: Julliard, 1983); English translation, *Memoirs. Fifty Years of Political Thought* (New York, London: Holmes and Meier, 1989), ch.III.
11. Aron delivers a first systematic critique in Raymond Aron, 'L'Allemagne. Une révolution antiprolétarienne: idéologie et réalité du national-socialisme', in E. Halévy

et al. (ed.), *Inventaires*, vol.I, *La crise sociale et les idéologies nationales* (Paris: Alcan, 1936), pp.24–55.

12. Especially those gathered around Léon Blum and his *Front populaire* and those who insisted on saving at any price the system of collective security based on the idealism of American President Woodrow Wilson after the First World War.

13. Aron (note 11).

14. Raymond Aron exposes his critique of the functionalists in Raymond Aron, 'Les racines de l'impérialisme allemand' (1943), in Bachelier (note 2), pp.596–607.

15. Raymond Aron, 'Introduction', in Miriam B. Conant (ed.), *Politics and History. Selected essays by Raymond Aron* (New York: Free Press, 1978), p.xxiii.

16. This is not Weber's own term but the one comtemporary sociology used to describe his methodology, as it is outlined in Max Weber, *Gesammelte Aufsätze zur Wissenschaftslehre* (Tübingen: Mohr, 1956).

17. Aron elucidates Weber's method in *German Sociology* (1934) (London: Melbourne, Toronto: Heinemann, 1957) ch.III, part 1 and 2, and in Raymond Aron, *Main Currents of Sociological Thought* (London: Weidenfeld and Nicholson, 1965) ch.3, part 2.

18. My translation from Raymond Aron, 'Tyrannie: rationalisation et déraison' (1940–41), in Bachelier (note 2), pp.415–518.

19. Ibid.

20. Ibid.

21. My translation from Raymond Aron, 'Le machiavélisme, doctrine des tyrannies modernes' (1940), in Bachelier (note 2), pp.417–26.

22. Raymond Aron, *Les guerres en chaîne* (Paris: Gallimard, 1951, p.50 ff), English translation, *The Century of Total War* (London: Verschoyle, 1954).

23. Raymond Aron, 'L'essence du totalitarisme selon Hannah Arendt', *Critique* (1954), reprinted in *Commentaire*, 28–29 (Winter 1985), pp.416–25.

24. My translation from the passage that inspires Aron in Max Weber, *Wirtschaft und Gesellschaft* (Tübingen: Mohr, 1956), pp.123–4.

25. Aron (note 21).

26. Aron (note 18).

27. Aron discusses the philosopher's commitment and the differences between Arendt's and his own approach in Aron (note 23).

28. Both Aron and Arendt criticise pure economic or neo-Marxist interpretation of fascist and communist regimes. See Aron (note 23) and Arendt (note 3).

29. Aron outlines his method of 'objective commitment' in his thesis from 1938, Raymond Aron, *Introduction à la philosophie d'histoire. Essai sur les limites de l'objectivité de l'histoire* (Paris: Gallimard, 1986), p.394, English translation, *Introduction to the Philosophy of History. An essay on the Limits of Historical Objectivity* (London: Weidenfeld and Nicholson, 1961).

30. For a good account of the differences between Arendt's and Aron's methodology, see Luc Ferry, 'Stalinisme et historicisme. La critique du totalitarisme stalinien chez Hannah Arendt et Raymond Aron', in Evelyne Pisier-Kouchner (ed.), *Interprétations du stalinisme* (Paris: PUF, 1983), pp.227–55.

31. Raymond Aron, *Leçons sur l'histoire* (Paris: Editions de Fallois, 1989), p.170ff. Aron refers to the debate beteeen scholars favouring 'covering' laws and scholars favouring 'individual understanding', and he shows how the Weberian method avoids these two opposite positions.

32. Aron refers to Weber's 'probabilism' in his thesis from 1938, Aron (note 29), p.202.

33. My translation from Aron (note 18).

34. Raymond Aron, 'Mythe révolutionnaire et impérialisme allemand' (1941), in Bachelier (note 2), pp.440–51.

35. Aron (note 2).

36. Ibid.

37. The term 'conservative' refers to the interstate level and is opposed to "revisionism', both terms developed in Aron (note 22).
38. Aron (note 34).
39. Aron (note 2).
40. Ibid.
41. Raymond Aron, 'La stratégie totalitaire et l'avenir des démocraties' (1942), in Bachelier (note 2), pp.559–71.
42. Aron, Introduction à la philosophie d'histoire (note 29), p.202.
43. Aron, Les guerres en chaîne (note 22), p.3.
44. Raymond Aron, 'A l'ombre de Bonaparte' (1943), Commentaire, 28–29 (Winter 1985), pp.359–68. According to Aron, 1815 definitely deprived Frenchmen of imperialist ambitions in Europe. Since then any 'new cesar' has had to commit himself to modern France's myth of origin, namely the Revolution of 1789 with its republican values.
45. Aron, Introduction à la philosophie d'histoire (note 29), pp.195–327.
46. Ibid.
47. Raymond Aron, 'Révolution et rénovation', in Bachelier (note 2), pp.869–88.
48. Ibid.
49. Ibid.
50. Raymond Aron, 'L'avenir des religions séculières', in Bachelier (note 2), pp.925–48.
51. Aron (note 22), p.142ff.
52. Aron (note 50).
53. Ibid.
54. Aron, Les guerres en chaîne (note 22), p.147
55. Ibid.
56. Raymond Aron, 'L'Allemagne enjeu ou arbitre' (20 October 1949), in Georges Henri Soutou (ed.), Les articles du Figaro (Paris: Editions de Fallois, 1990), vol.1, pp.299–302.
57. Aron (note 2).
58. Aron, Les guerres en chaîne (note 22), p.167.
59. This distinction becomes Aron's main characteristic of the East–West confrontation as to its ideological aspect. See Raymond Aron, Le Grand schisme (Paris: Gallimard, 1948), and Raymond Aron, Démocratie et totalitarisme (Paris: Gallimard, 1965), English translation Democracy and Totalitarianism (London: Weidenfeld and Nicholson, 1968).
60. Raymond Aron, 'Neutralité vers l'Est?', (4 May 1950), in Soutou (note 56), vol.1, pp.395–98.
61. Aron (note 2), p.199.
62. Ibid., p.178ff.
63. Raymond Aron, 'Remarques sur la gnose léniniste (1981) in The philosophy of Order, Essays on History, Consciousness and Politics, presented to Eric Voegelin, (Stuttgart: Klett-Cotta, 1981), pp.263–274
64. See Aron's polemical dialogue with the French political scientist Maurice Duverger on the interpretation of Soviet reform policy, in Soutou (note 56), vol.2.
65. Raymond Aron, Démocratie et totalitarisme (Paris: Gallimard, 1965).
66. Pierre Hassner on Aron's theory of totalitarianism, 'Le totalitarisme vu de l'Oeust' (1984), in Pierre Hassner, La violence et la paix (Paris: Edition Esprit, 1995), pp.221–58.
67. Aron is conceptually close to Emil Lederer, who also refers to 'totalitarianism' in his State of the Masses. The Threat of the Classless Society (New York: Howard Fertig, 1967). Lederer shows that the masses are products of the modern industrialised state and that they irrationally acclaim authoritarian leadership. In Aron's analysis it is the 'violent elites' that historically seize the opportunity to keep the peoples in unconscient and fearful masses.
68. Aron (note 22), p.154.

69. Ibid., p.152
70. Aron (note 50).
71. For the comparison between fascist and Soviet ideological strength, see Raymond Aron, *Le spectateur engagé* (Paris: Julliard, 1981), p.68, English translation, *The Committed Observer* (Chicago: Regnery Gateway, 1983).
72. Aron (note 23).
73. Raymond Aron develops this analysis in his articles from April 1950, in Soutou (note 56), vol.1, pp.370-91.
74. Aron (note 22), p.153ff.

9

The Establishment and Development of the Metaxas Dictatorship in the Context of Fascism and Nazism, 1936–41

MOGENS PELT

In October 1935, Italy launched a fully-fledged attack on Abyssinia, threatening Britain's position in Egypt and the supremacy of the Royal Navy in the eastern Mediterranean. Three years later, in 1938, Germany established her dominance over Central Europe in a series of short-of-war operations, incorporating Austria and the Sudetenland into the *Reich* by *Anschluss* and the Munich agreement.

The dismemberment of Czechoslovakia dealt a fatal blow to the French security system in south-eastern Europe, *la petite entente* with Prague serving as its regional power centre. While the credibility of France as a great power almost completely eroded overnight, Vienna and Prague suddenly provided ready-made platforms to an invigorated and resurgent Germany to project her power into south-eastern Europe, and to rearrange that area in line with Berlin's plans for a new European Order. This, in turn, gave a boost to national vindication in the revisionist states, Bulgaria and Hungary, while it generated shock waves of national insecurity and internal instability in the status quo states, Greece, Romania and Yugoslavia.

On 10 October 1935, only a week after the beginning of Mussolini's African enterprise, a military *coup d'état* in Greece reinstated the monarchy, which had been abolished in the wake of the First World War, and some ten months later, on 4 August 1936, King George II established what was meant to be a permanent dictatorship under the leadership of General Ioannis Metaxas, a prominent royalist. This article will examine and discuss the establishment and development of the Metaxas dictatorship. It takes as its point of departure that Greece was subject to a number of the same changes in *Realpolitik* which affected the relations between the European states during the 1930s. Greece, too, was affected by the rise of Nazism and fascism, and by the crisis of parliamentarism. In addition, the Great Depression, which had boosted Hitler's rise to power, also dealt a hard blow to the stability of the Greek economy, society and politics.

Where it concerns Greek relations with the great powers, focus will especially be on the repercussions of the rising power of Germany, and Italy's increasingly ambitious policy in the eastern Mediterranean. In order to understand the specific policies and *Weltanschauung* on which the Metaxas regime was based, it is also necessary to discuss the historical and national context in which Metaxas rose to power. This leads us back to the First World War.

A Legacy from the First World War: The National Schism

The immediate impact of the First World War on Greece was strong: it provoked a widening of already existing cleavages and turned politics into a zero-sum game. This divide, known as the National Schism, was generated by conflict wthin the political élite and among those competing for positions in the state and armed forces.

The cleavage originated from a bitter confrontation between King Constantine I and his Prime Minister, Eleftherios Venizelos. It was triggered by conflicting visions about how to bring Greece through the First World War, and to realise Greek national ambitions, known as the Great Idea – *i megali Idea*. In its most far reaching visions, it strived at the resurrection of a Greek Empire in the East – a new Byzantium – with the reconquest of the former imperial capital, Constantinople as its final goal.[1] The King wanted to keep Greece on a neutral course, while Venizelos opted for participation on the side of the *Entente* powers.

Germanophilia is often listed among the reasons for Constantine's stance. It is true that he was related to the German Kaiser by his marriage to Sophie, Wilhelm's sister. It is beyond doubt that he was an admirer of German militarism, of which he had a first-hand knowledge from both battlefields and school. As the commander-in-chief of the Greek armed forces in the 1897 campaign against the Ottoman Empire, the young Crown Prince had witnessed the efficiency by which the German-trained Turkish troops, in a stunningly brief span of time, managed to defeat his army in a devastating *Blitzkrieg*. Two years later, in 1899, he went to Germany to visit the same teachers who had instructed his enemies so well, entering the Academy of War in Berlin as a student. However, Constantine also feared British sea power, and owing to Greece's geopolitical position as a Mediterranean country he thought it too dangerous to ally with the Central Powers. On the other hand, siding with the Entente would expose Greece's recently conquered lands in Macedonia to claims from Bulgaria, who sided with the Central Powers in 1915.

Macedonia had a special symbolic value to Constantine: his triumphal entrance into Salonika, the prize of the Balkan Wars, did much to exonerate him in the eyes of the public from his ignominious defeat by the Ottomans in 1897. It earned him many devout supporters in both government and the military, and raised his popularity among the Greek public enormously. In 1913, at his moment of triumph and at a time when he was about to succeed his father on the throne, it was widely expected that he would adopt the style of Constantine XII, the successor of Constantine XI Palaiologos, the last emperor of Byzantium, to indicate that he was his direct successor and heir destined to return Constantinople to Greek hands.[2]

The protracted power struggle between the King and the Prime Minister propelled Greece into a state of civil strife, and divided the country into a royalist 'Old Greece' and a Venizelist 'New Greece' with two opposed governments, one under Constantine in Athens, another under Venizelos in Salonika. In 1917, the Entente powers intervened in the conflict on the side of Venizelos and forced Constantine to abdicate, while Greece entered the First World War under the leadership of Venizelos.[3]

As a victorious power at the peace conferences in Paris, not only was Greece allowed to keep her possessions in Macedonia, but she was also awarded former Bulgarian territory in Thrace and vast tracts of former Ottoman lands in Asia Minor. The latter offended Italian ambitions and laid the foundations of an uneasy relationship between the two states which was to last for the whole inter-war period; it further pitted Italy against Greece when Athens, on 19 May 1919, and with British consent, began to land troops in Izmir. In accordance with the St Jean de Maurienne agreement signed in 1917, the Entente powers had promised to give Izmir to Italy. Furthermore, the Greek landing in Asia Minor made it look as though Greece's moment in the Near East had come, and that it would emerge as a medium-sized, Mediterranean power on a par with Italy. For a short time it even appeared that Britain, or at least Lloyd George, was considering counting on Greece to act as its proxy in that area.[4]

However, in November 1920, Venizelos was surprisingly defeated at the elections by the royalists' parties, and shortly afterwards Constantine returned to Greece while Venizelos went into exile in Paris. This, in turn, transplanted the National Schism to the Greek communities in Asia Minor to the extent that the Holy Synod even considered the excommunication of King Constantine, while Athens retaliated by cutting all financial assistance to the Patriarchate in Istanbul.[5]

The Fall of the King and the Establishment of the Venizelist State

1922–23 constitutes a turning point in modern Greek history. During the summer of 1922, the Turkish nationalists, under the leadership of Mustapha Kemal, drove out the Greek army and, in its wake, more than one million Greek orthodox, all subjects of the defunct Ottoman Empire. It meant the end of the Great Idea as an active force. The disaster in Anatolia led to the influx of about 1.2 million refugees, and to an increase of the Greek population by more than 20 per cent. The short-term consequences were economic and political chaos and a need for immediate relief.[6]

The army and a huge part of the population and, in particular, the refugees who were mainly Venizelists, held the King responsible for the defeat. In the same year, a military government forced Constantine into exile, where he died shortly afterwards, and executed six leading anti-Venizelist politicians and army officers, whom they blamed for the disaster in Asia Minor. After an abortive royalist *coup d'état* in 1923, the Venizelists proclaimed a republic in 1924. In this way, the disaster in Asia Minor and its immediate political sequel became incorporated into the National Schism, while at the same time Venizelists and anti-Venizelists were divided into opposed camps regarding the constitutional issue.[7]

The armed forces played a crucial role in Greek politics.[8] After the disaster in Asia Minor and the abortive royalist *coup d'état*, Venizelist officers got full control of the army. Indicative of this is the fact that it was the army which transferred power from a military junta to parliament in 1924. As a result of elections held the same year, the Venizelists became preponderantly dominant by securing over 90 per cent of the seats.[9] During the following years, various Venizelist governments ruled the country, interrupted by a military government ruling from June 1925 to August 1926; hereafter the arena of politics was left to parliamentarians but remained under Venizelist dominance. However, in the wake of Great Depression and the signing of the so-called Ankara agreement in 1930, which caused a significant number of refugees to desert Venizelos, the Venizelists lost their parliamentary power.[10]

On 10 March 1933, the anti-Venizelists formed a government under the leadership of the moderate Panages Tsaldaris. This contributed significantly to the widening of the breach between army and government, and multiplied claims for an anti-Venizelist *reconquista* of the state. It led to a revival of the National Schism when the anti-Venizelists launched plans to reform the power structure in the army and to change the electorial system, in order to reduce the impact of the refugee vote. Furthermore, plans were worked out to curtail the power of the Senate, which was still dominated by the Venizelists.[11] This prompted the British minister in Athens to make the following note in his 1935 annual report to London: 'Greek politics are in reality nothing but a struggle between two factions for control of the armed forces ...'[12] Venizelist officers began to conspire against the government, while royalist officers, who had lost influence, positions and prestige after the abolition of the monarchy in 1923, were reactivated. Among whom was the would-be dictator, Ioannis Metaxas.

Metaxas and the Revival of the National Schism

Metaxas was a crucial player in the royalist camp. He was a strong supporter of the monarchy and had a long history as a devotee of Constantine, who was also his patron, dating back to the time before Constantine was King. Metaxas, who shared Constantine's admiration for Germany and the Prussian military machine, was sent to Germany to receive military training at the Academy of War. Metaxas returned to Greece imbued with German virtues, like discipline, *Ordnung* and *Ernst* [order and seriousness], and overwhelmed by his first-hand impressions of the results of *Bildung* [education and self-cultivation] and the achievements of state and society.[13]

Metaxas was soon adopted by a small circle of intimates around Constantine, the so-called 'Little Court'. Apart from army and navy officers, the group included the president of the powerful National Bank of Greece, by far the most important private institution in Greece, and several intellectuals. In the realm of *Realpolitik*, the 'Little Court' constituted the closest ties between Greece and Germany. During the decade before the First World War, Constantine and the 'Little Court' had attempted to reorganise and modernise the Greek army with German support, but with only little success.[14]

For a brief period during the First World War, Metaxas acted as the chief of the Greek general staff, but resigned as a protest against Venizelos's plans to commit Greek troops to the British campaign in Gallipoli. He resigned from the army in 1920 as a strong critic of the Greek military adventure in Anatolia. This, in turn, left Metaxas untainted by the disaster in Asia Minor. Metaxas's decision clearly reveals his pragmatic attitude to the Great Idea, and demonstrates that he was prepared to let professional judgements guide him even in situations where he was under strain from ideological pressure within his own camp. However, he remained a devoted royalist even after Constantine's death, and he was a leading figure in the ill-fated royalist *coup d'état* in 1923 which finally paved the way for the proclamation of the republic. He demonstrated his pragmatism by the fact that he was the first prominent royalist to recognise the republic by ostensibly declaring himself a republican, a decision that allowed him an early entry into politics in the Venizelist state. Nevertheless, at heart he continued to identify with the monarchy and remained a sworn enemy of the Venizelist state. He founded the Free Opinion Party, which, apart from the period following the elections in 1926, would remain only a minor factor in party politics.[15] After the formation of the Tsaldaris government, Metaxas became increasingly involved in a series of conspiracies, of an extra-parliamentary nature, instigated by radical anti-Venizelists.[16] In May 1934, Georghios Kondilis, a former Venizelist but then the anti-Venizelists' strongman, informed Metaxas that he was planning a *coup* for 15 August 1934, to enforce the executive power in order to overcome Venizelist resistance. He wanted Metaxas to become President and take charge of reforming the army.[17] By allying Metaxas with his cause, Kondilis had found a personality who, unlike himself, held an undisputed royalist reputation, and whose long and loyal relationship with the late Constantine could be expected to inspire the necessary trust in royalist officers needed for their support to purge the army from Venizelist dominance. As events transpired, Kondilis did not carry out the *coup*. Instead, on 1 March 1935, a group of Venizelist conspirators under the leadership of their hero from the 1922 revolution, Nikolaos Plastiras, attempted a *coup d'état*.[18] Greece was now precipitated into its worst national crisis since the *débacle* in Asia Minor. For more than a week the country was on the brink of a disintegration similar to the old cleavage between anti-Venizelist 'Old Greece' and Venizelist 'New Greece'.

However, it soon became clear that the conspirators had failed to muster sufficient backing from the army and from the population as a whole. Within the first 24 hours, loyalist troops re-established total control of Athens. On 8 March, Kondilis mustered an army of 45,000 to fight the rebels in northern Greece; within two hours he had managed to neutralise all resistance, and, on 10 March, Thrace and Macedonia were recovered. Finally, on the night of 11–12 March, Venizelos fled the country.[19]

In the aftermath of the attempted *coup*, Metaxas once more came to the fore among the radical anti-Venizelists when he proved his dexterity as a strongman by assisting Kondilis in a massive, and thorough, purge of Venizelist officers.[20] This, combined with the abolition of the Venizelist-dominated Senate, and a large-scale dismissal of Venizelists from the administration, resulted in an overwhelming anti-Venizelist dominance in the state apparatus and in the armed forces. When the Venizelists decided to boycott the election planned for on 10 June 1935, they lost all their influence in parliament, and a final blow was dealt to the Venizelist state.[21]

Metaxas and the Restoration of the Monarchy

Obviously encouraged by this development, and not least by his own role and increasing influence, Metaxas now gave signs that he wanted to enhance Greek–German relations. In May 1935, he established contact with Berlin via a middleman in order to let the German government know that he was interested in economic and political support from Germany, in order to build a strong army and to loosen France's grip on Greece should he come to power.[22] The Germans did not doubt that the middleman was acting on behalf of Metaxas. This took place only six months after the Nazi Party's foreign political office, *Aussenpolitisches Amt der NSDAP* (APA), had declared that for long-term German interests in Greece it was important to avoid a return to power of the Venizelists, and for that reason it recommended cautious German support for the royalists.[23]

However, as Metaxas did very poorly at the general election in June 1935 the German minister to Greece, Ernst Eisenlohr, did not see any reason to pursue the case any further.[24] Nevertheless, Metaxas clearly indicated that his ambitions were far-reaching, seeing himself in a role of influence regarding the rearmament of Greece, and declaring that he wanted Germany's support to realise these aims. Furthermore, although Metaxas failed utterly at the elections, his royalist cause got a strong boost when, on 10 July, Kondilis made the parliament pass a resolution providing for a plebiscite on the restoration of the monarchy to be held before 15 October. The parliament was then in recess until 10 October.[25] However, on the very day that parliament was due to convene, Kondilis and the three chiefs of the armed forces overthrew Tsaldaris and took control of the country using dictatorial powers. The junta abolished the republic and proclaimed the restoration of the monarchy

On 3 November, a rigged plebiscite ratified the restoration of the monarchy, with 97.87 per cent of the votes in favour.[26] Upon his arrival in Greece on 25 November, George II, who had been living in Britain for almost 12 years, turned out to be determined to reconcile the domestic political world. On 30 November, an uncompromising Kondilis decided to resign in protest over the attitude of the King. George II pardoned the Venizelist participants in the March *coup*, and appointed a caretaker government which was to stay in power until a political cabinet could be formed after the election slated for 26 January 1936.[27]

Kondilis's resignation has been seen as a result of his disagreement with the King over the latter's wish to placate the Venizelists, and grant an amnesty to those involved in the March uprising. It has also been suggested that the King would not agree to act as Kondilis's puppet.[28] Both explanations seem reasonable. It has to be stressed, however, that the King was as adamant as Kondilis in his rejection of the reinstatement of the Venizelist officers; apparently their disagreement did not estrange them irreparably, as both soon afterwards found sufficient grounds to plan joint action, should the Venizelist officers demand reinstatement. According to the counsellor at the German legation, Theo Kordt, the King held Kondilis in reserve should the attempted conciliation with the Venizelists fail.

Furthermore, Kondilis had told Kordt quite frankly that he was ready to obstruct any attempt to reinstate the Venizelist officers, if necessary even by a revolution, 'if some government should prove ready to readmit the "March traitors" into the Army'.[29]

This indicates that the King was ready to resort to heavy-handed government, if the situation so demanded. It should be noted that 12 years of absence from Greece had left George II out of touch with its current political world. Like Kondilis and Metaxas, he, too, nurtured an obvious and ill-concealed contempt for Greek party politics, confiding to the German minister that he simply saw politicians as 'a bunch of sick old men', while praising Kondilis for his loyalty.[30] However, the King soon lost the 'Kondilis option', when the general died in early 1936. This made Metaxas an obvious choice to succeed Kondilis as the King's strongman; Metaxas had already demonstrated his great zeal for creating an anti-Venizelist army. Furthermore, the need for the 'strongman option' increased after the elections on 26 January 1936, which ended in a political deadlock. Neither of the political blocs could form a majority government without the support of the Communist Party.[31] The deadlock soon turned into a prolonged political crisis.

The Establishment of the Metaxas Dictatorship

On 5 March 1936, as a reaction to rumours that the Venizelists and the Communists were negotiating, Minister of War Alexandros Papagos informed the King that the army would not accept a government formed by Communists and Venizelists. However, the King refused to tolerate such interference by the armed forces. He immediately dismissed Papagos and assigned the Ministry of War to Metaxas, who also became Deputy Prime Minister.[32] On 13 April 1936, Constantine Demerdzis, leader of the caretaker government, died, and a few hours later the King appointed Metaxas Prime Minister. According to Kordt, the King had done so in order to have a strongman at hand who was ready to act firmly should parliamentary chaos threaten Greece.[33] This observation seems to the point. On 30 April 1936, Metaxas suspended parliament for a period of five months.[34] On 22 July 1936, the leaders of the anti-Venizelists and the Venizelists informed the King that they were ready to form a government when parliament met again in October. The agreement was based upon the reinstatement of the purged Venizelist officers.

This, however, would spell trouble for the anti-Venizelist army, and could pose a serious threat to the power base of the King and, not least, of Metaxas. The following day, on 23 July, Metaxas told three of his close associates that the King had given him *carte blanche* to establish a dictatorship within ten to 15 days.

On 4 August 1936, Metaxas decided to act and established what became known as the Fourth of August Regime. His official justification for establishing the dictatorship was to forestall a Communist-inspired revolution. According to Metaxas, this was planed in connection with a 24-hour general strike declared for 5 August.[35] By cracking down on the Communists, Metaxas maintained, in an interview with the daily newspaper *Vradini*, that he had prevented bloodshed. Furthermore, he declared that in the long run he intended to win over followers from the Communist Party to his side.[36] According to contemporary diplomatic observers, however, the prospect of a Communist revolution was quite improbable.[37] These observations are supported by historians, who tend to explain the establishment of the dictatorship in terms of the protracted political crisis and the successive deaths of several leading political figures, such as Venizelos, Kondilis and Tsaldaris, within a short span of time.[38] As will be demonstrated below, the impact of German policy also played a significant role in this development, as well as in the decisions that resulted in the establishment of the Metaxas regime.

The establishment of the Metaxas dictatorship efficiently contributed to solidify anti-Venizelist power over the state, bringing to a successful end a process which had begun in 1933 when the anti-Venizelists won the elections. It cemented anti-Venizelist dominance in the armed forces. It symbolised the complete resurrection of the royalist faction in Greek politics, which just one decade earlier had seemed condemned to extinction after the death of the mythical, and unusually popular, Constantine I. However, the regime confronted an array of new and unsolved problems, created by the repercussion of the Great Depression, resurgent revisionism in Europe and a preponderant German influence on the Greek economy.

Fortifying Greece against Revisionism and Stabilising State and Society, 1936–38

The Abyssinian crisis of October 1935 unleashed a state of frenetic panic in the Greek armed forces, as it highlighted the fact that Greece was in no state of preparedness for modern warfare, let alone for defending its borders against weapons such as tanks, aircraft and gas. This sparked off a series of initiatives to redress this state of affairs, and to reorganise and modernise the Greek armed forces. In October 1935, the Greek general staff established a Special Office for Civil Mobilisation to study and organise industrial mobilisation. Emphasis was placed on safeguarding the supply of shells, gas masks, boots, medicines and so on. In November 1935, an investigation was initiated into the requirements for anti-aircraft defence, and in January 1936, it was decided to co-ordinate the control of the three services in a so-called Supreme Council for the National Defence.[39]

Greece turned to Nazi Germany, informing Berlin that 'Greece is in dire straits regarding war material' and that orders were expected to be in the range of 75–100m Reichsmarks.[40] (At this time Greece's outstanding account on the Greek–German clearing amounted to about 32m Reichsmarks).[41] In order to expedite the matter, the Greek Minister of Foreign Affairs, Ioannis Theotokis, turned to the head of the *Abwehr* [German intelligence], Wilhelm Canaris, and urged him to do what he could to hurry up deliveries. In return for this, he held out prospects of improvements in the relationship between Greece and Germany.[42] The confidential nature of the exchange shows that the Greek government still considered it necessary to keep the arms affair as secret as possible, perhaps because of competition between the Great Powers, but also because of the conflict between Venizelists and anti-Venizelists. Thus, the French Ambassador in Athens had warned the Greek government that France would regard Greek purchases of German war equipment as a violation of the Treaty of Versailles. Theotokis told the Germans that he had chosen to ignore this, because rearmament was of 'great importance' to Greece.[43] On 24 October, Theotokis informed the German minister that, 'the total financial power of the country will be put at the service of the concept of rearmament'.[44]

However, as a result of the restoration of the monarchy which had brought back George II from his long exile in Britain, and the political deadlock created by the elections on 26 January, the negotiations on German armaments deliveries came to a standstill. Obviously, as long as the outcome of the political crisis remained uncertain, none of the leading personalities in politics or the army would risk making decisions that might tie them to any promises that could destroy their careers if the Venizelists came back into power.

Basing national rearmament on German support could be expected to arouse an incoming Venizelist government and defy the Great Powers, Britain and France, who had been the main foreign sources of military hardware and know-how in the Greek armed forces since Venizelos had sided with the Entente during the First World War. In this situation Berlin placed strong pressure on George II, and threatened to sever German imports of Greek tobacco unless Greece finally decided to place large orders for war material with German firms.[45]

The rising political power of Metaxas coincided in a spectacular manner with a substantial breakthrough in Greek–German arms negotiations. One week after his appointment as Minister of War, and in connection with Germany's termination of the Locarno agreement and the German march into the Rhineland, the Greek government was at pains to assure Germany that Greece intended to remain uninvolved in Central European affairs and distance itself from the French-dominated Little Entente.[46] Kordt, in turn, hailed Metaxas's presence in the cabinet and told the *Auswärtiges Amt* that Metaxas was an asset to German interests, and one of Germany's most reliable friends. Referring to the Greek government's refusal to make the Balkan Entente dependent on the Little Entente, Kordt concluded: 'We have several important friends in the cabinet who will not allow the Balkan Entente to be taken in tow by the Little Entente, that is, by France.'[47]

Less than a month after his appointment as Minister of War, Metaxas initiated a series of negotiations which would finally lead to an agreement on 22 July 1936 that resulted in massive Greek rearmament based on German materials and expertise.[48] It should be noted that it took place on the same day that the Venizelists and their opponents had declared that they were ready to form a government and agreed to the reinstatement of the purged Venizelist officers, and that a renewed Venizelist presence in the armed forces could be expected to pose a serious threat to the agreement with Germany. However, given his *carte blanche* from the King to establish a dictatorship, Metaxas found a way to eliminate this danger and to achieve massive rearmament based on German war material and technology.

This, in turn, provided for a liquidation of Greek assets on the clearing account in Berlin, and created the basis for maintaining Greek tobacco exports to Germany at a high level. In this way, Metaxas's prompt intervention in the arms negotiations solved several pending problems, which had faced Greece since the Great Depression and Italy's attack on Abyssinia. It also worked to stabilise the social and political situation in the tobacco growing areas in northern Greece.[49]

In the same period, the Greek armament industry expanded by leaps and bounds, and in 1939 it had turned into the most important modern armaments complex in the Balkans and the Near East. This development was based on co-operation between the Greek business tycoon, Prodromos Bodosakis-Athanasiades, owner of the Powder and Cartridge Company, and the German firm Rheinmetall-Borsig, which by 1938 had come under the total control of Hermann Göring.[50] This co-operation was the first German encroachment on the position held by the French steel industry in south-eastern Europe. Schneider-Creusot served as France's industrial spearhead in the area. The French firm controlled Skoda, the leading Czechoslovakian company for steel and armaments production. France also controlled the industry in both Romania and Yugoslavia.[51]

In the second half of 1937, Rheinmetall-Borsig judged that it had no stronghold in the world to compare with its position in Greece.[52] This must be explained by the fact that the French steel and armaments industry still had a firm grip on the rest of south-eastern Europe. It was not until Germany's domination of Central Europe, following the 1938 *Anschluss* and the Munich agreement, that Berlin achieved a major breakthrough in these countries. According to the same assessment, the breakthrough for the German armaments industry in Greece, and the subsequent consolidation of its position, was primarily due to internal political factors: the restoration of the monarchy in 1935 and the establishment of the Metaxas dictatorship in 1936.[53]

Thus, just months after the King had appointed Metaxas Prime Minister, it was clear that George II had found a strongman who was able to cope with the two major problems pending since the Great Depression and the beginning of Italy's aggression in Africa: the issue of rearmament and the huge frozen Greek credits on the clearing account in Berlin. However, Metaxas's role in the development of Greek–German relations was more one of a restoration rather than an innovation, containing as it did obvious elements of continuity connecting Metaxas's efforts to those of Constantine's 'Little Court'. Nevertheless, in his efforts to develop the dictatorship beyond being a mere *ad hoc* response to specific pending problems and into a permanent feature of Greek politics and society, Metaxas soon faced problems to which neither anti-Venizelist customs nor Greek tradition could provide the answers. Accordingly, Metaxas began to look for models outside Greece, and, primarily, he turned to Nazi Germany. Metaxas made this clear to Berlin from the beginning. On 29 September 1936, he informed the German Minister of Propaganda, Josef Goebbels, that he admired National Socialism's achievements in Germany, privately confiding to Goebbels that he would like to achieve something similar in Greece while at the same time maintaining friendship and peace with both Britain and Germany.[54]

The Fourth of August Regime: Political Methods and Reforms

Metaxas suspended democratic rights and introduced strict censorship.[55] The Security Police was reorganised and began an efficient and brutal persecution of all opponents to the regime, especially the Communists.[56] The regime strived to promote itself as 'anti-plutocratic', as an alternative to trade unions, political parties and professional and industrial bodies. The First of May became a national holiday, rebaptised and celebrated by the regime as the 'National Day of Celebration of Work'. New labour legislation was passed which sanctioned compulsory arbitration and increased the minimum wage, as well as improving social welfare provision. The regime paid great attention to the actual enforcement of the labour legislation, and the Ministry of Labour did not refrain from fining employers if working hours in offices or factories were exceeded.[57] According to official figures, 616,000 workers and 141,000 public servants were covered by the labour legislation in 1939.[58] Wages increased by a nominal rate of 50 per cent from 1935 to 1940, although real growth was hardly more than five per cent owing to an increase in consumer prices.[59]

Job creation was of central importance to the regime. According to the German Embassy, the Greek government succeeded in bringing down unemployment from 128,000 to 26,000 during its first year in power, and in 1939, according to the same source, unemployment was down to 15,000.[60] The key factors, according to the German Embassy, were state-sponsored stimulation of industrial growth and efficient implementation and surveillance of labour legislation; the latter had set the working day for industrial workers at eight hours and for office workers at seven hours.[61] The above figures, however, should not be taken at face value, and should be treated with considerable caution due to the desire of the regime to promote itself as 'pro-labour', and as an alternative to communism and free trade unions. However, it is a fact that the period under Metaxas was one of sustained industrial growth. This is particularly true in terms of the armament industry.

Propaganda and Ideology of the Fourth of August Regime in the Context of Hitler's New European Order

On certain occasions, the propaganda used by the regime aped the methods of Mussolini and Hitler. Metaxas gave himself symbolic titles, such as 'First Worker' (*Protos Ergatis*) and 'First Peasant' (*Protos Agrotis*), founded the national youth organisation EON (*Ethniki Organosis Neoleas*) which resembled the Hitler Youth, and introduced the 'Roman salute'. However, observers inside and outside Greece agreed that Metaxas failed to generate genuinely popular support.[62]

Moreover, these were not symbols of unity rooted in an original mass movement, and Metaxas's road to power was very different from both Hitler's and Mussolini's. The fact that the regime was not based on a mass movement indicates that it would be wrong to call the dictatorship 'fascist'.[63] Moreover, the regime did not have any plans for territorial expansion: these had been buried in the wake of Greece's disastrous campaign in Asia Minor in 1920–22.

However, all such observations on the Metaxas dictatorship pertain to a regime in its early infancy. The fact that Metaxas obviously intended the regime to be a permanent one makes it necessary also to evaluate the institutions and symbols which Metaxas created in regard to their potential significance and meaning in a long-term context. Seen from this point of view, Metaxas was clearly attempting to transform the Greek mind, and create a generation of new and regenerated Greeks. These efforts were in line with the ones undertaken by Hitler, Mussolini and Stalin to create a 'new man'. The ideological content of Metaxas's reforms, however, had much in common with Fascism and Nazism, and can be seen as an attempt to reorient Greece in a direction which would also make it conform with the planned Axis 'New Order' in Europe.[64]

The fight against communism was the area in which the shared ideological interests of the two regimes were most significant and successful for both parties. The oppression of political opponents, and in particular of the Communists, during the Metaxas regime was, in terms of determination and efficiency, without precedent in Greek history. In November 1936, on the initiative of the Gestapo,[65] and as the result of an inquiry from the German legation in Athens, Metaxas declared that he approved the Greek Security Police and the Gestapo joining forces to exchange information as a defence against 'Bolshevik agitation'.[66] According to a German assessment, it was because of Metaxas that only a year after the establishment of his regime, communism lost its most important stronghold in the Near East.[67] At the end of 1937, the British legation acquired an item of correspondence dated May the same year between Heinrich Himmler, head of the SS, and Konstandinos Maniadakis, the Secretary of Security. This stated that Maniadakis accepted an invitation on behalf of the Greek police to participate in a congress about methods to fight communism.[68] In this way German assistance also played a part in Metaxas's fight against internal enemies. It is notable that the British Foreign Office learned from sources in Germany that ten per cent of the value of the German arms trade to Greece went to Metaxas. The money was used for the establishment of Metaxas's party machinery and propaganda for the regime.[69] The British legation in Athens did not doubt the validity of the information, and in their eyes the crucial question was whether Metaxas would finally manage to claim supremacy and thrust the King into the background.[70]

During the initial phase of the dictatorship, Metaxas made it clear to the public that he did not hold anti-Semitic views. According to Kordt, this reverberated in the censored Greek press, which stressed that the Jews in Greece had the same status as any other citizen, and that anyone in Greece who entertained anti-Semitic feelings was a bad Greek.[71] This stance was also noticed abroad. The *Jewish Chronicle* in London printed a short article in September 1937 which praised Metaxas for prohibiting the publishing of anti-Semitic writings.[72] However, this public image contradicts the impression Goebbels gained from his talks with Metaxas in September 1936, which prompted him to characterise Metaxas as 'strongly anti-Semitic'.[73] This conversation, of course, was private, and Metaxas might have attempted to please Goebbels by expressing such views. Nevertheless, it indicates that Metaxas found it opportune to convey the impression to Berlin that he held anti-Semitic views. The regime also made some groundwork in institutionalising overt and state-sponsored anti-Semitism, as well as *untermenschen* ideology. Application for membership of the EON, established with an eye to creating a new stock of regenerated Greeks, required the individual to be a Greek Christian. No Jews, Muslims or other minorities were permitted.[74] At its peak, the EON had more than one million members.[75] The frequent, and massive, book-burnings organised by the state included works by personalities whom Nazi anti-Semites systematically identified as exponents of international Judaism, namely Stefan Zweig and Sigmund Freud.[76]

Whether or not this state-sponsored anti-Semitism arose from heart-felt convictions, we should note that it does provide some evidence that Metaxas's Greece was a seriously race-conscious state that would form part of a future Axis-dominated New European Order. Moreover, in general the regime placed much emphasis on creating a national identity based on cultural and ethnic homogeneity. To this end, Turkish-speaking Muslims, Slavophones and Albanian-speaking minorities were forced to compromise their beliefs, and instruction of Greek became mandatory in minority schools.[77] The regime also clamped down on the subculture of the refugees from Asia Minor, in regard to certain manifestations of their specific identity. This, in particular, found an expression in the *rembetika* tradition: certain songs were prohibited, while the police closed down clubs and even imprisoned performers on the grounds that they were politically or morally subversive.[78]

The regime wanted to create a modern, and culturally heterogeneous, Greece in the image of classical Hellas and Byzantium, and introduced a cultural and national policy of integration. Metaxas ascribed paramount symbolic significance to a militaristic and oligarchic Sparta, and depicted Sparta as the first of three Greek civilisations. The two others were Byzantium, representing the Christian Orthodox ideal, and Metaxas's own regime, portrayed as 'the Third Greek Civilisation'. Metaxas believed that after 400 years of Turkish domination, Greek civilisation was totally obliterated, and he saw the ideal of classical Greece as a means to elevate twentieth-century Greece from its present level, as a 'bastard culture' of idle individuals, into a 'pure race' of disciplined and uncorrupted men and women working for the common cause of creating a 'new Greece'. It is notable that Metaxas did not see classical Greece merely as an ideal to be passively admired, but rather as a method for political action to modernise society and culture. This conception of Hellas probably stemmed from his admiration for German culture. His views to some extent resembled whose of Wilhelm von Humboldt, the architect of the German restoration after the Napoleonic Wars, who authorised the instruction of the classical Greek language and culture as a means of purging German culture and society from French influence and raising Germany to a higher level of civilisation.[79] If one believed that the extraordinary achievements of modern Germany were the results of the Humboldtian reformation, then the high level of German culture and society would appear to be the result of the implementation of the ideals of ancient Greece. Or, to put it differently, of a process in which Germans were to become transformed into ancient Greeks;[80] this is, perhaps, *the* key to understanding Metaxas's deep admiration for German culture.

German admiration for Greek antiquity and the Humboldtian credo, in turn, gave Greek–German relations an emotional quality, which did not exist in German relations with other countries in the region, but which was somewhat similar to the sentiments the National Socialists nurtured for the Nordic countries out of racial attachment to its peoples, whom they believed to be of an especially pure Aryan stock. According to the British minister to Greece, Sir Sidney Waterlow, the National Socialists saw an intellectual affinity between the ancient Greeks and the modern Germans, or, as he expressed it, between Pericles and Hitler.[81] Albert Speer noted that Hitler was primarily influenced by Greek architecture, and regarded Greek culture as an expression of the highest imaginable perfection.[82] From the diaries of Goebbels it is possible to discern the feelings that were aroused in the German Minister of Propaganda during his first visit to Greece. In the following notes he describes how the dream of his youth came true in the airspace above Mount Olympus: 'There towers Mount Olympus and there Parnassus. It makes one warm. Old memories from my youth emerge. A dream comes true. The sun sets beautifully. Over eternal Greece'.[83] On the second day of his visit, Goebbels went to the Acropolis. The minister described it as the happiest morning of his life: 'Yesterday: one of the most beautiful and most significant mornings of my life. On the Acropolis. Only a few people. And I wandered about for hours in these noble places of Nordic art.'[84]

It is interesting that Goebbels depicts Greek antiquity as a part of the pre-Christian Nordic world, a fact that reveals that he subscribed to the views of racial 'history' propagated by people like Guido von List, who believed that the Aryans originally stemmed form the North Pole but had spread to the Mediterranean and bred the race of the ancient Greeks.[85] It was in this spirit that Goebbels wrote: 'My soul is filled with beauty. Blessed antiquity, which lived in eternal joy free from Christianity. An evening stroll through the town. This joyful highest life. This smell of happiness. How pleased the Fuehrer would be if he were here with us!'[86] His joy at seeing the Acropolis again in 1939 inspired Goebbels further: 'On Acropolis. O, this shattering view! The cradle of Aryan culture.'[87]

Metaxas Takes over Control from the King

Metaxas was a central figure in Greek relations with Germany. This, and the fact that the armed forces, the tobacco industry and a growing section of business, in particular, the armaments industry, increasingly depended on these relations, in turn provided Metaxas with a power base which made him less dependent on the King. Soon after he was installed in power, Metaxas established a number of new ministries and secretariats, or created parallel ones to already existing ones, to which he appointed people who owed him their loyalty. From this platform, and by creating a *Herrschaftsanarchie*, Metaxas began to expand his power to the detriment of the King. In addition, his contacts with Germany, in particular in the realm of trade and armaments, depended on 'unofficial' contacts like Bodosakis, the deputy-director of the Bank of Greece, Kiriakos Varvaressos, and the private institution, the National Bank of Greece. There is strong evidence from German provenance that, at least well into 1937, Metaxas deliberately toned down his pro-German tendencies *vis-à-vis* the public, and attempted to keep the King in the dark.[88] Furthermore, the same evidence demonstrates that Berlin equally regarded this to be in the interest of Germany. Thus, Goebbels wrote in his diary that the cordiality of relations between Greece and Germany must be toned down, otherwise Metaxas could encounter trouble with Britain.[89] However, within months of Germany's conquest of Central Europe Metaxas swung into action, and in November 1938 he emerged victorious from a power struggle with the King.[90]

This in turn necessitates a correction of evaluations which analyses of Greek–German relations based on British evidence have produced. This is true, in particular, regarding Koliopoulos, an authority on Greek–British relations, who concludes that 'Metaxas could not credibly match the King's British connection with a German one'.[91] However, Koliopoulos, who does not use German evidence, evaluates Greek–German relations rather exclusively on the basis of reports from Waterlow. The British minister indeed believed that the King was in charge of the government, and that he had Metaxas firmly under his control. Assertions that Greece had entered on a pro-German course were linked by Waterlow to the fact that the British community in Athens consisted mainly of business people, and that Britain's commercial interests in Greece were negatively affected by German trade policy.[92] This would also mean that, for some time at least, it would be in Waterlow's own interests to stress the significance of his relationship with the King. The American ambassador to Greece, Lincoln MacVeagh, suggests this explicitly in a letter to the State Department: 'Sir Sidney's [Waterlow] confidence in His Majesty and estimate of his personal influence and ability run far ahead of anything I would care to hazard. Indeed, in the light of the record, his attempt ... to guide the King in his choice of advisers, takes on a decided aspect of the blind leading the blind.'[93]

It is notable that the American ambassador did not regard the King as a central element in Metaxas's power base. In words more appropriate to a description of criminal circles, MacVeagh outlined the following persons and institutions as central to Metaxas's position: 'about and behind the Dictator [are] – Drossopoulos of the National Bank, Kanellopoulos of the Youth Movement, Diakos, "the eminence grise", Maniadakis the sardonic reincarnation of Fouché, Bodossakis, the arms merchant et al.'.[94] In June 1939, the Foreign Office replaced Waterlow with the considerably younger Michael Palairet because he had lost his influence with the King and had a poor relationship with Metaxas.[95]

Greece in Search of an Ally, 1939–41

Since the time of the Abyssinian crisis, Greece saw Italy as its main threat. After the *Anschluss* and the Munich agreement, Greece increasingly feared Bulgaria and even the creation of an alliance between the Slavic countries Bulgaria and Yugoslavia.[96] In May 1938, the Greek government contacted Britain to obtain a guarantee against Bulgaria, but in vain. After the Munich agreement, Athens contacted

London twice, on 3 and 16 October, to seek an alliance with Britain in case of war between Italy and Britain. But again it was in vain. Metaxas now warned London that should Britain decline his request, Greece would have to observe a stance of strict neutrality; Metaxas also told the British that only an alliance with Britain would make it possible for Greece to escape the German economic 'stranglehold' on Greece.[97] Throughout this time every indication is that the Greek government paid an increasing political regard to Germany. On 8 October, before the meeting with Waterlow, Metaxas declared to the German minister in Greece, Prinz Victor von Erbach-Schönberg, that in the event of a Great Power conflict he would try to keep Greece neutral as long as possible. The German minister told the *Auswärtiges Amt* that, in his opinion, it was quite likely that Greece would join Britain in case of war. For this reason, according to Erbach, Greek neutrality was the most that Germany could hope for in this eventuality.[98] In a note from Metaxas's diary dated 20 October 1938, it appears that the Greek dictator had another meeting with Erbach just after the meeting with Waterlow, apparently in order to explain the situation to the German minister; the note reads: 'Negotiations with Waterlow. My suggestions [concerning a Greek–British alliance]. I am sure that they will not be accepted. But I am relieved.'[99] At the same time Metaxas asked the King to visit Hitler, something, however, George II managed to avoid.[100]

In this situation, London ordered Waterlow to put pressure on the King to get rid of Metaxas, because, according to London, the King was becoming a hostage of Metaxas, and because the regime was becoming increasingly totalitarian and fascist. However, Waterlow acted in vain and only contributed to make the King move closer to Metaxas.[101] According to the American ambassador, Britain made this move because Metaxas was expanding his control of the state to include foreign policy, and because not only was Metaxas 'a German sympathiser personally' but 'politically' a firm believer in the advisability of neutrality for his country. At the beginning of 1939, the influence of the King further eroded to the extent that MacVeagh stated that the King was now completely dominated by his 'Fascist Frankenstein, the German-educated General Metaxas'. According to MacVeagh, British attempts to liberate the King from this 'monster' should be seen as endeavours to stop the influence that foreign totalitarian states like Germany had gained during the dictatorship.[102]

At the same time, the British attempts to force the King to get rid of Metaxas made Goebbels contact Metaxas via Kostas Kodzias. Kodzias was one of Metaxas's men, and the only one from the regime who had met Hitler. The British often referred to him as the Göring of Greece. Goebbels wanted to know whether the King was ill-disposed toward Germany and if Greece had submitted herself to Germany's enemies.[103] Metaxas rejected the German assessment of the King, informing Goebbels that foreign policy was the responsibility of the Greek government and not the King, indicating that he would not allow the pro-British George II to influence his policy *vis-à-vis* Germany. At the same time, Metaxas emphasised that Greece had friendly relations with all Great Powers and intended to remain strictly neutral.[104] Metaxas repeated these points to Goebbels at a meeting held in Athens on 1 April 1939. From Goebbels's diary it is clear that he believed that Metaxas intended to keep Greece on a neutral course, and that he was convinced that the Greek dictator wanted friendship and peace with Germany.[105] Metaxas obviously attempted to balance Greek interests between several Great Powers to avoid unilateral dependence on Germany.

However, Britain proved reluctant, if not impotent, to counterbalance the rising German influence: it was not until 1939 that Britain granted Greece a £2m credit to buy British arms, a relatively modest amount compared to the Greek–German arms trade. London almost completely failed to assist Greece in taking some of her tobacco exports; after one year of fruitless negotiations with the British government, Athens was giving up the hope of even limited British assistance in this field.[106] The defeatist attitude of the Greek administration is reflected by Simmonds, trade secretary at the British legation, in his description of a meeting with Apostolides, the Greek Minister of Finance, on 28 March 1939:

> I went to see Monsieur Apostolides this morning about commercial affairs and found him in a state of great depression … He asked me not to mention the question of British buying of Greek tobacco as he was sick of hearing about it – he knew it would lead to nothing but more talk … He referred to the recent German economic arrangement with Romania and said that, as far as he could see, Romania had given away almost everything. What was more, he added, was that Greece's position was as hopeless as that of Romania and she might be called on to make a similar or worse agreement.[107]

In the wake of Italy's occupation of Albania on 7 April 1939, and after the outbreak of the Second World War, Greece moved somewhat closer to Britain, but Metaxas was extremely careful not to estrange Germany. On the occasion of the unilateral British guarantee to Greece against Italian aggression in April 1939, the Greek government was at pains to convince Berlin that the guarantee was merely a result of unilateral British conduct, and that the Greek government would defend its harbours against any aggressor.[108] After the outbreak of war, the Greek government concluded a War Trade Agreement with Britain, while private Greek shipowners reached an understanding with London regarding the provision of about 500,000 tons of shipping.

However, in the wake of Germany's successful *Blitzkrieg* in Europe, and after the fall of France, at a time when fear was rising that Italy would enter the war, Metaxas let Berlin know through his 'unofficial' German connections that he had warned Britain that he would not give up the smallest island or piece of land even to Britain or France without fighting. Metaxas also asked the German authorities to force Italy to stay out of the Balkans, and refrain from violating Greek territory. Metaxas's explanation for this 'unofficial' procedure was to avoid the British reprisals that would have been likely as the result of an open and official request to this effect. In fact, he wanted Berlin to know that he was 'dying for' Germany to guarantee Greek borders: 'The German government can be assured that such a guarantee will be received with enthusiasm by the Greek government as well as by the majority of the Greek people.'[109] However, in view of the unofficial character of the request, the *Auswärtiges Amt* informed Metaxas that the Greek government would be better off to declare her adherence to the Axis powers openly.[110]

In this period, Greece and Romania came under heavy pressure as Berlin made an unsuccessful attempt to make certain Greek officers persuade Metaxas to adopt an overt, pro-Axis policy,[111] and the Axis powers forced Bucharest to conform to revisions to which Stalin had also agreed, and surrender lands it had gained after the First World War to Bulgaria, Hungary and the Soviet Union. On 1 July 1940, Romania renounced a British guarantee and complied with Soviet and Bulgarian demands. With the Second Vienna Award signed on 30 August 1940, an international court created an intra-European legal system conforming with the interests of the revisionist states. As a consequence, Transylvania was ceded to Hungary, while Italy and Germany guaranteed the rest of Romania.[112] A few days before, on 29 July 1940, Metaxas received information from the Greek ambassador in Berlin that the general attitude in Germany was that Greece would only obtain German support against Bulgarian demands for revision if she adjusted to the 'new situation' and joined the Axis.[113] Nevertheless, Metaxas would not believe these reports regarding Germany's attitude to Greece, and was, therefore, convinced that Hitler's love of ancient and modern Greek culture meant that Germany would never support such demands by Slavic Bulgaria. Moreover, Metaxas was sure that an 'honest and sincere' Greek neutrality was appreciated by the German government, and that there was an understanding of the difficulties which Greece's geographical position entailed. For these reasons, Metaxas refused to abrogate the British guarantee.[114] However, from August 1940 onwards, Greece began to violate the Greek–British War Trade Agreement entered into in January of the same year.[115]

At the same time, Italy was searching for ways to provoke a *casus belli* with Greece. In this situation, and in spite of Metaxas's refusal to comply with the demands from the Axis powers, in particular Italian ones, Germany did intervene twice in August towards Mussolini on the behalf of Greece, stressing that a disruption of peace in the Balkans was against German interests. In this capacity, Germany functioned as a kind of protector to Greece.[116] In spite of that, on 28 October 1940, Italy presented Metaxas with an ultimatum demanding access to Greek territory on the grounds that Rome was now the rightful executor of Albanian claims to Greek territory. However, Metaxas rejected Mussolini's demands out of hand by his famous *megali ochi* (Big No), and successfully resisted the invading Italian army, forcing Mussolini's troops to retreat into Albania. Mussolini's Greek débacle, and the need to secure its south-eastern flank, finally made a reluctant Germany decide to undertake a military intervention to bring the hostilities to an end and re-establish 'peace in the Balkans'. To obtain these ends Hitler decided to occupy not only Greece but also Yugoslavia.[117] Following the German victory, both countries were split up and forced to cede lands which were claimed by the revisionists powers in the region, Bulgaria and Albania.

Metaxas died in January 1941 before German troops arrived on the Greek borders, and before British forces were dispatched to

Greece. In the wake of Germany's occupation, the Greek government fled to Egypt to form the backbone of the British-supported Greek government-in-exile. This made it necessary to conform to British values and to abandon its former Nazi and fascist dispositions. The policy of the Metaxas regime can best be described as one of national efficiency, modernisation and integration, implemented through the extensive use of brutality and at the expense of parliamentary principles and democratic rights. In its focus on rearmament and its attempts to establish a corporate organisation of the labour market, as well as by its vision to organise the political apparatus and society according to the same principles, it departed from policies led by previous governments.

Metaxas's reliance on certain aspects of National Socialism and fascism must be seen as an expression of a more general tendency among Europeans, who felt that the Great Depression had widely shown parliamentarism and liberal economic philosophy to be impotent in coping with the new problems of a modern world. However, we should also see Metaxas's reforms as an attempt to prepare Greece for a New Order in accordance with Hitler's visions of a Europe under German leadership. This was especially true after Germany's conquest of Central Europe in the autumn of 1938, at a time when it appeared impossible to contain Germany and far from preordained that it would be defeated, should war come.

However, due to the short duration of the regime, Metaxas's reforms of state and society never took root, and only left a more lasting impression on Greece in the realm of legislation and military matters. Metaxas's foreign policy goals were to protect Greek national integrity and to retain her sovereignty as much as possible. This made it necessary to navigate carefully between the Great Powers. In the realm of trade and rearmament, he made Greece increasingly dependent on Germany. Regarding strategic policy, Metaxas was searching for protection against revisionism and especially against Italian aggression. To this end he approached Britain and Germany, but in vain. After Mussolini's attack on Greece, Germany began to plan a military action to restore 'peace in the Balkans' should the war between Greece and Italy drag on. Britain, in turn, decided to send a token contingent of troops to boost Greek morale.

NOTES

1. For a discussion of the Great Idea and its significance in the early twentieth century, see Michael Llewellyn Smith, *Ionian Vision: Greece in Asia Minor 1919-1922* (London: Hurst, 1973).

2. George Th. Mavrogordatos, *Stillborn Republic: Social Coalitions and Party Strategies in Greece 1922-1936* (Berkeley: University of California Press, 1983), pp.55-64.

3. Ibid.

4. Llewellyn Smith (note 1), pp.12-18; 77-85; 282-3.

5. Alexis Alexandris, *The Greek Minority of Istanbul and Greek–Turkish Relations* (Athens: Centre for Asia Minor Studies, 1983), pp.22-4, 70-1.

6. John A. Petropoulos, 'The Compulsory Exchange of Populations: Greek–Turkish Peacemaking, 1922-1930', *Byzantine and Modern Greek Studies* 2 (1976), pp.135-60.

7. Mavrogordatos (note 2), pp.55-64.

8. Thanos Veremis, 'The Officer Corps in Greece, 1912-1936', *Byzantine and Modern Greek Studies* 2 (1976).

9. Mavrogordatos (note 2), p.31.

10. Ibid., pp.182-225.

11. Ibid., pp.315-18; Veremis (note 8), p.118.

12. Annual Report 1935, FO 371/2 0392, Public Record Office (PRO).

13. Cf. P.J. Vatikiotis, 'Metaxas the Man', in Robin Higham and Thanos Veremis (eds.), *The Metaxas Dictatorship 1936-40: Aspects of Greece* (Athens: ELIAMEP, 1993), pp.189-91. For the early career of Metaxas, see P.J. Vatikiotis, *Popular Autocracy in Greece 1936-41: A Political Biography General Ioannis Metaxas* (London: pub?, 1998).

14. Konstantin Loulos, *Die Deutsche Griechenlandpolitik von der Jahrhundertwende bis zur Ausbruch des Ersten Weltkrieges* (Frankfurt am Main, Berne, New York: Peter Lang, 1986), pp.82-8.

15. Mavrogordatos (note 2), p.35.

16. Ibid., pp.315-18; Veremis (note 8), p.118.

17. Thanos Veremis, *I epemvasis tou stratou stin elliniki politiki, 1916-36* [The Intervention of the Army in Greek Politics 1916-1936] (Athens: Odysseas, 1983), pp.195-8.

18. Ibid., p.183; Mavrogordatos (note 2), p.318.

19. Annual Report 1935 (note 12).

20. Ibid.

21. The Venizelists declared the election invalid on the ground that the state of emergency was lifted too late.

22. Geneva, 4 May 1935, Politisches Archiv des Auswärtigen Amtes (PAAA), Pol.Abt.II, Pol.2, Balkan, 1089.

23. 24 October 1934, Abteilung Süd-Ost in Aussenpolitischen Amtes der NSDAP (APA). Wolfgang Schumann and Ludwig Nestler (eds.), *Weltherrschaft im Visier. Dokumente zu den Europa- und Weltherrschaftsplanen des deutschen Imperialismus von der Jahrhundertswende bis Mai 1945* (Berlin: 1975), p.238.

24. Athens, 19 June 1935, PAAA, Pol.Abt.II, Pol.2, II Balkan 1462 Gr.; II, Balkan, 1089 Gr.

25. Mavrogordatos (note 2), pp.48-51.

26. Ibid.

27. Hary Cliadakis, 'The Political and Diplomatic Background to the Metaxas Dictatorship, 1935-36', *Journal of Contemporary History* 14/1 (January 1979), p.127.

28. Everett J. Marder, 'The Second Regime of George II: His Role in Politics',

Southeastern Europe 2/1 (1975), p.58.

29. Kordt to Auswärtiges Amt (AA), Zum Tode des General Kondilis, Athens, 1 February 1936, Abschrift von II Balk 282 Gr., PAAA, Abt.IIb Gr. Pol.11–14, Militär.

30. Eisenlohr to AA, Athens, Akten zur deutschen auswärtigen Politik 1918–45, 12 December 1935, ADAP, C, IV, 459.

31. Mavrogordatos (note 2), pp.227–79.

32. John S. Koliopoulos, Greece and the British Connection 1935–1941 (Oxford: Oxford University Press, 1977), pp.39–40.

33. Kordt to AA, Athens, 15 April 1936, PAAA, Abt.II, Gr. Pol.7, Ministerien Bd.2.

34. Istoria tou ellenikou ethnous [History of the Greek Nation], IE (Athens: Ekdoti Athinon, 1978), p.378.

35. Griogrios Dafnis, I Ellas metaxi dio polemon [Greece between two wars] II, second edn. (Athens: Ikaros, 1975), p.432. Dafnis uses material from a conversation with Diakos, one of Metaxas's intimate friends.

36. Ioannis Metaxas, To prosopiko tou imerologhio tou [his personal diary] IV (Athens: Ekdosis Gnovosti, 1960), pp.232–3.

37. Koliopoulos (note 32), pp.44ff.

38. Ibid., p.52.

39. Alexandros Papagos, O ellinikos stratos ke i pros polemon proparaskevi tou [The Greek Army and its Preparation for War] (Athens: 1945), pp.130–1.

40. Frohwein to the Legation in Athens, Berlin, 21 October 1935, ADAP, C, IV, 369.

41. Mogens Pelt, Tobacco, Arms and Politics: Greece and Germany from World Crisis to World War, 1929–1941 (Copenhagen: Museum Tusculanum Press, 1998), pp.143–4.

42. Personal letter from Theotokis to Canaris, Athens, 18 October 1935, PAAA, Geheimakten II FK118, Aus- und Einfuhr von Kriegsgerät nach den Balkanländer.

43. Eisenlohr to AA, Athens, 19 October 1935, eilig und geheim, PAAA, Geheimakten II FK118, Aus- und Einfuhr von Kriegsgerät nach den Balkanländer.

44. Eisenlohr, Athens, 20 November 1935, geheim, PAAA, Geheimakten II FK118 Aus- und Einfuhr von Kriegsgerät nach den Balkanländer.

45. Pelt (note 41), p.140; on the full course of Greek–German arms negotiations, pp.133–51.

46. Gesandtschaftsrat Kordt to AA, Athens, 13 March 1936, ADAP, C, V, 97. See also Berlin, 14 March 1936 ADAP, C, V, 110. Aufzeichnung des Vortragenden Legationsrat von Renthe-Fink.

47. Kordt to AA, politischer Bericht, Athens, 18 March 1936, PAAA, Abt.II, Pol.7, Gr., Ministerien Bd.2.

48. Pelt (note 41), pp.124–6.

49. Ibid., pp.124–6, 142–51.

50. Mogens Pelt, 'Bodosakis-Athanasiadis, a Greek Businessman from the East: A Case Study of the Interrelationship between State and Business', in Lars Erslev Andersen (ed.), Middle East Studies in Denmark (Odense: Odense University Press, 1994). On Göring's role, see Pelt (note 41), pp.91–101, 110–12, 161–76, 241–6.

51. Alice Teichova, An Economic Background to Munich: International Business and Czechoslovakia 1918–1938 (Cambridge: Cambridge University Press, 1974), pp.200ff. An agreement made by the International Steel Cartel assured the Czechoslovakian steel industry a share of 70 per cent of the south-eastern European markets in Albania, Yugoslavia, Bulgaria and Romania through the trade cartel Zentraleuropäische Gruppe der internationalen Rohstahlgemienschaft. This agreement provides one of the best examples of power policy put forward by the Treaty of Versailles. Alice Teichova, Kleinstaaten im Spannungsfeld der Großmächten (Munich: 1988), pp.169ff.

52. Rheinmetall-Borsig, confidential Aktennotiz, Sophia, 9 October 1937, Imperial War Museum (IWM), Speer Documents, FD790/46.

53. Ibid.
54. Joseph Goebbels, *Die Tagebücher* II *1931-1936* (Munich: K.G. Saur Verlag, 1987), p.687.
55. Spiros Linardatos, *I 4e avgoustou* [The Fourth of August] (Athens: Themelio, 1966), p.77. Censorship made it illegal even to comment on the foreign trade, a matter that had stirred public opinion earlier.
56. David H. Close, *The Origins of the Greek Civil War* (London: Longman, 1995), pp.32-59. Yannis Andricopoulos, 'The Powerbase of Greek Authoritarianism', in S.U. Larsen *et al.* (eds.), *Who were the Fascists?* (Bergen: Bergen-Oslo-Tromso Universitetsforlaget, 1980), pp.568-84.
57. Henry A. Hill, *The Economy of Greece: Prepared for the Coordinating Committee of American Agencies in Greece* II (New York: n.d.), p.45.
58. Erbach to AA, Athens, der 1. Mai in Griechenland, 10 May 1939, PAAA, pol.IV, Po.5, Gr. Bd.1.
59. Linardatos (note 55), p.121 n.1.
60. Griechenlands nationale Widergeburt. Zum ersten Jahrestag der Einführung der autoritären Regierungsform, PAAA, Pol.IV, Po.5, Gr. Bd.1.
61. Erbach to AA, der 1. Mai in Griechenland, Athens 10 May 1939, PAAA, Pol.IV, Po.5, Gr. Bd.1.
62. Annual Report 1937, FO 371/23371; Annual Report 1938, FO 371/23777; Political Review of the Year 1938, FO 371/24914 R441, all PRO.
63. Various frequently-cited scholars have suggested that the regime was a Fascist one; Nikos Psiroukis, *O fasismos ke i 4e augoustou* [Fascism and the 4th of August] (Athens: Ekdosis, 1974); Linardatos (note 55); and Heinz Reichter, *Griechenland zwischen Revolution und Konterrevolution, 1936-1946* (Frankfurt am Main: Europäische Verlagsanstalt, 1973).
64. On Hilter's New European Order, see Mark Mazower, *Dark Continent: Europe's Twentieth Century* (London: Penguin, 1998), pp.141-84.
65. The Gestapo's aim was to make Berlin a so-called 'centre for the prevention of political crime'. The purpose was mainly propagandist and to show foreign countries that National Socialism had saved Europe from the Bolshevik danger. Agreements with the secret police in Italy, Hungary and Finland had already been made, and a practical co-operation agreement with Poland and Yugoslavia was instituted. Note by Heinrich Himmler's Deputy State Secretary, Berlin, 8 October 1936, PAAA, Inland IIg, Polizei Abkommen mit Griechenland und Bulgarien.
66. Erbach to AA, Telegram No.143, geheime Reichssache, Athens, 27 November 1936, PAAA, Inland Iig, Polizei Abkommen mit Griechenland und Bulgarien.
67. Erbach to AA, politische Behandlung der zum Jahrestag der Errichtung des autoritären Staats in Griechenland, politischer Bericht, Athens, 28 July 1937, PAAA, Pol.IV, Po.5, Gr. Bd.1.
68. FO 286/1142/71/71/49/37, PRO.
69. The source for this was from Mr Bartlett, agent for the Bristol Aeroplane Company in Europe. He gained the information during a stay in Germany. According to the same source, the Greek King found out and consulted Göring. Southern Department to the Embassy in Berlin, London, 17 March 1938, FO 371/22354/R 2314/18/19, PRO.
70. Athens, 23 March 1938, FO 371/22354, PRO.
71. Kordt to AA, die innerpolitische Entwicklung in Griechenland, Athens 17 September 1937, PAAA, Pol.IV, Po.5, Gr. Bd.1.
72. *The Jewish Chronicle*, no date, 1937, A/8/3, Greek Ministry of Foreign Affairs, 1937, A8/3.
73. Goebbels (note 54), II, p.687.
74. Jon V. Kofas, *Authoritarianism in Greece: The Metaxas Regime*, East European

Monographs (New York: Colombia University Press, 1983), p.89. See also Constantine Sarandis, 'The Ideology and Character of the Metaxas Regime', in Higham and Veremis (note 13), pp.147–77.

75. Close (note 56), pp.32–59.
76. Kofas (note 74), p.85.
77. Ibid., pp.89ff.
78. Gail Holst, Road to Rembetika: Music of a Greek Sub-Culture, Songs of Love, Sorrow and Hashish, 1st edn. (Athens: Limni, 1975), p.39 and passim.
79. On Humboldt's Bildung, see Suzanne L. Marchand, Down from the Olympus: Archaeology and Philhellenism in Germany, 1750–1970 (Princeton: Princeton University Press, 1996), pp.25–32.
80. On Humboldt's Hellenic ideal, see Stathis Gourgouris, Dream Nation: Enlightenment, Colonization and the Institution of Modern Greece (Stanford: Stanford University Press, 1996), pp.122–4.
81. Annual Report 1935 (note 12).
82. Renate Meissner, 'I ethnikososoalistiki Germania ke i Ellada kata tin diarkia tis metaxikis diktatorias' [National Socialist Germany and Greece during the Metaxas dictatorship], in Hagen Fleicher and Nikos Svoronos (eds.), Ellada 1936–1940, diktatoria – katochi – antistasi (Athens: 1989), pp.50–7.
83. Goebbels (note 54), II, p.682.
84. Ibid., II, p.683.
85. Birgitte Hamann, Hitlers Wien: Lehrjahre eines Diktators (Munich: Piper, 1996), pp.293–311.
86. Goebbels (note 54), II, p.684.
87. Ibid., III, p.586.
88. The German legation to AA, Politischer Bericht, Geheim, Deutsche Kulturpolitik in Griechenland. Ein Bericht des Griechischen Gesandten in London, Athens, 10 March 1937, Bundesarchiv Koblenz (BAK), R43 II/1445.
89. Goebbels (note 54), III, p.108.
90. Pelt (note 41), pp.185–91.
91. John S. Koliopoulos, 'Metaxas and Greek Foreign Relations, 1936–1941', in Higham and Veremis (note 13), pp.90–1.
92. Pelt (note 41), pp.104–7.
93. John O. Iatrides (ed.), Ambassador MacVeagh's Reports (Princeton: Princeton University Press, 1980), pp.151–2, MacVeagh to State Department, Athens, 31 January 1939.
94. Ibid., pp.148–9.
95. Koliopoulos (note 32), pp.107–8.
96. Pelt (note 41), p.108.
97. Koliopoulos (note 32), pp.89–90. See also Dimitris Kitsikis, I Ellas tis 4s Avgoustou ke i megale dinamis (Athens: Ikaros, 1974), p.76; and Pelt (note 41), pp.222–5.
98. Erbach to AA, vertrauchlich, Politischer Bericht, Athens, 8 October 1938, ADAP, D, V, 233.
99. Metaxas (note 36), IV, p.311.
100. Kitsikis (note 96), pp.74–7.
101. Pelt (note 41), pp.185–91, 225.
102. Iatrides (note 93), p.156.
103. Rizo-Ragavis to Metaxas, Berlin, 6 March 1939, Metaxas Archive, fak.30.
104. Metaxas to Rizo-Ragavis, Athens, 6 March 1939, Metaxas Archive, fak.30. In the commentary to Metaxas's diary, the event has been dated to 9 March 1939, Metaxas (note 36), IV, pp.335–6. However, as this must be the same event, the discrepancy may have occurred as a result of the publisher printing 6 upside down.
105. Goebbels (note 54/87), III, p.587.

106. Pelt (note 41), pp.214–21.
107. Athens, 28 March 1939, FO 371/23776, PRO.
108. Erbach to AA, Athens, 19 April 1939, ADAP, D, VI, 231.
109. Aufzeichnung für den Reichsaussenminister, Berlin, 4 June 1940, ADAP, D, IX, 384.
110. Ibid.
111. Pelt (note 41), pp.231–2.
112. Ibid., pp.202–3.
113. Ragavis to Metaxas, Berlin, 25 July 1940, Greek Ministry of Foreign Affairs, 1940/A Pol/A/4.
114. Metaxas to Ragavis, coded, Athens, 27 July 1940, Greek Ministry of Foreign Affairs 1940/A Pol/A/4.
115. Memo by Morath, Berlin, 2 December 1940, PAAA, Handakten Clodius, Gr. Bd.4. Koliopoulos claims that Greece was able to live up to the Anglo–Greek War Trade Agreement, Koliopoulos (note 91), p.99. However, this is contradicted by German calculations concerning deliveries of chrome, which concluded that Greece had complied with the war trade agreement in the period between January 1940 and 1 September 1940 and had delivered only 1,073 tons of chrome to Germany in spite of the 15,730 tons agreed upon. On the other hand, it was apparent that the agreed tonnage was delivered to Germany in the period from August 1940. Memo by Morath, Berlin, 2 December 1940, PAAA, Handakten Clodius, Gr. Bd.4.
116. Pelt (note 41), pp.232–6.
117. Ibid., pp.206–10.

Abstracts

'Opposing the past': Danish Radical Conservatism and Right-Wing Authoritarianism in the Inter-War Years

ADAM HOLM

Never a country of political extremism, Denmark still saw its fair share of right-wing ideas during the 1920s and 1930s. Although neither Italian-style fascism nor Nazism played any significant part in Danish political life, such values as democracy, parliamentarism, nation and equality were furiously debated at a time when democratic structures were emasculated all over Europe and replaced by various forms of authoritarian regimes. The parliamentary system remained intact in Denmark, but it was increasingly subjected to heavy criticism from right-wing intellectuals. Writing in magazines and newspapers, and publishing numerous books and leaflets, this group, though far from homogenous, attacked the pro-liberal and pro-democratic parties and institutions for being weak, obsolete and incapable of producing the results needed to tackle the socio-economic crisis. Bearing affinities to the 'Conservative Revolution' of the Weimar Republic, the Danish intellectuals were placed between traditional conservatism and right-wing extremism. Their main objective, not withstanding their internal differences, was to delegitimise the liberal-democratic establishment. In their view the salvation of the nation hinged upon its unity, thus calling for 'strong solutions'.

The Dual State and Fascism

GERT SØRENSEN

Starting with Fraenkel's *The Dual State* (1941), based on the author's experience with the Nazi regime, this article examines to what extent the concept of the dual state can be applied to Italian Fascism. Elaborating on Carl Schmitts's concepts of mandatory and of absolute dictatorship, Fraenkel defines the dual state as an unifying complexity of structures and methods that combine normative and prerogative power.

The dual state in Fascist Italy is an example, to almost the same degree, of emergency measures being undertaken to prepare the conditions necessary for the further development of a fascist revolution. This article, therefore, suggests that the concept of the dual state is more adequate for analysing, for example, relations between the monarchy and Fascism from the 'March on Rome' onwards, than concepts such as 'diarchy' (in the words of Mussolini), which does not embrace the complex reality of the subordinated role of the king, and of normative traditions represented by the *statuto*.

The Strategy of Fascist Italy: A Premise

LUCIO CEVA

In Fascist Italy, the political and military leader was one individual, Mussolini. His foreign policy from 1922 to 1940 was aggressive, according to his personal political and moral structure. His true nature could be made explicit only after the break in the European balance, when a regime similar to Fascism seized power in Germany in 1933. Fascist Italy accomplished its political goals through military force only when the opponents were harmless or inferior (such as the Libyan *mugiahidin*, Ethiopian partisan troops, Albanian and Republican Spanish soldiers). Otherwise, Fascist imperialism relied on the widespread fear of Nazi weapons, both when they were not yet powerful enough (during the controversy with Great Britain and the League of Nations over the war in Ethiopia in 1935–36) and when they were really effective (during the 1938 crisis, postponed by the Munich agreement, and on the occasion of Italy's entering the war in 1940). Mussolini sacrificed Italy and the Italian people in favour of his personal inclinations and connivance, even though he was growing aware that there were only two possible outcomes to the war: either Italy would be defeated or it would become subservient to Germany.

Mussolini, Franco and the Spanish Civil War: An Afterthought

MORTEN HEIBERG

On the basis of fresh documents from Italian and Spanish archives this essay discusses two important aspects of the Italian intervention in the Spanish Civil War: 1) Mussolini's decision to send combat troops to Spain in the autumn of 1936, and 2) Italian attempts to 'fascistise' Nationalist Spain in 1936–37. It holds that the existing historiography, beginning with the studies of John Coverdale and Renzo De Felice, has only scratched the surface of these questions. One might argue that the two historians each in their own way underestimate the imperialistic aggressiveness of Italian Fascism. With regards to Spain, Mussolini's aggressiveness showed itself in two different projects, to which historians have failed to take heed: the possibility of an armed intervention already in September 1936 and Mussolini's interference in the unification-process of the Spanish political parties during the spring of 1937.

'The war that we prefer': The Reclamation of the Pontine Marshes and Fascist Expansion

STEEN BO FRANDSEN

The reclamation of the Pontine Marshes in the 1930s was a huge success for Mussolini. It strongly impressed Italians and foreigners alike with the Italian dictator in his proclaimed reconstruction of his country. Even after the fall of Fascism it was considered to be one of the more positive deeds of the regime. Little attention has been given to the fact that the creation of a new society in the countryside south of the capital brought together several of the most important aspects of Fascist politics. Among them were the autarchic economy, the ideal of a future peasant-civilisation, demographic politics and the organisation of a strongly hierarchic and militarised society. This article particularly stresses the close connection between domestic and foreign policy and argues that the organisation of the new province must be considered as a training ground for the imperialist expansion to come.

The Papacy in Two World Wars: Benedict XV and Pius XII Compared

JOHN F. POLLARD

This article will examine the similarities and differences between the response of Popes Benedict XV and Pius XII to total war. In particular, it will consider the influence of Benedict's experience of the First World War on Pius's conduct of Vatican policy during the Second. It will also assess the impact made by the intervening experience of the rise of fascist regimes in Italy and Germany, and the double polarisation of international relations in Europe during the 1930s – between the democracies and the dictatorships on the one hand, and between the Soviets and the rest on the other – on Pius XII's policies during the Second World War.

The Sentinel of the Bravo: Italian Fascism in Mexico, 1922–35

FRANCO SAVARINO

The main theme of this article is the impact of Italian Fascism on Mexico between 1922, the year of the March on Rome, and 1935, the year of the Ethiopian campaign. It introduces two key aspects: the fascistisation of the Italian-Mexican community and Mexican political reactions in the face of the birth and development of the nationalist revolution in Italy. Finally, it addresses the theme of diplomatic relations between the two governments, pointing out the complex problems that faced Fascist Italy in Mexico and Latin America as a whole within the context of the foreign policy of the regime, underlining the possibilities and the limitations of this on that continent. This article introduces some preliminary results of research on the theme of the Italian–Mexican political and diplomatic relationship, and on the impact of Italian Fascism on Mexico.

Defence of a Concept: Raymond Aron and Totalitarianism

TRINE M. KJELDAHL

French sociologist Raymond Aron was among the first scholars to establish the concept of totalitarianism. He described, explained and discussed how and why fascist and communist ideologies took the form of anti-human regimes. This article recommends Aron's critical use of the concept for future studies of authoritarian government. Aron did not aim to establish either a systematic or a general descriptive theory, but suggested a dynamic use of the concept on the basis of Max Weber's historical sociology. Aron's originality lay in the way he combined political theory, a study of international relations and history writing. Totalitarianism was a guiding concept in Aron's liberal interpretation of history and in his pragmatic policy recommendations to French governments from the 1930s to his death in 1983.

The Establishment and Development of the Metaxas Dictatorship in the Context of Fascism and Nazism, 1936–41

MOGENS PELT

The Metaxas dictatorship was established in the context of a national crisis which had split the Greek political world into two antagonistic blocs: Venizelists and anti-Venizelists. Metaxas belonged to the latter bloc, and his way to power was achieved by extra-parliamentary manoeuvring and by the intervention of the King. Although a product of the Greek political world, Metaxas soon departed from Greek traditions in his efforts to reconstruct state and society. In these efforts, Nazi Germany in particular served as a model. Imitating Germany could also serve as a method for adapting Greece to Hitler's New European Order. At the same time, Metaxas attempted to steer Greece on a neutral course in the escalating Great Power conflict. This was especially true after the successful German *Blitzkrieg* in 1940. However, Italy's ambitions in the eastern Mediterranean forced Greece into the Second World War, and made Hitler decide, albeit reluctantly, to invade Greece in April 1941.

About the Contributors

Lucio Ceva is a Professor of the History of Military Institutions in the Faculty of Political Science at Pavia University. His works include: *La Condotta Italiana della guerra 1941–42* (1975), *Le Forze Armate* (1981), *Africa Settentrionale 1940–1943* (1982), *Guerra mondiale. Strategie e industria bellica 1939–1945* (200); and, as co-author, *La meccanizzazione dell'esercito italiano dalle origini al 1943* (1989) and *Industria bellica anni Trenta* (1992).

Steen Bo Frandsen is a researcher at the Carlsberg Foundation. He has spent several years in Italy as Jean Monnet Fellow at the European Institute in Florence and as Vice-Director at the Danish Academy in Rome. His research has focused on civic and regional identities in the nineteenth century and aspects of Fascism such as urban planning and the scenography of power in Rome. His publications also include books and articles on Danish–German relations, regional questions in Danish and Italian history.

Morten Heiberg received his PhD in 2002 and is an Assistant Professor in the Department of Romance Languages and Literature, University of Copenhagen. He has published articles in three languages on Italian and Spanish history in the inter-war period.

Adam Holm, MA, is a Research Assistant at the Department of History, University of Copenhagen, and the Opinion Editor at the Danish newspaper *Politiken*. He has written numerous articles and reviews for Danish and international magazines and anthologies.

Trine M. Kjeldahl holds a DEA in Political Philosophy from Brussels Free University and a PhD in Roman Philology from the University of Copenhagen. Attached to the Danish Institute of International Affairs, she contributes to a government report on Denmark during the Cold War.

Mogens Pelt holds a PhD from the University of Copenhagen, and an MA in history and BAs in Latin and Modern Greek from the same place. He is Associate Professor at the Department of History, University of Copenhagen. He has been a visiting fellow at the Department of Near Eastern Studies, Princeton University, Deputy-Director at the Danish Institute at Athens and a Research Fellow at the Department of Middle Eastern Studies at the University of Odense, Denmark. His works include *Tobacco, Arms and Politics: Greece and Germany from World Crisis to World War, 1929–1941* (1998), and *Tying Greece to the West: American–West German–Greek Relations, 1949–1974* (forthcoming), along with contributions to the journals *Middle East Studies in Denmark* and *Journal of the Hellenic Diaspora*.

John F. Pollard was educated at Trinity Hall, Cambridge University and took his doctorate at Reading University. He has written extensively on the history of Italy and the Papacy in the nineteenth and twentieth centuries. His most notable publications are *The Vatican and Italian Fascism, 1929–32: A Study in Conflict* (1985), *Papal Diplomacy in the Modern Age*, edited with Peter Kent (1994), *The Fascist Experience in Italy* (1998), and *The Unknown Pope: Benedict XV and the Pursuit of Peace, 1914–1922* (1999) (translated into Italian as *Il Papa Sconosciuto*, 2001). He is currently writing *Money and the Rise of the Modern Papacy: The Finances and Financiers of the Vatican, 1870–1945*, to be published in 2003.

Franco Savarino was born in Torino, Italy, but is now a Mexican citizen. After receiving his PhD at Genova University in 1995, he undertook post-doctorate work at Leiden University and the University of Torino. He is Professor of Contemporary History at the Escuela Nacional de Antropologia e Historia, Mexico City. His main publication is *Pueblos y Nacionalismo, del régimen oligárquico a la sociedad de masas en Yucatán, 1894–1925* (1997).

Gert Sørensen is Senior Lecturer in the Department of Romance Languages and Literature, University of Copenhagen, responsible for Italian history and culture. Among his publications are *Antonio Gramsci og den moderne verden* (1993), *Den dobbelte Stat. Krønike om magtens hemmeligheder: Italien* (1998), and *Kairos. Humanisme og posthumanisme i italiensk politisk tænkning*, to be published in 2002.

Index

Books of Related Interest

Faith, Hope and Nazism
Selected Essays

Uriel Tal
With a Foreword by **Saul Friedlander**

This book comprises a representative selection of the essays –
many of them difficult to find – of the late Uriel Tal. There has
scarcely been another scholar who was as keenly aware of what
German National Socialism owed to a combination of bowdlerised
Christianity and bastardised science, a view he argued with great
cogency and formidable scholarship. The cultural depth, clarity of
exposition and scholarly richness of Tal's essays will establish
formidable standards for the future volumes in this series. This
volume also contains a personal memoir of Uriel Tal by Saul
Friedlander.

240 pages 2002
0 7146 5185 0 cloth
0 7146 8190 3 paper
Totalitarian Movements and Political Religions Series

FRANK CASS PUBLISHERS
Crown House, 47 Chase Side, Southgate, London N14 5BP
Tel: +44 (0)20 8920 2100 Fax: +44 (0)20 8447 8548 E-mail: info@frankcass.com
NORTH AMERICA
5824 NE Hassalo Street, Portland, OR 97213 3644, USA
Tel: 800 944 6190 Fax: 503 280 8832 E-mail: cass@isbs.com
Website: www.frankcass.com

Totalitarian Democracy and After

International Colloquium in Memory of Jacob Talmon

Yehoshua Arieli (Ed)

Jacob Talmon was Professor of Modern History at the Hebrew University, Jerusalem, and a long-standing member of the Israel Academy of Sciences and Humanities until his death in 1980. This book, first published in 1984, contains the principal papers from a distinguished colloquium held in his honour in 1982. Its avowed aim was to investigate further the notion of 'totalitarian democracy' that Talmon brought to the fore in his influential first book *The Origins of Totalitarian Democracy* (1951), and to look at its repercussions in the contemporary world.

420 pages 2002
0 7146 5184 2 cloth
Totalitarian Movements and Political Religions Series

FRANK CASS PUBLISHERS
Crown House, 47 Chase Side, Southgate, London N14 5BP
Tel: +44 (0)20 8920 2100 Fax: +44 (0)20 8447 8548 E-mail: info@frankcass.com
NORTH AMERICA
5824 NE Hassalo Street, Portland, OR 97213 3644, USA
Tel: 800 944 6190 Fax: 503 280 8832 E-mail: cass@isbs.com
Website: www.frankcass.com

Contrasting the French and Italian Communist Parties

Comrades and Culture

Cyrille Guiat, *Heriot-Watt University, Edinburgh*

This is a systematic comparative study of the French and Italian Communist Parties in the period ranging from the early 1960s to the early 1980s. Unlike most studies of these parties, which usually adopt a macro-political approach, this book focuses on the municipal level, through the careful examination of the cultural policies implemented by these parties in two communist strongholds, Ivry-sur-Seine (France) and Reggio Emilia (Italy).

In Ivry-sur-Seine, the French Communist Party implemented a highly ideological cultural policy of attempted indoctrination of the local population, a policy primarily aimed at promoting the image of 'really existing Socialism' and strengthening the 'counter-society' dimension of French Communism. In the case of Reggio Emilia, however, the main goal of the Italian Communist Party was to create a comprehensive, modern network of cultural services and facilities made widely available to the local population, and there was no orthodox Marxist-Leninist thrust to cultural policy-making as was in the case of the French Communist Party.

256 pages 2002
0 7146 5332 2 cloth
Totalitarian Movements and Political Religions Series

FRANK CASS PUBLISHERS
Crown House, 47 Chase Side, Southgate, London N14 5BP
Tel: +44 (0)20 8920 2100 Fax: +44 (0)20 8447 8548 E-mail: info@frankcass.com
NORTH AMERICA
5824 NE Hassalo Street, Portland, OR 97213 3644, USA
Tel: 800 944 6190 Fax: 503 280 8832 E-mail: cass@isbs.com
Website: www.frankcass.com

The Secret File of Joseph Stalin
A Hidden Life

Roman Brackman
With a Foreword by **Harold Shukman**

Starting with Stalin's early years, the book reveals the bitter family conflicts caused by the suspicion that Stalin was the child of an adulterous affair. He would grow up into a brutal and cunning criminal, and became an agent-provocateur of the tsarist secret police, the Okhrana, which afforded him protection in exchange for information on the activities of the revolutionary underground. The book reconstructs Stalin's rivalry with Roman Malinovsky, the top Okhrana agent inside Lenin's Bolshevik organization, and reveals Stalin's provocation to expose Malinovsky, which threatened to blow up into a great state scandal in 1913. It also explains why Stalin was not exposed after the collapse of the tsarist regime and tells of the discoveries in the archives of Stalin's Okhrana files after his rise to power. Most important of all, the book traces the history of Stalin's St Petersburg Okhrana file.

The author also reveals the important roles Soviet officials of Polish and Jewish ethnic origin played in the story of this file, inspiring Stalin's hatred for these two groups, and igniting the irrational motives to destroy them that led to the Soviet pact with Hitler in 1939.

496 pages 20 illus 2001
0 7146 5050 1 cloth

FRANK CASS PUBLISHERS
Crown House, 47 Chase Side, Southgate, London N14 5BP
Tel: +44 (0)20 8920 2100 Fax: +44 (0)20 8447 8548 E-mail: info@frankcass.com
NORTH AMERICA
5824 NE Hassalo Street, Portland, OR 97213 3644, USA
Tel: 800 944 6190 Fax: 503 280 8832 E-mail: cass@isbs.com
Website: www.frankcass.com